CHURCHYARDS
OF ENGLAND AND WALES

Culbone, Somerset

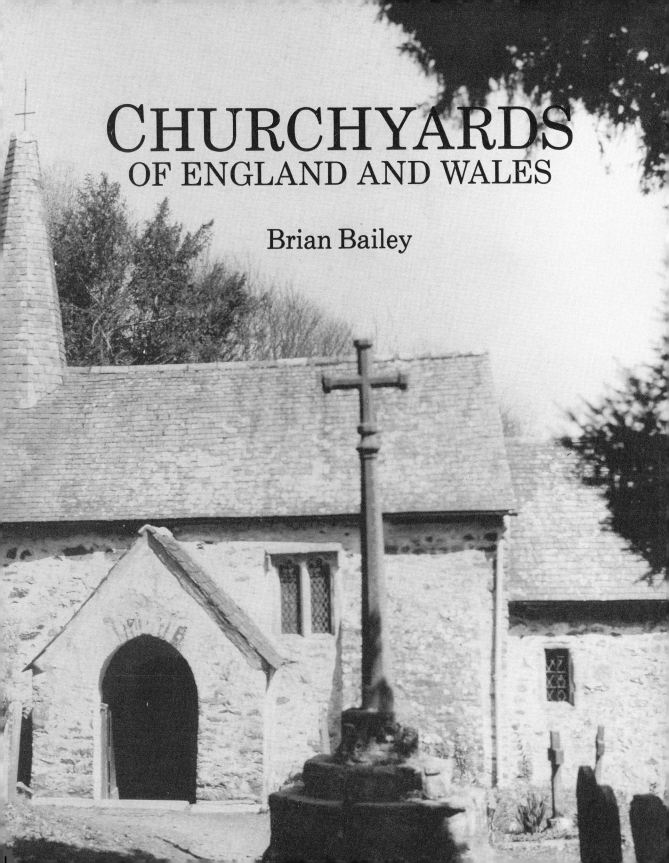

CHURCHYARDS
OF ENGLAND AND WALES

Brian Bailey

© *Brian Bailey 1987*
First published in Great Britain 1987

Robert Hale Limited
Clerkenwell House
Clerkenwell Green
London EC1R 0HT

Bailey, Brian J.
Churchyards of
England and Wales.
1. Tombs—England
I. Title
942   DA90

ISBN 0-7090-2948-9

Photoset in Century Schoolbook by
Derek Doyle & Associates, Mold, Clwyd.
Printed in Great Britain by
WBC Printers Ltd., Bristol
and bound by WBC Bookbinders Ltd.

Contents

List of Illustrations   9
Introduction   15

1 God's 25,000 Acres   19

2 Gatherings from Graveyards   51

3 Ghosts, Graves and Robbers   81

4 The Business of Burial   111

5 Here Lies Buried …   141

6 The English Way of Death   163

Appendix: Some notable burials in English and Welsh churchyards   187
List of Sources   233
Index   235

To
the children
of the silent cities

Illustrations

Black and white illustrations

	Culbone, Somerset	*frontispiece*
1	March, Cambridgeshire	14
2	St Mary's, Whitechapel, London	16
3	Cartmel, Cumbria	18
4	Rudston, Humberside	23
5	Nevern, Dyfed	25
6	Bewcastle, Cumbria	26
7	Ampney Crucis, Gloucestershire	29
8	Bitterley, Shropshire	29
9	Barfreston, Kent	31
10	Painswick, Gloucestershire	32
11	Pickworth, Leicestershire	34
12	Staunton Harold, Leicestershire	36-7
13	Clophill, Bedfordshire	39
14	Sarratt, Hertfordshire	42
15	Paddington Green, London	43
16	Lychgate at Harpsden, Oxfordshire	45
17	Anstey, Hertfordshire	48
18	Flowering Sunday in Wales	50
19	The Smithfield Dole	52
20	Dole table, Powerstock, Dorset	54
21	Gargoyle, Fairford, Gloucestershire	56

22	Sheela-na-gig, Kilpeck, Hereford & Worcester	57
23	West Wycombe, Buckinghamshire	59
24	The Village Pastor	62-3
25	Haworth, West Yorkshire	65
26	Almshouses, Mancetter, Warwickshire	66
27	Sundial, Eyam, Derbyshire	69
28	Sundial, Elmley Castle village churchyard, Hereford & Worcester	70
29	Ship's figurehead, Morwenstow, Cornwall	71
30	Holy well, Whitstone, Cornwall	72
31	St Mary's, Bow, London	74-5
32	Poor souls' light, Bisley, Gloucestershire	76
33	Female fertility figure, Braunston, Leicestershire	78
34	Stoke Poges, Buckinghamshire	80
35	Combe Florey, Somerset	84
36	*Bleak House*	86
37	Haworth, 1875	88-9
38	Watch hut, Warblington, Hampshire	93
39	'Body-snatchers' cage', Henham, Essex	95
40	Chest tomb, Loversall, South Yorkshire	98
41	Dr John Dee	101
42	*The Woman in White*	102
43	Romsey, Hampshire	106-7
44	Baldwin family tomb, Madeley, Shropshire	110
45	Madeley, Shropshire	112
46	'Bodystone', Westerham, Kent	114
47	William Penn's grave, Jordans, Buckinghamshire	116
48	Mickleham, Surrey	117
49	Long Melford, Suffolk	118
50	Mass-produced angel, Awliscombe, Devon	119
51	Swithland, Leicestershire	120
52	Mayfield, East Sussex	123
53	Diagram of types of monument	124
54	'Bale tomb', Burford, Oxfordshire	126-7
55	Pyramid at Painswick, Gloucestershire	130
56	Hardenhuish, Wiltshire	132
57	Nancy Mitford's grave	133
58	The postman's bell, Heanton Punchardon, Devon	134
59	Edith Sitwell's grave	136
60	Eric Gill's grave	137
61	Hannah Twynnoy's gravestone	140
62	Wasdale Head, Cumbria	143
63	A village funeral	146-7
64	No names, no pack-drill	153
65	Bonnie Prince Charlie's daughter?	158
66	Eyam, Derbyshire	160

67	Grave of Mrs Humphry Ward	162
68	Sheepstor, Devon	165
69	The Anglican burial service	169
70	Powerstock, Dorset	172-3
71	South Molton, Devon	175
72	Kensal Green cemetery	177
73	South Molton pavement, Devon	178
74	Beaconsfield, Buckinghamshire	182
75	Cerne Abbas, Dorset	185
76	Sir Richard Burton's great stone tent	186
77	Lord Burnham's chest tomb	189
78	Basil Liddell Hart's grave	192
79	John Ruskin's monument	195
80	T.E. Lawrence's grave	200
81	C. Day Lewis's grave	201
82	Warren Hastings' grave	203
83	St John's Wood	211
84	Randolph Churchill's grave	216
85	J.K. Jerome's grave	218
86	George Orwell's grave	219
87	Unity Mitford's grave	220
88	Funtingdon churchyard	224-5
89	Bread prices, Great Wishford, Wiltshire	228

Picture Credits

Mary Evans Picture Library: 10, 18, 24, 69. Rita Bailey: 11. Van Phillips: 15. The Mansell Collection: 19, 37, 42, 43, 63, 72, 83, 88. Derek G. Widdicombe: 21, 89. All other photographs and sketches by the author.

Colour Plates

Between pages 40 and 41

1   St Michael of the Rock, Brent Tor, Devon
2   Oakwoodhill, Surrey
3   Stoke Poges churchyard by moonlight
4   St Enodoc, Trebetherick, North Cornwall

Between pages 104 and 105

5   The ancient site of Knowlton, Devon
6   Bridell, Gwynedd
7   *Home from the Sea* by Arthur Hughes
8   Churchyard yews at Painswick, Gloucestershire
9   Cross and churchyard at Snowshill, Gloucestershire

Between pages 152 and 153

10   Whippingham, Isle of Wight
11   St Just-in-Roseland, Cornwall
12   *East Bergholt churchyard* by Constable
13   John Peel's gravestone, Caldbeck, Cumbria
14   Arncliffe, North Yorkshire

Between pages 184 and 185

15   Escomb, County Durham
16   Llangelynin, Gwynedd
17   Sir John Gilbert's painting of *Bettws-y-Coed*
18   Holmbury St Mary, Surrey

Picture Credits

Roy J. Westlake: 1, 4, 11. Derek G. Widdicombe: 2, 13-14, 16, 18. The Mansell Collection: 3. Rita Bailey: 5, 8-10. Roger Worsley: 6. The Ashmolean Museum: 7. Victoria and Albert Museum: 12. Joy Wotton: 15. Guildhall Art Gallery/Bridgeman Art Library: 17.

God's Acre

Morning up the eastern stair
Marches, azuring the air,
And the foot of twilight still
Is stolen toward the western sill.
Blithe the maids go milking, blithe
Men in hayfields stone the scythe;
All the land's alive around
Except the churchyard's idle ground.
There's empty acres west and east,
But aye 'tis God's that bears the least:
This hopeless garden that they sow
With the seeds that never grow.

A.E. Housman

Introduction

Churchyards, it seems to me, possess that curious quality of being at once forbidding and irresistible, so that one might at one time have hesitated to linger *too* long in them, for fear of being considered morbid or suspected of poetic pretensions. But now that we have outlived so many of the old superstitions, and have decreed that 'death shall have no dominion', and do not believe in ghosts, we can dwell in churchyards with a little more peace of mind, and look upon them not fearfully as habitations of the dead, which is how they were seen not so long ago, but with fascination as open-air museums of the past.

Not least of the many attractions of churchyards is their peacefulness. Even in the middle of a big town, if you want a few minutes respite from the thundering traffic, the crowded shops and the heat of the day, you should always head for the churchyard; for even when it is only just off the busy main street, it seems a magical haven, unreal like a fairy grotto, where you suddenly feel inclined to whisper instead of shout, and there is always the cool shade of an old tree.

Dickens described the typical nineteenth-century city churchyard in *The Uncommercial Traveller*: 'The illegible tombstones are all lop-sided, the grave-mounds lost their shape in the rains of a hundred years ago, the Lombardy Poplar or Plane-Tree that was once a drysalter's daughter and several common-councilmen, has withered like those worthies, and its departed leaves are dust beneath it. Contagion of slow ruin overhangs the place.'

Yes, but ruin implies neglect, and it is the very air of neglect that imparts to churchyards their serenity. These places of the past have

St Mary's, Whitechapel,
London

nothing to do with commercialism and computers. They have defied the influence of 'progress', as we are inclined to call the rat-race outside the gates, and so they afford us pleasurable moments of quiet reflection. The former churchyard of St Botolph Aldersgate, opposite the post office in central London's King Edward Street, is known as Postman's Park, the workers very sensibly crossing the street to relax there during their breaks from duty.

Country churchyards, of course, are even more tranquil and, in my own view (though this is heresy), are all the better for being neglected, with the gravestones peeping out from long grass, weeds and wild flowers, instead of standing stark naked and stone cold on wide expanses of immaculately mown lawns with gravel paths between them. However, as the majority of regular visitors to churchyards are either those tending to graves of the recently dead or those seeking the burial places of the famous, it has to be admitted that tidiness is generally more helpful, if less romantic.

No one person could write a book with everything of interest about the country's churchyards in it, even if he spent half a lifetime on it, and in spite of extensive travelling and observing, I do not claim to have done anything more than scratch the surface to reveal a little of what might be discovered. For it is a curious fact that, whilst a vast number of books has been written and published about churches, relatively little has been written about the burial grounds which have surrounded them from time immemorial and may indeed have been there first in many cases. There have been plenty of books about epitaphs, of course, but there is a great deal more to churchyards than these fairly recent expressions of personal feeling, as I hope to show, and there is not a churchyard in England that does not have something of interest in it. Furthermore, churchyards are freely accessible to everyone, unlike stately homes, museums and many other places of social or historical interest. To those whose further curiosity is aroused, having picked up some clues, I hope, as to what sort of things are worth looking for, there is only one appropriate piece of advice: seek, and ye shall find.

I ought to add that it is inevitable in a book of this kind that some errors creep in. Time forbids the possibility of checking and rechecking every churchyard mentioned. I trust the mistakes are few, and crave the reader's indulgence and the critic's absolution.

1

God's 25,000 Acres

...rtmel, Cumbria. The
...urchyard is probably
...ich older than the
...urch, which was the
...urch of Cartmel Priory
...fore the Dissolution

An estimate of the area of land used for burial purposes in England and Wales puts the figure at about 25,000 acres, or one in every 1,500. This figure includes cemeteries as well as churchyards, but it is a startling statistic – nearly forty square miles of ground. In these times of land scarcity it is hardly surprising that some people argue that the land taken up by churchyards could be put to better use than what modern materialism sees merely as rubbish disposal.

Were it not for two other important statistics, the area might have been even greater. First, bodies have been piled up on top of one another in churchyards over the centuries, a space-saving device similar to modern city tower-blocks, only going down instead of up. This practice has resulted in raising the level of the ground to such an extent that the floors of old churches are now generally lower than the ground outside. The seventeenth-century author and physician Sir Thomas Browne reckoned that more than a thousand cartloads of bones from the charnel-house at St Paul's were buried beneath mounds of earth at Finsbury Fields, about a mile to the north, and raised the ground level to a height sufficient for windmills to be built on it. The ground is now part of the Bunhill Fields Cemetery, the name coming from 'bone hill'.

The second reason is that the dramatic increase in cremation in the present century has reduced the possible demand for burial space by about half, modern folk having come round to the view, evidently, that the soul can ascend to Heaven as easily from a heap of smouldering ashes as from a pile of rotting bones. This, or something like it, was the expressed opinion of Napoleon (among others), who was not, however, allowed to be cremated, the ostentatious tombs of national heroes being useful to governments as morale-boosters in bad times. (Napoleon was buried in six coffins like a set of Chinese boxes.)

We shall come to these various facts in a little more detail later, but I mention them at the outset to show that churchyards and cemeteries between them constitute a not insignificant part of England's land usage, deserving serious attention. Yet it is a fact that, despite the vast literature on our churches and their contents, relatively little has been devoted to the consecrated ground around them. Between churchyards and cemeteries there is, of course, a big difference. Churchyards are centuries old, like the churches themselves, and their interest is far from being confined merely to the graves and monuments in them. Cemeteries, on the other hand, are only a nineteenth-century solution to the problems of pressure on graveyard space and the demands of Nonconformists for separate burial grounds, so they have no history, either social or religious, to speak of. This book is almost exclusively devoted to churchyards.

The origin of the churchyard is obscure. Christianity was well established in Britain by the time the Roman legions departed in the fifth century, but the conflicts arising from the chaotic condition of the island, left defenceless against Picts and Scots, Angles and Saxons, left Christianity also divided until Gregory the Great sent the monk Augustine on his mission from Rome to convert the recalcitrant natives. In 601 Pope Gregory sent his famous advice to his missionaries, via the Abbot Mellitus, not to destroy the pagan temples but to convert them into Christian churches.

The English took a long time to adopt the new religion wholeheartedly, and there were few permanent churches at first, but the population was caught in a sort of missionary pincer movement between the Roman monks operating from Kent and the Irish ones working from Iona.

The establishment of churchyards in England is usually credited to Cuthbert, Archbishop of Canterbury, who sought and obtained the approval of Rome in 752 for setting them up around city churches. Gregory the Great had in fact advocated them long before, so that prayers for the dead would be the more likely as the faithful passed them in going to church; it was believed by many that souls remained in purgatory unless frequent Masses were offered for them. The proximity of the dead to the place of worship also served to remind the living, of course, of their own physical mortality and, in theory at least, put them in the right frame of mind as they entered the church. The size of the area consecrated as a churchyard varied until the tenth century, when the practice of enclosing one acre was introduced, with the church at its centre. Hence the common nickname 'God's Acre'.

It is probable that in many cases churchyards were considerably older than the first churches they contained, since the Romans venerated their dead and erected monuments to them in cemeteries, generally preferring their burial grounds to be well away from their places of worship. With their passion for straight lines, the Romans substituted for the circular mounds and burial sites of earlier peoples the rectangular graveyard which is still to be seen around most churches. Certainly many churchyards *now* are much older than the churches in them, for the first churches were built of wood and eventually had to be replaced.

It is anybody's guess how many Christian churches in England stand on the sites of pagan temples or sacred places, but we know of quite a number that certainly do. Sometimes the churchyards around them are circular, as if the church had literally usurped a pagan enclosure. It would have been easy for church-builders to follow Gregory's advice if they found suitable pagan sites near a thriving centre of population, and could utilize ground previously levelled, and even make convenient use of building materials already on the site. (The words 'pagan' and 'heathen', sometimes used to refer to uncivilized and unenlightened barbarians, are used here only to denote non-Christians.)

Among the best-known examples of churches on pagan sites are those of Knowlton, Dorset, and Cholesbury, Buckinghamshire. Both are within large circular earthworks surrounded by banks and ditches. The church at Knowlton, on Cranborne Chase, is now a ruin, but it was built at the centre of a circle which was originally the middle one of three, known as the Knowlton Rings. Their purpose is unknown, but they date from the Bronze Age (*c*.1800-500 BC), and the church-builders clearly thought it proper to take advantage of the local population's lingering reverence or superstition. The site may originally have had a circle of standing stones on it. There are no gravestones here because the church has been deserted since 1647, the village it served having disappeared. Even the church's dedication is unknown, and a strange air of mystery seems to envelop the place.

The church and churchyard at Cholesbury are still in use and stand within the south-western perimeter of a hill-fort of the Iron Age (after *c*.500 BC). This was occupied by Belgic settlers and was not a sacred site, but the church-builders cannot have been ignorant of the pagan associations of this earthwork protected by double and triple ramparts.

The famous stone circle at Avebury, Wiltshire, was a pagan sanctuary, though there the modern village's churchyard is just outside the circle. Wiltshire has at least one other churchyard occupying ground with pre-Christian associations, however. At Ogbourne St Andrew, near Marlborough, the churchyard embraces a large bowl barrow which excavation proved to contain an intrusive Saxon burial.

The churchyard of St Dennis in Cornwall occupies the inner circle of an Iron Age hill-fort high up on the downs above St Austell. There were two circular ramparts defending the fort, and the churchyard wall defines the inner area. The dedication of the church might well be derived from the Celtic *dinas* (fort) rather than from some forgotten saint.

Ozleworth, Gloucestershire, is another place where the high ground on which the small Cotswold church stands was probably a pagan sacred site. The churchyard of St Nicholas, surrounded by a dry-stone wall, is circular, following the prehistoric earthwork, and the church itself has an ancient and unusual hexagonal tower indicating its antiquity. It is said that the last man hanged in England for highway robbery was buried here.

The church of St Michael at Winwick in Northamptonshire stands in a circular churchyard and provides an important clue to which churchyards are most likely to occupy pagan sites. For we find that many hilltop churches are, like this one, dedicated to St Michael, who was a pagan deity before he was an avenging Christian demi-god. The church at Glastonbury Tor is a case in point. The origin of St Michael as prince of the angels and leader of the heavenly host is obscure, but he may bear some relation to the Roman Mercury, being adapted to Christian themes via a Celtic god Michael who escorted souls to paradise and is thus easily associated with hill-tops. His supposed victory over a dragon is clearly pre-Christian.

Another circular churchyard is at Cranwich in Norfolk, and at Stowlangtoft, Suffolk, the churchyard stands within a rectangular earthwork believed to be Roman. In Wales the churchyard at Ysbyty Cynfyn, not far from Aberystwyth, had ancient megaliths still in evidence from the former stone circle it occupies, whilst a boulder in the churchyard at Maentwrog, Gwynedd, is said to have been hurled by St Twrog to destroy a pagan altar on the site of the present church.

Bolterstone, a village near Sheffield, has two large stones in its churchyard which may be the remains of a stone circle, one of them having mortice holes, like the lintels of Stonehenge. Latton, Wiltshire, has fragments of Roman columns in its churchyard, and a lingering belief about a stone in the churchyard at Bungay, Suffolk, reckoned to be 2,000 years old and called 'the Druids' Stone', is that if you dance or run round it twelve times you are sure to raise the Devil.

Churches which have a very common legend attached to them, about the Devil moving the stones during the night to some place other than where the medieval masons had intended to build the church (usually to the top of a hill), are fairly sure to be on pagan sites. Breedon-on-the-Hill in Leicestershire is one such case, where weird Saxon friezes inside the church seem to confirm pagan origins. The church and its graveyard occupy an Iron Age site on top of a windy hill which the villagers formerly had to climb by a steep and winding path. Doubtless here and elsewhere the legend grew in the minds of parishioners of later centuries who could not fathom why any sane man would build a church in such an inaccessible spot, but the origin of such tales is probably to be found in

Monolith at Rudston,
Humberside

the conflict between sacred and profane preferences in the sites of places of worship.

The Norman church of flint at Checkendon, Oxfordshire, was originally intended to be where an old stone quarry was surrounded by yew trees, but the materials were moved to a different site every night until the masons finally gave way. The quarry area is known as 'the Devil's Churchyard'. This legend seems to be a reversal of the usual tale, since the church was moved *away* from what was obviously the pagan site. Perhaps it was the villagers themselves who objected to the original choice, the pagan site thus being attributed to the Devil.

The most famous and spectacular ancient stone in a Christian churchyard is the one at Rudston, Humberside. This is the largest standing stone in Britain, six feet wide and more than twenty-five feet high. Because of the type of stone, Carboniferous sandstone or 'millstone grit', it is known that this colossal monolith of twenty-six tons was brought here specially, from at least ten miles away, and erected on what was obviously a place of some religious significance to the people of around 2000 BC who went to such lengths to obtain it. Other ancient relics have also been found in the churchyard, and it is clear that when the first church was built here, within a few yards of the giant stone, the builders deliberately aimed at capitalizing on the strength of association already existing between place and people.

The pagan worship of stones caused much concern to the Church fathers during the early centuries of Christianity. They issued edicts forbidding such practices, threatening the guilty with excommunication and giving instructions that, as far as practicable, stones and other natural objects of veneration should be hidden or destroyed. But ancient superstitions were too deeply rooted to be easily abolished, and it may be that the churchyard cross came into being as a compromise between an old pagan habit of regarding monoliths as the repositories of spirits of the dead, and the Church's insistence on total submission to its doctrines.

Crudely shaped stones with crosses or the Chi-Rho symbol may have been pagan idols converted, as it were, to orthodox use, the Christian Chi-Rho sign (Greek letters forming a monogram for Khristos) at once overpowering the evil spirits in the stones and at the same time retaining the local people's superstitious reverence for the objects – which was a useful missionary tactic. Thus eventually stones carved with crosses or crucifixes supplanted in people's affections stones inscribed with mazes or fertility figures. They were still only stones, but at least they were sanctified by Christian adaptation to circumstances.

In time, after centuries had passed, people forgot the ancient beliefs and dreamed up new superstitions to account for what they could not otherwise explain. Thus the Rudston monolith was believed to have been hurled by the Devil to demolish the church, missing it – as can easily be seen – by no more than a few feet! If only some monk or priest had had the wit to carve a cross on it, people throughout the Middle Ages and beyond would have revered the stone as an early Christian monument, as they have done with mazes.

Just outside the churchyard gate at Shebbear, Devon, is a massive boulder which is involved in an unusual ritual on 5 November each year. (No one can explain its origin or meaning, and it has nothing to do with Guy Fawkes.) Village men ring a peal of bells in the church, then come to the stone and turn it over, using crowbars, before going back to the church and ringing the bells again. The tradition in the locality is that if this ceremony is not performed, the parish will come to some harm, presumably at the hands of the Devil.

Inscribed ancient stones, particularly of Saxon origin, can be found in several churchyards around the country, but especially in Cornwall, such as at Cardinham and Marazion (where a reference to the Emperor Constantine dates the inscription to the early fourth century).

Several Celtic turf mazes survive in England and are usually known as

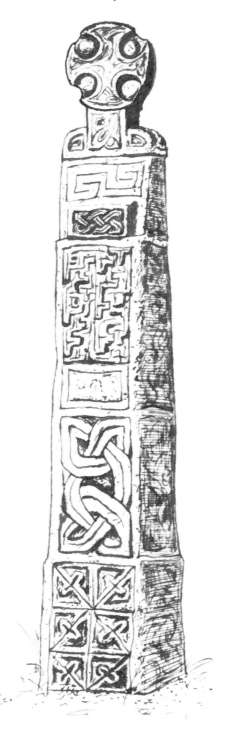

Nevern, Dyfed. The Celtic high cross in the churchyard bears inscriptions as yet undeciphered. Note the labyrinth design near the top of the shaft

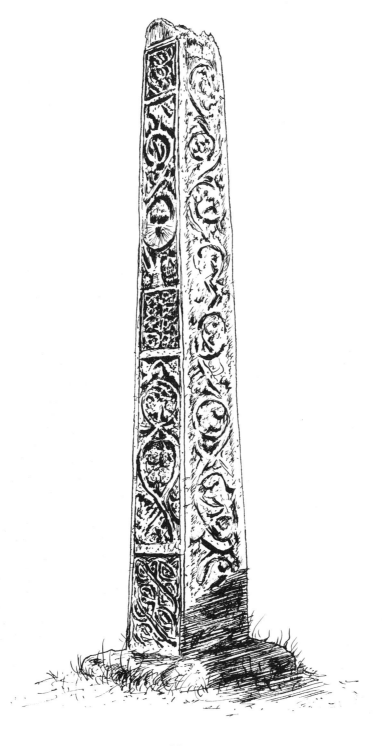

Bewcastle, Cumbria. Th[
ancient churchyard cross

Troy Town or City of Troy, though they have more to do with the Cretan labyrinth in which Theseus killed the Minotaur than with wooden horses. Why anyone should seriously believe they have anything to do with Christian ritual is baffling but, because they are often found near churches, folklore sometimes accounts for them by saying that they were invented by the Church as an instrument of symbolic penance for sinners, who had to tread the maze on their knees to the centre. Actually, they are further evidence of churches being built on or near pagan sites. There were once a great many more of these turf mazes than remain now, and they were the scenes of a pagan ceremony at Easter, a spiral dance connected with fertility, like dancing round the maypole. The name Troy Town probably derives from the tradition that heroes from the Trojan War founded Britain and France.

The most sensational evidence of the Church tolerating and then embracing these pagan survivals is to be found at Alkborough, Humberside, where a maze to the south-west of the Anglo-Saxon church is called Julian's Bower. Julus was the son of the Trojan hero Aeneas. In the south porch of the church, the pattern of this maze is copied in the floor, and there are two other other modern copies of the maze, one in a stained glass window, one in the gravestone of a village squire buried in 1922.

To return to the churchyard cross, however, it seems that it may have originated as a marking stone, for places of worship, before churches were built, and only later became the sole memorial for the poor of a parish, who did not have individual gravestones before the seventeenth century.

Many ancient and some famous churchyard crosses survive, the most remarkable of them undoubtedly being in the churchyard of St Cuthbert at Bewcastle, Cumbria. This is generally thought to date from the seventh or early eight century and commemorates a king of Northumbria. As the inscription is in runes, on one of the cross's four sides, the exact meaning and date of the cross have been disputed, but there is no doubt that this sandstone monument, which has stood here and survived the harsh northern climate for something like 1,300 years, is one of the outstanding examples of Anglo-Saxon art. The head of the cross was intact until the seventeenth century, when it was sent to the antiquary William Camden for investigation and was never returned. The shaft – $14\frac{1}{2}$ feet high – is carved on all sides; Christ, John the Baptist and John the Evangelist are depicted on the side with the runic inscriptions, and the other sides are incised with birds and beasts, vines, scrolls and geometric patterns.

Another famous cross is in the churchyard at Gosforth, on the western fringe of the Lake District. This one is neither as old nor as artistically accomplished as the one at Bewcastle but is still a remarkable and important survival. Dating from the tenth century, the Gosforth cross is a slender column, complete with head, and stands fifteen feet high. The carving was influenced by the Danish infiltrations which had occurred since the Bewcastle cross was made and, apart from a crude crucifixion scene, the representations on it are pagan.

These two Cumbrian crosses are rare enough in remaining so relatively complete and *in situ*, many fragments of ancient crosses having been moved inside their respective churches for preservation, but at the village of Irton, just south of Gosforth, is yet another churchyard survival, a smaller cross dating from the ninth century and still with its original head intact. This one is smaller than the other two, at ten feet, and its design shows Irish influence.

Several good Saxon crosses partially survive farther south, a notable one being in the churchyard at Bakewell, Derbyshire. Only part of the shaft remains here, but the carving of humans and animals on it is well preserved. Also in Derbyshire, Eyam's cross is of similar date and retains its head, while that at Brailsford is somewhat later. There are two Anglo-Saxon crosses in the churchyard at Ilam, Staffordshire.

Other interesting Anglo-Saxon crosses can be found at Masham, North Yorkshire; Halton and Whalley, Lancashire; Rothley, Leicestershire; Stapleford, Nottinghamshire, and Llanivet and Sancreed, Cornwall. The cross at Stapleford dates from only a few years before the Norman Conquest. At Fletton, Cambridgeshire, a Saxon cross seems to have been turned into a memorial for an individual, having Norman lettering on a shaft with earlier animal carvings, one of them no doubt the symbolic lamb of the *Agnus Dei*.

The reasons for so few really ancient crosses remaining are that most of the earliest ones were probably made of wood, and many of those that *were* made of stone were destroyed by the Puritan iconoclasts. Cornwall is unusually rich in churchyard crosses, but they are made of granite, which is as hard to destroy as to carve, so they tend to be of simpler design than those in other parts of England made of softer stone, though Breage has a very worn old cross of sandstone.

Medieval churchyard crosses are naturally more numerous, though complete survivals *in situ* are still comparatively rare. The church at Headless Cross in Hereford & Worcester is a Victorian building, but the name of the place speaks for itself. Rocester, Staffordshire, has a thirteenth-century stepped cross with part of its original head intact and Norman decoration on the shaft. Gloucestershire has some notable medieval crosses, the one at Ampney Crucis being especially fine. This fifteenth-century monument on a stepped base can be dated confidently to around the first years of Henry V's reign by the man in armour carved on one side. The cross-head has a gabled top with the traditional crucifix on one side and the Virgin Mary on the other. The head of the statue was found walled up inside the church, where it had no doubt been hidden from the idol-smashers, and it was replaced on the shaft in the

Left: The medieval cross at Ampney Crucis, Gloucestershire

Right: Bitterley, Shropshire. The churchyard cross with alleged 'sighting hole'

nineteenth century.

Still in Gloucestershire, Iron Acton has a remarkable cross of similar date, but this is an elaborate structure which may have been a memorial to a local bigshot; Ashleworth's fourteenth-century cross is another interesting survival. Good medieval crosses can also be seen at Higham Ferrers, Northamptonshire; Cricklade, Wiltshire (St Mary's); Dorchester, Oxfordshire; Somersby, Lincolnshire, and Stoke-sub-Hamdon, Somerset. Ripley, North Yorkshire, has a 'weeping cross' with holes made in its base so that penitents could kneel and pray but, alas, neither its head nor its shaft survives. The remaining base of the cross at Exford, Somerset, was used by the parish beadle at one time as a platform from which to issue his proclamations and became known as 'the Crying Stone'. The cross at St Mary's, Ross-on-Wye, in Hereford & Worcester, is a memorial to 315 local people killed by a visitation of the plague in 1637. The sandstone cross by the lychgate at Claverley, Shropshire, is a memorial to victims of the Black Death.

The slender shaft of the old cross in Bitterley churchyard, Shropshire, has a hole through it which some say is a 'sighting hole' by means of which 'leys' could be followed. The theory of leys is that prehistoric and later buildings on important sites were deliberately arranged in straight lines. However, all you can see through the hole in the Bitterley cross is the wall of the church, and if that were not in the way, the hill behind it would be. The hole, which occurs in a few other cross shafts, served some other purpose, undoubtedly connected with a religious ceremony.

Apart from the individual memorials and gravestones which began to proliferate from the seventeenth century, the other ubiquitous and ancient resident of the English churchyard is the yew tree. There is some slight mystery about why yews were the first choice for planting in churchyards. Many churchyard yews are in the region of a thousand years old, and a few may be considerably older. That is to say, they were planted before the Norman Conquest, and the practice continued after 1066.

It is often said that the yew was favoured as an appropriate symbol of everlasting life. Its longevity and the fact that it is an evergreen seem to support this idea, taken at face value; but in fact to the pagan world the yew was the tree of death, sacred to Hecate, a goddess of death, ghosts and witchcraft. Shakespeare knew this well enough, for his three witches in *Macbeth* include in their noxious brew

> … slips of yew
> Sliver'd in the moon's eclipse …

In Herefordshire, a girl who picked a twig of yew from a churchyard outside her own parish, and took it to bed with her on Hallowe'en, would be sure to see her future husband in a dream.

Probably one of the functions of the churchyard yew in very early times was to protect the community against evil spirits. Even in the seventeenth century one dabbler in the occult, Robert Turner, wrote that the yew 'attracts and imbibes putrefaction and gross oleaginous vapours exhaled out of the Graves by the setting Sun …'.

A yew in the churchyard at Nevern, Dyfed, is known as 'the bleeding yew', since a reddish resin is sometimes seen to ooze from it, and this has naturally been interpreted in tree-lore of the past as a 'sign', being associated particularly with menstruation, a well-known source of superstition to primitive peoples. And in Devon the massive old yew in the churchyard at Stoke Gabriel is associated with fertility. Both men and women can take advantage of its magical properties, women by walking forwards and men backwards round its girth.

Taken together with the yew's poisonousness and pagan associations, the Christian belief in it as a symbol of immortality, and the old story that it gave shelter to Christian missionaries before churches were built, seem to be cases of Christians making a virtue out of necessity. The trees *may* often have sheltered preachers simply because they (the trees) were there first, growing at pagan sacred sites where churches were eventually built; rather than the yews being planted in churchyards, churchyards may often have been planted round the yews.

The yew's Latin name *taxus* is related to the Greek *toxicon pharmakon* meaning 'poison for arrows' and *toxon* for bow, and the yew was already known to the ancient world for its strong, springy wood, ideal for making bows. The medieval English armies relied on yew for their longbows, and their expertise in using them gave English archers their reputation as the finest infantry in Europe. It has been disputed whether yews were ever planted in churchyards primarily to provide wood for bows, but it does not seem unlikely, although the best bows were certainly made from superior wood imported from overseas. The church and churchyard were, along with the village green, the centres of most community activity, and archery practice was expected of all able-bodied men from the time of Edward III, in readiness for conscription in the national service. Butts

Barfreston, Kent. The churchyard yew with a belfry

were often set up in the churchyards of villages where there was no other convenient place, and grooves in the church walls at Aston upon Trent, Derbyshire, for example, are commonly believed to have been made by archers sharpening their arrows.

Yews have also provided some protection to the fabric of churches and often sheltered their porches a little from the elements, and Edward I decreed that they should be planted for this purpose. They can also be something of a liability, however. In 1878 the church authorities at Amersham, Buckinghamshire, were held liable for damages when a farmer's cattle died after eating the young foliage of a yew hanging over a field from the neighbouring churchyard.

The oldest and biggest churchyard yews are mostly in the south and west of England, although Darley Dale in Derbyshire has the remains of one which had a girth of thirty-three feet. The ancient trees are often

hollow but live on regardless, often propped up against collapse like old men on crutches. Those at Crowhurst, Surrey, and Much Marcle, Hereford & Worcester, have seats built inside their hollow trunks and are reckoned to be about a thousand years old. The churchyard yew at Barfreston, Kent, is not so massive, but it has the church bell in its branches, since there is no belfry there. At Broughton, Shropshire, a large

...pping the Church at
...nswick,
...ucestershire. This old
...otograph shows children
...ircling the church in an
...ient ceremony
...bably derived from
...gan ritual

yew shades the ruins of the old church.

Some other very large and venerable yews are at Brockenhurst, Corhampton and Selborne in Hampshire; Tandridge, Surrey; Aldworth, Berkshire, and Woolland, Dorset. The yew at Selborne is well known from the writings of the Reverend Gilbert White, who is buried there. William Cobbett measured the tree's girth in 1823 and found it to be twenty-three feet eight inches.

The parish records of Denbury, Devon, include a bill from the village blacksmith in 1876 with the item 'to healing the yew tree, 2s 6d'. A large bough had been broken off by a gale, and the smith applied a mixture to the wound which saved the tree. The huge old yew propped up in the churchyard at Stoke Gabriel was once reckoned the second largest in England.

Many churchyards throughout the country are well planted with trees, though not always yews, of course. There are over a hundred fine clipped yews at Painswick, Gloucestershire, though these are mere striplings of two or three hundred years, but many of them form fine shady avenues through the churchyard and have naturally inspired legend, such as the popular belief that there are only ninety-nine of them, all attempts to grow a hundredth having come to nothing, allegedly due to Satanic influence. Legend ascribes the origin of the yews at Preston, Leicestershire, to the Garden of Gethsemane. The churchyard at Ospringe, Kent, has fine yews and cedars, while Barham is noted for its beeches. Bullington, Hampshire, and Sharnford, Leicestershire, are better known for limes, an avenue of which also forms the path to the doorway of the parish church at Stratford-on-Avon, Warwickshire. There are twelve on each side, said – naturally enough – to represent the twelve tribes of Israel and the twelve apostles. One of the apostles stands slightly out of line and represents in popular fancy Matthias, who replaced Judas Iscariot. Holbeach, Lincolnshire, and Holy Trinity at Huddersfield are among other churchyards worth noting for their trees – birch, beech and catalpa in the former case. There is a fine avenue of beeches in the churchyard at Chawleigh, Devon, and the yews and limes at Kerry, Powys, are well known.

At Stanhope, Durham, the seven-foot stump of a fossilized tree stands by the churchyard wall. It was taken from a quarry and placed there in 1964 as a monument to the village's industrial origins from mining and quarrying. The stump is reckoned to be many millions of years old.

Occasionally one comes across a church and churchyard which are surrounded by trees so completely as to be almost hidden from view, though this cannot have been the intention when the trees were first planted. Examples are at Wasdale Head, Cumbria; Ford, West Sussex; Whitchurch, Warwickshire, and Fishlake, South Yorkshire.

The trees, shrubs and long grass to be found, especially in most rural

The ruined arch at
Pickworth, Leicestershire

churchyards, provide a habitat for many wild flowers, birds, insects and small animals, if maintenance is not over-zealous, and wild orchids and other rare species sometimes thrive in churchyards when they have disappeared everywhere else through modern agricultural techniques. It may seem an irreverent thought to some, but it is unarguable that a churchyard is richer in good fertilizer than a garden full of modern chemicals, and in town and city churchyards selective weedkillers have to be used to suppress the rampant growth fuelled by bonemeal.

Thomas Hardy, as always, had some interesting thoughts on this, called 'Transformations':

> Portion of this yew
> Is a man my grandsire knew,
> Bosomed here at its foot:
> This branch may be his wife,
> A ruddy human life
> Now turned to a green shoot.
>
> These grasses must be made
> Of her who often prayed,
> Last century, for repose;
> And the fair girl long ago
> Whom I often tried to know
> May be entering this rose.
>
> So, they are not underground,
> But as nerves and veins abound
> In the growths of upper air,
> And they feel the sun and rain,
> And the energy again
> That made them what they were!

So many churchyards are noted for their plants and flowers that it is invidious to make a short list, but few would argue with St Just-in-Roseland, Cornwall, Easthorpe in Essex and Warmington, Warwickshire, being cited as examples. The churchyard at Navestock, Essex, has a rose garden made in the crater caused by a land-mine which exploded in 1940 and did much damage to the church. Mallwyd, Gwynedd, is noted for the daffodils that bloom among the gravestones of local grey slate in the spring.

Overleaf: Staunton Harold, Leicestershire. The church and its walled churchyard were built defiantly during the Commonwealth in the grounds at Staunton Harold Hall

The proverbial church mouse is as likely to be a fieldmouse or vole living in the churchyard as the more familiar house mouse; and the black 'churchyard beetle' got its common name from its liking for the dark cavities in the ground beneath stone structures. Flying insects inhabiting

the churchyard provide food for swallows and bats in the belfry. The quiet churchyard at Waxham, Norfolk, is a nesting place for local geese.

The situation and enclosure of a churchyard can be of considerable interest, quite apart from the possibility that it occupied a pagan site. Lords of manors often built churches in (or surrounded them with) their own private grounds, and several parish churches remain in private parks today, with a right of way making them accessible to the parishioners. The church at Brancepath, Durham, is inside the grounds of the medieval castle, while that at English Bicknor, Gloucestershire, is on the site of a motte-and-bailey castle, and mottes partly occupy the churchyards at Earls Barton, Northamptonshire, and Chipping Norton, Oxfordshire. The churchyard at Stokesay, Shropshire, is separated from the medieval castle only by a moat, while at Datchworth, Hertfordshire, the churchyard is itself surrounded by a moat which also originally enclosed the manor house, as is still the case at Great Chalfield, Wiltshire. The churchyards at Harewood, West Yorkshire; Exton, Leicestershire; Knebworth, Hertfordshire; Tawstock, Devon, and Upper Shuckburgh, Warwickshire, among many others, are in the grounds of the local lords' mansions.

Some churches were built on island sites on village greens, as at Great Asby, Cumbria; Elsdon, Northumberland; Hawkedon, Suffolk, and Kew, London, but in one or two cases the churchyard gradually encroached on the green and eventually took it over entirely. Thus at Snowshill, Gloucestershire, the former Cotswold village green is now the churchyard.

Churchyards in one or two medieval 'new towns' fill a whole square of the town's grid pattern. Such is the case with St Thomas's at Winchelsea, East Sussex, and St Lawrence's at Ludlow, Shropshire. Near the Winchelsea churchyard an ash tree used to stand where John Wesley preached the last of his outdoor sermons, in 1790. The Ludlow churchyard contains the ashes of A.E. Housman, who wrote a characteristic poem on 'God's Acre', which he called 'idle ground':

> There's empty acres west and east,
> But aye 'tis God's that bears the least:
> This hopeless garden that they sow
> With the seeds that never grow.

Sometimes churches and their churchyards are remote from any centre of population. This is usually because they are the only buildings remaining from deserted medieval villages, the inhabitants having been killed by the Black Death or driven off by economic necessity or a ruthless landowner. The church was probably the only building of stone in the village, and the houses built of wood have disappeared long since. Sometimes the churchyards have disappeared too, as at Pickworth, Leicestershire, where on ground known as 'the old foundations' only a

Clophill, Bedfordshire.
The churchyard is still in
se beside the long-ruined
church

single Gothic arch remains to identify the spot which moved John Clare to write an elegy on the ruins where

> The dust of many a long-forgotten grave
> Serves to manure the soil from whence it grew.

Archaeologists working at the deserted village of Wharram Percy in North Yorkshire discovered a large number of skeletons, clearly identifying the former churchyard during their excavations, but a more common occurrence is for the churchyard to remain around a completely ruined church, as at Clophill, Bedfordshire, and Layston, Hertfordshire, where what is left of the old church is still used as a cemetery chapel.

All churches did not automatically acquire churchyards in medieval times. The parish church at Market Harborough, Leicestershire, has never had a churchyard because it was founded as a daughter-church of Great

Bowden, where all burials took place long after Market Harborough had overtaken Great Bowden as an important market town. Many churches founded as chapels-of-ease (chapels built for communities which had grown up at a location too distant from the parish church for regular attendance) acquired their own graveyards as a result of the Black Death in 1349. The Bishop of Lincoln spoke to the parishioners of Great Easton, Leicestershire, of 'a mortality of men such as has not been seen or heard aforetime from the beginning of the world, so that the old graveyard of your church is not sufficient to receive the bodies of the dead'. The old churchyard belonged to the mother-church at Bringhurst, a mile away.

Where an ancient church has fallen into ruin or disrepair and a new one has been built a few yards away from it, the churchyard may still contain parts of the old one as well. Thus at Cheam, Surrey, the so-called Lumley Chapel, standing in the churchyard of the Victorian parish church of St Dunstan, is actually the chancel of the medieval church. At Walton, Suffolk, and Salthouse, Norfolk, lesser fragments of former churches remain, as is the case at Thorney, Nottinghamshire; but at Sand Hutton in North Yorkshire the ruins of the Norman church of St Leonard stand behind the nineteenth-century church of St Mary. There are Saxon foundations in the churchyard at Bockleton, Hereford & Worcester.

Eccleston, Cheshire, has the remains of an early nineteenth-century church which was demolished in 1900 to be replaced by a new church built by the Duke of Westminster, the lord of the manor, and at Thurstaston, Merseyside, a tower remains from a rebuilding of the old church in 1824, similarly displaced by a later model.

Two churches occupying one churchyard can be seen at Swaffham Prior, Cambridgeshire, and Antingham, Norfolk. At Swaffham Prior, the older of the two – St Mary's – is still in use, the other – St Cyriac's – having been repaired after falling into dereliction and now in use as a church hall. In medieval times the two churches served separate parishes which became one in the seventeenth century. A similar situation occurs at Antingham, where St Mary's is again the survivor, its neighbour St Margaret's being a ruin.

At Willingale, Essex, the churches of St Christopher and St Andrew occupy one churchyard and are both still in use, serving the adjoining parishes of Willingale Doe and Willingale Spain respectively. At Alvingham, Lincolnshire, two churches occupy a churchyard accessible only through a farmyard. The explanation of these occurrences is probably that the soil and underlying rock were judged the most suitable in the vicinity for bearing the foundations of such big buildings, so the churches were built alongside each other flanking the parish boundaries. Trimley, Suffolk, is a similar case, though there each church occupies its own churchyard, side by side. There used to be two churches in the churchyard at Wantage, Oxfordshire – the antiquary Leland commented

High on Brent Tor
stands the church of
St Michael of the Rock,
near Tavistock, Devon

The little forest church
of Oakwoodhill, Surrey

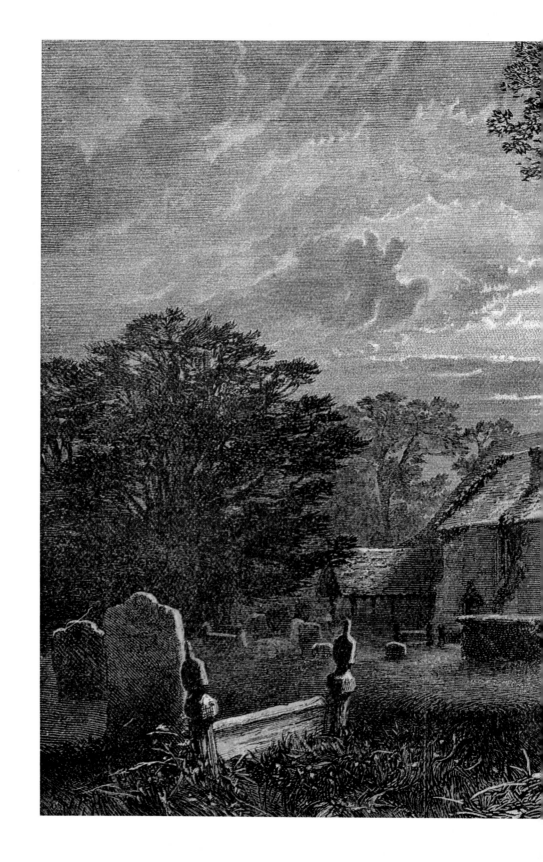

The scene of Gray's
Elegy. Stoke Poges
churchyard by
moonlight

An aerial view of St Enodoc, 'the church in the dunes',
Trebetherick, North Cornwall

on the fact. But one of these buildings was demolished in 1850, having served latterly as a grammar school.

Much more unusual – not to say bizarre – is the situation at Treyford, West Sussex, where there are two churchyards with not a single church between them. Treyford is a village on the South Downs between Elsted and Didling. The old church of St Mary was left derelict when, in the mid-nineteenth century, a large new church was built to serve all three villages. St Mary's was subsequently demolished, leaving only a few wall fragments in its small, overgrown churchyard. In due course, however, the new church of St Peter, which had been dubbed 'the cathedral of the Downs', was also razed to the ground, after 102 years, having become unsafe, and Elsted's old church was repaired and restored to take over the parish, leaving Treyford with two vacant churchyards.

Another churchyard without a church can be seen at Kinoulton, Nottinghamshire, where the original church on Kinoulton Wolds, above the village to the west near the Roman Fosse Way, was replaced by a more convenient church in the late eighteenth century.

The churchyards of ruined churches can be quite as interesting as those still in use. I recall hearing, as I approached the tiny ruin along a quiet lane at Bix Bottom, Oxfordshire, a murmur which I took to be the ghost of a long-dead incumbent preaching the gospel to a congregation of sparrows, but it turned out to be the local apiarist's beehives in the overgrown churchyard, where flattened headstones were buried beneath grass and weeds. You can feel these hidden gravestones beneath your feet at Dishley, Leicestershire, too. The agricultural pioneer Robert Bakewell was buried in the church that is now a forgotten ruin. A flock of pigeons took off from the conifers round it when I disturbed the ground there some years ago, and one of the half-buried gravestones had served as a sacrificial altar, for the feathers of one of the pigeons' brethren were strewn upon it, left there by a fox or the farmyard cat.

Many churchyards in England and Wales occupy positions which afford splendid views, but there is space to mention only a handful of them here. The view of Tintern Abbey from the village churchyard of St Mary's, on the hillside high above, is worth seeking out, while at Corfe, Dorset, the churchyard is the best vantage point in the village for looking up at the spectacular ruins of Corfe Castle. Villagers must have stood here aghast in the seventeenth century when Parliamentarian soldiers blew up the castle and great chunks of stone walls rolled down the hillside in clouds of dust and smoke.

The graveyard at Thorney, Cambridgeshire, is said to have been the scene of an event peculiar to the watery Fens in 1834. The ageing Thomas Telford had been at work supervising the drainage of the North Level, a large area of Fenland at the centre of which stood Thorney. The digging of new ditches took four years, but they were completed on a Sunday

morning, with dramatic results, and the news reaching the church during
divine service, the priest and the whole congregation rushed outside to see
the water, which had for so long been lying stagnant, suddenly beginning
to flow away.

The view from the churchyards of St Just-in-Roseland, Cornwall,
Ashingdon, Essex, and Selworthy, Somerset, are among well-known ones
in the south. The churchyard at St Just-in-Roseland occupies such
steeply sloping ground above a stream that the lych-gate stands above the
level of the church tower. The Midlands have Rockingham, Northamptonshire, and Hanbury, Staffordshire, overlooking the valleys of the Welland
and Dove respectively. In the north, Hawkshead, Cumbria and
Middlesmoor, North Yorkshire, are among the many churchyards
enjoying fine views.

The little churchyard at Culbone, Somerset, containing what is reputed
to be England's smallest church, lies in a deep wooded valley with a
stream tumbling beside it towards the sea, only a stone's throw away. At
Eyam, Derbyshire, the churchyard is beside the row of cottages where the

Sarratt, Hertfordshire.
The churchyard is some
distance from the moder
village which has migra
from its original centre

plague epidemic broke out in 1665, and contains the graves of some of those who died.

The obverse of this coin is, of course, that many churchyards in industrial areas are in surroundings which hardly assist any awareness of ground hallowed by centuries of religion and reverence for the dead. The churchyard at Goole, Humberside, is overlooked by dockyard cranes and buildings and the superstructure of ships. That at Burslem, Stoke-on-Trent, has surviving old bottle-ovens of the Potteries as its grimy neighbours. Many a churchyard in Greater Manchester has the shadows of cottonmill chimneys moving across it as well as that of the church

Old gravestones lined up at Paddington Green, London

steeple. Churchyards in South Yorkshire and chapel burial grounds in South Wales often look down on grim coal-mining scenes where religion came *after* the rise of capitalism, not before it.

Railways, too, have intruded on the clean peacefulness of many town churchyards. The one at Yarm, Cleveland, is overlooked by the great brick viaduct of forty-three arches built in 1849 to carry the railway across the Tees. The parish church of St Peter in Leeds is separated by the railway from the city centre, and part of the railway embankment is covered with old headstones from the churchyard. I retain a vivid mental image of a funeral in the Welford Road cemetery in Leicester, which is beside the main railway line to London. It was a foggy morning in November, and fog blanketed the noise of city traffic so that the world seemed to stand in reverential silence, but just as the minister was commending the departed soul to heaven, a train thundered past and carried it off, as it were, second class to St Pancras.

There are some more unusual sites for churchyards. At Gunwallow, Cornwall, the church is on the beach, built up against a rocky headland for protection from the sea, with an ancient cross and some headstones in its little churchyard. It dates from 1320 but there was another church here before it, built – it is said – in 570. At Dartmouth, Devon, ships used to tie up to the churchyard walls of St Saviour's, before new quays and embankments separated the church from the river bank.

At Dunwich, Suffolk, several churches, along with other buildings of the former cathedral city, have gone over the crumbling cliffs into the sea, the last only in 1904, when All Saints began to disappear from sight. Some old churchyard remains can still be found in the undergrowth above the beach, where pieces of masonry and occasional human bones are revealed by the tides.

The approach to a churchyard is often by means of steps or a short path from the town or village street, and so is unremarkable (though the forty steps leading up to the churchyard at Warmington, Warwickshire, deserve mention!), but there are plenty of more evocative approaches, sometimes by an attractive avenue, such as Nun Monkton, North Yorkshire, and Bredwardine, Hereford & Worcester. St Andrew's at Bredwardine was the church of the Reverend Francis Kilvert, the remarkable diarist, for the two years prior to his death in 1879, and he was buried in the churchyard. The avenue leading to it is best seen in spring, when the path is flanked by carpets of daffodils.

The path to the churchyard at East Coker, Somerset, passes a row of stone-built seventeenth-century almshouses and is the approach to the big house as well. T.S. Eliot's ancestors came from this village, and the poet made it the subject of one of his *Four Quartets*. The churchyard at Eccleston, Cheshire, has an avenue of lime trees leading to the porch, and yews flank the paved path to the porch at Woodchurch, Merseyside.

The many churchyards approached from village greens always seem to have an additional air of peacefulness about them, tucked away just a little more securely from the noise of modern traffic.

The actual enclosure of a churchyard is most likely to be by means of a stone wall in rural areas. It may be a dry-stone wall in western and northern England – pale limestone in the Cotswolds; darker sandstone in the Pennines; slate in the Lake District. Dry-stone walls of slate in

The timber lychgate at
Harpsden, Oxfordshire

herringbone pattern can be found surrounding churchyards in Cornwall, as at Tintagel.

Elsewhere walls may be of dressed stone with mortar joints, and in the south-east and East Anglia, possibly flint. In areas such as these, where there is little readily available stone, brick walls or iron railings may surround the churchyards. Stone walls are always best, weathering to complement the old churches themselves and gathering lichens and ivy as they age. One of the most unusual churchyard walls is at Titchmarsh, Northamptonshire – a ha-ha wall, separating the burial ground from the adjacent land but invisible except at close quarters. In the same county, the churchyard at Castle Ashby, beside the great house, has a monument in the wall itself, to the fourth Marchioness of Northampton. At Sonning, Berkshire, one wall of the churchyard is built largely of sixteenth-century bricks, from the former palace there owned by the bishops of Salisbury.

Notable railings surround the churchyards at Hampton Lucy, Warwickshire, and St Paul's at Bedford. The Hampton Lucy cast-iron railings came from the Coalbrookdale ironworks in Shropshire around 1825. Those at Bedford are older, and several fine eighteenth- and nineteenth-century iron gates still grace the entrances to churchyards around the country.

Starting in the south, the gates to St John's churchyard at Hampstead were acquired from the Duke of Chandos's palace at Stanmore, when it was sold in 1747 after the Duke's death. The splendid gates at Hatfield, Hertfordshire, are often said to have come from St Paul's Cathedral, part of a huge quantity of ironwork made in Sussex to Wren's order and eventually dismantled, mostly to be sent to Canada, only to sink to the bottom of the Atlantic when the ship was wrecked. There is no real evidence that these Hatfield gates were Wren's, however.

In Buckinghamshire the wrought-iron gates to All Saints churchyard at High Wycombe date from 1762 and came from Wycombe Abbey (which never was an abbey and is now a school). Somerset has some good gates, at Huntspill and Wincanton, those at Huntspill having been made at Coalbrookdale early in the nineteenth century. The gates at Abbey Dore, Hereford & Worcester, and a little farther north at Leominster, are of eighteenth-century wrought iron and nineteenth-century cast iron respectively, while in East Anglia gates at Woodbridge, Suffolk (St Mary's), and King's Lynn, Norfolk (St Nicholas), are worthy of note.

At Stapleford, Nottinghamshire, the churchyard's iron gate is Victorian and was brought here from Wellington College; but at Ashbourne in neighbouring Derbyshire the fine gates of wrought iron date from around 1700. It is not generally claimed that these gates are by the master of wrought-ironwork, Bakewell of Derby, but the one to the village churchyard at Foremark, south of Derby, is his. North Yorkshire has good iron gates at York (St Margaret).

It will be noticed that the majority of the fine iron gates mentioned here are in towns, as might be expected, but perhaps the most surprising story of churchyard gates concerns the rather more modest gates at Ayot St Lawrence, Hertfordshire. They are of wrought iron and were placed at the entrance to the churchyard from the village centre in 1948, though the church itself has long been a ruin. The occupant of the New Rectory was invited to unveil the new gates, and he did so with the words: 'This is His house, this is His gate, and this is His way.' Nothing very surprising about that, one might think, until learning that the speaker was the ninety-two-year-old sage George Bernard Shaw, who left in his will, two years later, a more characteristic note that he did not want to be commemorated by a 'cross or any other instrument of torture or symbol of blood sacrifice'.

The lych-gate by which a great many churchyards are still entered is an ancient invention taking its name from the Old English word for corpse – *lic*. The function of these covered gateways was to shelter a coffin and its bearers at the edge of consecrated ground while awaiting the arrival of the priest to conduct the burial procession. All lychgates would formerly have had a stone or timber ledge or shelf for the coffin to be rested on, but these have often been removed. The actual gates may be single or double, or – as at Chalfont St Giles, Buckinghamshire – a pivoted swing gate which is a great attraction to local children, blissfully unaware of the gloomy import of their plaything.

A number of medieval lychgates survive in more or less unaltered form. Beckenham (St George) and Boughton Monchelsea in Kent have examples of medieval carpentry, and the gate at Limpsfield, Surrey, dates from the fourteenth century. The lychgate at Hartfield, East Sussex, is an early sixteenth-century gate with a timber-framed cottage beside it, the upper floor of which is partly above the gate; and the gate of later date at Long Compton, Warwickshire, is actually inserted into the space made by removing part of the ground floor of the cottage above and beside it. At Llangennith in West Glamorgan the lychgate is carved with scenes from the life of St Cenydd, to whom the church is dedicated.

At Wendron, Cornwall, the lychgate has a little parish meeting-room built over it, while the consecrated ground at St Leven is protected by a cattle grid at the lychgate. Tintagel, too, has old cattle grids of granite at the entrances to its large, bleak churchyard, devoid of trees.

At Anstey, Hertfordshire, a tripartite fifteenth-century lychgate was altered around 1830 to convert a third of it into the village lock-up. The *Hertfordshire Mercury* of 1831 reported that, 'A few nights ago Thomas Edwards, a man confined therein for disorderly conduct in a public house, effected his escaped by pushing one side of the building down.' The report is dated 27 December – Tom obviously got drunk at Christmas. Perhaps the churchyard ghosts helped the ale to reinforce his strength. The rebuilt lock-up still stands there.

Isleham, Cambridgeshire, still has its medieval lychgate, as do Llanwarne and Whitbourne in Hereford & Worcester, while the modern church of All Saints at Brockhampton-by-Ross has a lychgate with a thatched roof, like the church itself. In Shropshire, Oswestry (St Oswald) and Clun have fine lychgates of the seventeenth and eighteenth centuries respectively, and there is a fine seventeenth-century gate at Burnsall, North Yorkshire.

Anstey, Hertfordshire. The lychgate with village lock-up attached

Notable lychgates of more recent construction can be seen at Dorchester, Oxfordshire; Thixendale, North Yorkshire, and Heaton Mersey, Greater Manchester.

As well as the traditional lychgates, iron gates and more modest and simple entrances to churchyards (including stiles in some places), there are a few slightly more unusual ways of entering consecrated ground. In Berkshire, for instance, St Nicholas's churchyard at Newbury is entered from the main street by two pointed archways; at Bray, a half-timbered medieval gatehouse with brick infilling guards the churchyard and was here when Symon Symonds, the most celebrated vicar of Bray, kept changing his religion from Papist to Protestant and back again to suit the prevailing Tudor climate, so as not to lose his living. Gatehouses like this, and cottages with lychgates incorporated in them, were usually built to provide a home for the church sexton or clerk.

Owston Ferry, Humberside, has an elaborate Victorian tripartite gateway of stone, and Thornton Hough, Merseyside, has a hexagonal modern gateway, designed in Norman style, to the Congregational churchyard (St George) built by Lord Leverhulme.

These, then, are some of the variations on the standard themes of churchyards – the boundaries, entrances, crosses, trees and situations that might provide one or more interesting aspects of almost any churchyard we care to enter in town or village. But even before we start to consider the graves and burial customs which are the whole *raison d'être* of churchyards, there are many other rather less obvious, and occasionally very surprising, contents and practices to consider.

2

Gatherings from Graveyards

Whether or not medieval archers cut their longbows from churchyard yews, God's acres came to be associated with several other more or less practical customs over the centuries, and remnants of some of them survive here and there. An annual ceremony called 'Clipping the Church', for instance, took place in many churchyards at one time, when parishioners joined hands to encircle the church itself and dance round it in a ritual derived from some pagan festival probably connected with ideas of purification and fertility, since it usually took place in the spring, at Easter or on Shrove Tuesday. The popular name of the ceremony may possibly result from a Christian re-interpretation confused with annual clipping of the churchyard yews. The ritual survives in a watered-down version at Painswick, Gloucestershire, and Guiseley, West Yorkshire, where local children dance round the churches in late summer. It has also been revived from time to time in two or three Midland villages.

The former tradition of eating 'puppy-dog pies' at Painswick – plum pies with little china dogs inside them like the coins in a Christmas pudding – lends support to the theory that 'clipping the church' is a relic of a Roman expiation ceremony called 'Lupercalia' which took place on 15 February and involved the sacrifice of a dog. The naïve Christian explanation at Painswick, however, is that so many crowds came to the village to watch the ceremony that the local inns had to resort to pies made of dog-meat to feed them!

Great Wishford, Wiltshire, is noted for an ancient churchyard custom observed on the Monday of Rogation Week, in which the grazing rights on land owned by the parish church are auctioned for the season. Shortly

...wering Sunday in a ...lsh churchyard in the ...eteenth century

51

The Smithfield Dole. Poor widows receiving sixpence and a hot cross bun in the
churchyard of St Bartholomew the Great, London

before sunset, the parish clerk walks up and down between the churchyard gate and the church door, carrying the key. Farmers bid for the rights while he does so, but the moment the sun disappears below the horizon, the clerk raps the gate with the church key, like an auctioneer closing the sale with his gavel, and the last bid before he does so is successful. What happens, however, when it is cloudy?

In some parts of Wales and western England, it was an old custom to dress graves with flowers on Palm Sunday. The occasion was known as Flowering Sunday (*Sul y Blodau* in Wales) and in earlier times graves were tidied and dressed on other days as well as Palm Sunday. It was an occasion for cleaning up graveyards generally, in preparation for the Easter festival, as if that were a time when it was important for the dead to be seen at their best. Large numbers of people gathered in churchyards on these days, and even the neglected graves of the forgotten were tended in the ritual revival.

Graveside doles were fairly common at one time, when benefactors concerned for the good of their souls willed that their posthumous hand-outs should be made at their gravesides. Twenty-one poor widows of the City of London used to receive sixpence each on Good Friday, over a grave in the churchyard of St Bartholomew-the-Great (London's oldest church) at Smithfield. The origin of this old charity was unknown in the nineteenth century, but it was updated by one Joshua Butterworth and is now called the Butterworth Charity.

The Borrington Dole, at Ideford, Devon, dating from 1585, provided for twenty poor people to be given a shilling each on Maundy Thursday, the receivers having to pick up their shillings from the benefactor's gravestone where the coins were laid in the presence of the rector.

These churchyard rituals were not, of course, examples of generosity without self-interest, designed as they were to ensure that those receiving charity should be mindful of their benefactors and remember them in their prayers, but some such doles had further strings attached. Poor boys at Wotton, Surrey, could benefit to the tune of 40 shillings each under the will of William Glanville, who died in 1717, provided they could recite the Lord's Prayer, the Ten Commandments and the Apostles' Creed, whilst standing in the churchyard with the palms of their hands laid on the benefactor's tombstone. They also had to read and write a passage from the scriptures. This ludicrous and indeed vile examination was meant to take place on the anniversary of the founder's death, 2 February, when the gravestone was liable to be icy cold and the churchyard deep in snow.

A rather more touching if mysterious legend is connected with the grave of Sir Harry Coningsby at Areley Kings, Hereford & Worcester. A five-foot block of sandstone nearby is inscribed with the words '*Lithologema Quaere? Reponitur Sir Harry*.' This curious mixture of Greek and Latin seems to mean something like 'If you seek a monument, here is Sir

The 'dole table' in the churchyard at Powerstock Dorset

Harry's'. Sir Harry is wrongly said to have left a request in his will that when the walnut trees were in fruit, local boys should crack the nuts on his tomb. Sir Harry had long before been the accidental cause of his infant son's death. He never fully recovered from his grief and died a recluse. The origin of this curious bit of folklore is lost, but the block of stone is known locally, at any rate, as 'the Coningsby Wall'.

At Powerstock, Dorset, the churchyard contains a thirteenth-century dole table, which looks at first glance like a table tomb. Gifts of bread used to be given to the poor of the parish from this slab. The BBC, in a programme broadcast some years ago, thought this village one of the least affected by the twentieth century but it is a sign of the times that the dole has been changed from bread to coal. Other dole tables occur at Potterne, Wiltshire; Dundry, Avon, and Saintbury, Gloucestershire.

Some wealthy people were cautious about such distribution because they feared abuse of the graveside dole, for it was by its very nature a fairly hit-and-miss method of ensuring that the poor received their due. Richard Clarke of Lincoln bluntly rejected any 'penny dole dolt for me at my burial', which took place in 1528, and asked instead that a hundred poor people be selected to receive a groat each. Protestants subsequently condemned the distribution of doles altogether, as 'superstitious and heathenical', but, of course, this did not put an end to them, any more than Protestant revulsion at the Popish symbolism of plants has prevented people today from putting wreaths of flowers on coffins and graves.

If the graves in the churchyards were the medieval villagers' books of local history and biography, the churches themselves were their books of art and philosophy, written, as it were, on stone, like the Mosaic Law, that the peasants might recognize their permanent values; for they could not understand the priest's Latin any better than the lord of the manor's French.

In regions where the local building stone lent itself to fine carving, masons and sculptors lost no opportunity to people the churchyards with symbolic figures looking down from the walls and towers of their buildings. God's acres were overlooked by signs which were not lost on the illiterate masses. Their meanings may often be obscure to us now, but they were not just art for art's sake – the parishioners were meant to learn moral lessons from them, and sculptors were given free rein in ramming the lessons home as dramatically or as humorously as they were able to do. Gargoyles and grotesque figures might serve practical architectural purposes as waterspouts to carry rainwater clear of the church walls, or as decorations on string courses, etc. They also represented well-known proverbs and folk sayings, or might be magic symbols to keep away evil spirits, or public mockery of the Devil and all his works. Masons and sculptors, as well as parsons and schoolmasters, were among the great educators of the populace, particularly in rural England, warning the village poacher of the nightmares of conscience, the village prostitute of the wages of sin, and the village idiot of the dangers of temptation. Nightmare images outside the church were doubtless intended to incite sinners to hasty repentance within and were thus a useful compromise by the early Church between the sacred new religion and the profane old beliefs.

A great many church exteriors have gargoyles and grotesques of wondrous variety, of course, but some specially interesting riots of uninhibited stone-carving overlook the churchyards of Adderbury and Bloxham, Oxfordshire; Chalk, Kent; Barnby Dun, South Yorkshire; Elkstone, Winchcombe and Aldsworth, Gloucestershire; Theddlethorpe (All Saints), Lincolnshire; Patrington, Humberside; Evercreech, Somerset. The gargoyles looking down on the churchyard at Braughing, Hertfordshire, have been described as 'grinning', though they seem to be shocked, rather, by the life they see going on beneath them. One of the old timbered cottages below was used by the village's poorer newly-weds for their receptions, and one room was specially reserved for the bridal bed.

Nowhere is there more vivid stone-carving than in the churchyard at Kilpeck, Hereford & Worcester. The outside of the Romanesque church is like a child's picture-book in which practically every picture is meant to teach as well as entertain. Dragons and serpents join with human figures and natural animals and birds in a riot of symbolic sculpture round the south door and the corbel table. A hare and a hound forsake their natural enmity, just as Isaiah says 'the wolf shall dwell with the lamb, and the leopard shall lie down with the kid'. There is a pair of figures which some say are wrestlers and others believe to be lovers embracing; more likely the latter, frowned upon and re-interpreted by the puritanical. Most famously, or notoriously, there is a 'sheela-na-gig', a female exhibitionist figure, perhaps intended as a warning against the sins of the flesh.

Gargoyle at Fairford, Gloucestershire

Kilpeck, Hereford &
Worcester. The
sheela-na-gig overlooking
the churchyard

Attempts to re-interpret this figure, which also occurs on several other churches in Britain, verge on the farcical. Grotesquely caricatured women, the figures are usually of hideous aspect, with legs wide apart and bent so that the hands can pass underneath to hold open an enormously exaggerated vulva. Victorian puritans were apt to describe them as men with holes in their chests, showing the way to their hearts!

The figures are often said to be Celtic, partly because they are found more frequently in Ireland, and the usual name for them is Irish, meaning 'Cecilia of the breasts', apparently, although breasts are their least evident attributes and the authenticity of the name is much doubted. In England, at any rate, the figures have often been called 'the idol' or 'the whore' and variously identified as the great Earth Mother, still furtively venerated by primitive Christians, like the standing stones we noticed earlier; as a protective device against the 'evil eye'; as a satirical figure holding up to ridicule the doctrine of the Immaculate Conception, and so on.

The 'sheela-na-gig' is probably a Saxon image readily perpetuated by the Normans among all the other reminders of eternal damnation and the tortures of hell which were intended to help in keeping the people in line. The proliferation of the figure by the Normans would explain its widespread appearance on castles in Ireland as well as churches. Many 'sheelas' were undoubtedly destroyed in the seventeenth century. Of the few that survive, a large proportion is tucked away among the hills of the Welsh Marches, where village churches in thinly populated areas escaped the attention of the zealous. Some of the remaining examples are *inside* the churches, but churchyards where the ever-open whore can still be found include (besides Kilpeck), Holdgate and Church Stretton, Shropshire; Whittlesford, Cambridgeshire, and Buckland, Buckinghamshire. At Whittlesford, the sheela is accompanied by an unidentifiable beast with erect penis. Many of these carvings are of different stone, or stone of different weathering, from that around them. That is to say, they are probably older than the churches themselves and have been set in these walls from earlier buildings or removed from other sites.

A rather different sort of paganism impresses itself on church-goers at West Wycombe, Buckinghamshire, where the hilltop churchyard of St Lawrence is overlooked not by strange medieval carvings but by a huge golden globe on the church tower. This site, too, was an Iron Age hill-fort (and is thick with yews), but the old church was rebuilt in the eighteenth century by Sir Francis Dashwood, Tory MP, sometime Chancellor of the Exchequer, and founder and chief priest of the so-called 'Hell-Fire Club'. The gilded sphere on the church was entered by an iron ladder and contained seats where Dashwood and his cronies held drinking-parties – 'the best Globe Tavern I was ever in', John Wilkes called it; but the poet Charles Churchill commented accurately on the church itself that it was

> A temple built aloft in air
> That serves for show and not for prayer.

Notwithstanding all this intimidating stuff, churchyards came in time to be used for village fairs and dancing. Morris dancers, though re-enacting a pagan ritual, were frequently to be seen performing in country churchyards with the incumbent's blessing, and although the Statute of Winchester, dealing with matters of public order in 1285, banned fairs and markets in churchyards, the customs were too deeply ingrained for the ban to have much effect, and in some places, such as parts of South Wales and at Laughton-en-Morthen, South Yorkshire, the local traditions were kept up into modern times. The churchyard was, after all, sometimes the only convenient place for community gatherings in villages with no green or square. Most space would usually be available on the north side of the church, for reasons we shall discover.

West Wycombe,
Buckinghamshire.
The golden globe on the
church tower

Apart from the annual fairs, a frequent excuse for revelry in the churchyard was the so-called 'church ale', commonly held at Whitsun but sometimes on other holidays during the year as well. It began as a means of raising money for the poor, repairing the church, supporting the priest and other such purposes, and was eventually made redundant by the introduction of parish rates. In 1497 a church ale at Bassingbourn, Cambridgeshire, raised over £14 towards the purchase of a new church bell.

The antique origins of the church ale were the 'love-feasts' (*agape*) whose purpose was to increase mutual love among rich and poor Christians alike, the rich providing for the poor in a community meal associated with the Lord's Supper. '*Agape*' comes from the Greek meaning 'brotherly love', but some participants soon put a broader interpretation on the event, their unseemly behaviour being condemned in the Epistle of Jude and by the Council of Carthage in 397. At the later church ales, the churchwardens provided ale which was sold largely for the benefit of the poor 'according to the Christian rule', as John Aubrey put it, 'that all festivity should be rendered innocent by alms'.

Church ales were not wholly affairs of Christian virtue, however, any more than their ancient models. The hanky-waving Morris men would do their routines, the villagers would elect a Lord and Lady, or King and Queen, of the Whitsun Ale, in an arbour made of branches and garlands in the churchyard, which they called the Summer Bower, or Robin Hood's Bower, and sometimes even a maypole was put up near the church door where village maidens danced and collected alms for the poor – all good old pagan stuff perforce tolerated by the Church until the seventeenth century – which inevitably led to country folk taking the occasion as a licence for drunken and bawdy merriment.

Some parsons took a dim view of this old custom, including the one at Storrington, West Sussex, who told his parishioners in 1623 that their expectation of bread and cheese and a barrel of beer on Easter Day after evening prayer was unlawful. And even before the Puritan purges, one Robert Deryck was hauled before the church court at Boughton, Nottinghamshire, for setting up a maypole in the churchyard. Still, as Sir Thomas Overbury wrote, the average parson 'allows of honest pastime, and thinks not the bones of the dead anything bruised, or the worse for it, though the Country Lasses dance in the churchyard after Evensong'.

Gossip has always been a by-product of the churchyard after the service inside the church, though Addison raised it to more dignified status in one of his essays on Sir Roger de Coverley: 'A Country-Fellow distinguished himself as much in the Churchyard, as a Citizen does upon the 'Change; the whole Parish-Politicks being generally discussed in that Place either after Sermon or before the Bell rings.'

Sports and games were also played in churchyards in the Middle Ages, in addition to the obligatory archery practice, and itinerant mummers and jugglers gave their performances in the churchyard if there was nowhere else. Wrestling, fives, marbles and even cock-fighting were popular churchyard pastimes in some places, and the village parson was not slow to join in if the mood took him. Alsop en le Dale, Derbyshire, was but one place where a cockpit existed in the churchyard, and Penrith, Cumbria, another, while several places in Wales had churchyard cockpits.

The ecclesiastical courts were clearly more zealous in some places than in others. Several men were condemned at Durleigh, Somerset, in 1623 for playing fives against the church wall on Sundays and holidays. In the previous year at Boxgrove, West Sussex, two old churchwardens were admonished for encouraging boys to play cricket in the churchyard, where they were liable to break the church windows and 'a little child had like to have her braynes beaten out with a cricket batt.' Churchyard football hooligans were dealt with at Great Baddow, Essex in 1598; and at Flamborough, North Yorkshire, in 1567 a man was censured for tossing the caber in the churchyard there. Churchyard tennis and bowls were both condemned at Stogumber, Somerset, in 1623.

Although the Church made increasing efforts to ban such unseemly activities not only from churchyards but everywhere else as well, particularly on the Sabbath, James I defended the people's customs with unarguable logic: 'For when shall the common people have leave to exercise, if not upon the Sundays and holidays, seeing they must apply their labour and win their living in all working days?' But the Puritan revolution threw a thick blanket of solemnity and gloom over the Sabbath, and the new look to an English Sunday survived the Restoration and lasted, in some respects, right up to the present.

Meanwhile, the ecclesiastical courts dealt harshly with moral offences committed in churchyards as well as elsewhere. Misdemeanour on consecrated ground was regarded throughout the Middle Ages as so heinous that the Church's abhorrence was reinforced by the State. An Act of Edward VI's reign introduced severe penalties for polluting holy ground with fighting and other offences, and a churchyard so affected became subject to an act of purification before another religious ceremony could take place in it. In Manchester a man was excommunicated in 1592 for talking in the churchyard during the sermon, and two other men were brought before the court for the same offence at Childwall in the same year.

Many culprits were ordered to do penance for offences such as brawling, drunkenness and swearing. (Dickens refers to such an incident in *David Copperfield* when David's friend Traddles is humiliated by the beadle before the congregation for supposedly laughing in church, though in fact the culprit was Steerforth.) Boys were brought before the courts for

The Village Pastor. This engraving, after a painting by W.P. Frith, depicts social intercourse in an eighteenth-century rural churchyard

breaking windows or roof tiles by throwing stones; the churchwardens presented parishioners for allowing their pets to make nuisances of themselves in the churchyards. At Porlock, Somerset, in 1623, a woman named Alice Sundell was excommunicated for 'easing herself in open show' in the churchyard, and in 1811 one Joseph Wiggins was presented in Oxfordshire 'for a Nucence a Privey neere the Churchyard' (this occurred at Pishill). In the churchyard at North Stoke in the same county, in 1584, Henry White got into trouble for 'runninge after maydens', and at Little Thurrock, Essex, and Minster, Kent, early in the seventeenth century, offenders put horns on or near the churchyard gates as indecent insults to couples getting married.

Sexual offences, needless to say, were the most shocking and the most severely punished. Minor offences might result in a fine or a penance, the offender, draped in white and holding a candle, having to stand in the church porch while fellow parishioners entered and left. But sexual offenders risked excommunication or physical punishment, such as being whipped whilst walking three times round the church.

Although the village stocks were probably used more by the lord of the manor and later by the secular courts, the church courts used them as well, and sets of stocks remain in or near several churchyards; for instance at Grappenhall and Ashton-upon-Mersey, Cheshire; Marsden, West Yorkshire; South Elmham St Margaret and Ufford, Suffolk; Cranworth, Norfolk; Harting, West Sussex, and Marsden, Kent; at St Leonard's church at Shoreditch, London, the stocks and whipping post are housed in a structure with a thatched roof. Parham, Suffolk, has preserved its stocks in the roof of the lychgate. In St John's Church at Hackney, London, as well as a whipping post there is the ducking stool on which malicious gossips were liable to be given an unpleasant drenching in the village pond, and at Tollesbury, Essex, the village lock-up is inside the churchyard.

At the same time, throughout the Middle Ages, the churchyard as well as the church was regarded as a sanctuary where fugitives from justice could linger with impunity, at least for forty days, as long as they did not commit sacrilege. If such felons went before the local coroner in sackcloth, confessing their guilt and promising to leave the country, they were free from arrest and trial. This procedure was known as 'abjuration of the realm', and only a royal pardon could permit the offender to return to his country. The ancient right of sanctuary lasted until the seventeenth century, when it was abolished under James I. Some places had rituals of sanctuary, like Ravenstonedale in Cumbria, where the fugitive had to ring the old church's 'refuge bell' before his pursuers caught up with him. Others had a 'frith' or 'frid' stool for the criminal to sit on, as at Chewton Mendip, Somerset; Hexham, Northumberland, and Beverley Minster, Humberside. But reaching the churchyard itself was sufficient in law to

Keeping the churchyard
grass down at Haworth,
West Yorkshire

ensure the fugitive's safety.

The maintenance of churchyard boundaries and paths was a matter of concern to the church authorities. At Tenterden, Kent, in 1502, the records show that pigs were getting in the churchyard because the fencing was inadequate, and offenders were frequently reprimanded here and there for some activity that blocked paths to the church doors. No paths through churchyards are public rights of way in law, unless recognized as such by ancient custom, and no right of way can be established through consecrated ground without a 'faculty', a dispensation granted by the Consistory Court on behalf of the bishop, who has jurisdiction over all churchyards in his diocese as far as ecclesiastical matters are concerned.

Some places customarily made local landowners responsible for maintaining the boundary walls or fences of churchyards, and as far apart as Shropshire and Sussex there remains evidence of this in the churchyards of Church Stretton and Cowfold (where the surrounding cottages turn inward towards the church). The wall in the one case and the fence in the other bears the names or initials of the householders responsible for the relevant section of the boundaries.

Despite the objection in principle to animals wandering freely over consecrated ground, it gradually became common for local incumbents to

Almshouses in the churchyard at Mancett Warwickshire

allow sheep or goats to be grazed in their churchyards to keep the grass and weeds under control, and although the church courts occasionally fined parish priests for allowing sheep, horses or cattle to defile graves, they generally relaxed their opposition to such practices after the Reformation, and some customers left requests in their wills that their graves should be protected from animals with brambles or withies. One such was Matthew Wall, of Braughing, Hertfordshire. The *Churchwardens' Guide* of 1895 was followed by the *Parson's Handbook* of 1932 in allowing that there could be no objection to sheep being put to pasture in churchyards, and the *Churchyards Handbook* of 1976 recommends sheep for keeping down churchyard grass, with geese or even cattle as other possibilities, or tethered goats as a last resort. Horses occasionally had the run of churchyards in some places. The vicar at Lydden, Kent, built a stable for his own horse in the churchyard in 1603, while at East Peckham there is still a building at the churchyard gates put up as stabling for parishioners' horses whilst they (the parishioners) were in church. Mounting-blocks or stones still remain at churchyard gates here and there, as at Exford, Somerset, and Adderley, Shropshire, and a stable and mounting platform still stand by the northern entrance to the churchyard at Wingfield, Suffolk.

At Itchingfield, West Sussex, there is a priest's house in the churchyard. It is a little timber-framed house of the fifteenth century and may have been built originally as a lodging for a priest who travelled there to conduct services before the village had its own incumbent. It was altered later and used as an almshouse. Itchingfield is not the only village with an almshouse in its churchyard. There is also one at Mancetter, Warwickshire, built there in 1728. At Abingdon, Oxfordshire, almshouses surround St Helen's churchyard on three sides.

The churchyard at Dale, Derbyshire, also has a house in it, this one attached to (or semi-detached from) the church, while Hemingstone, Suffolk, has a detached building mysteriously known locally as 'Ralph's Hole'. The legend is that it was built by a Roman Catholic, Ralph Cantrell, a member of an important local family, who declared that he would never go into a Protestant church. Since he stood to lose his property if he failed to attend church services, this little building apparently enabled him to observe the letter of the law without going back on his word.

Some churchyards have separate chapels or detached parts of church buildings in them, and even church towers are detached in one or two cases, usually because of marshy ground unable to support the weight of such structures. Elstow and Marston Moretaine in Bedfordshire are examples. Detached bell-houses occur at Pembridge, Hereford & Worcester; Middleton-in-Teesdale, Durham, and East Bergholt, Suffolk. The latter is a sixteenth-century timber structure with a steeply pitched tiled roof. The one at Pembridge is a spectacular three-tiered medieval tower, in the Scandinavian style, with a ground floor of stone and massive timbers supporting the structure inside.

Separate chapels can be seen at Bray, Berkshire; Bodmin, Cornwall, and Prestbury, Cheshire. The Prestbury chapel is the nave and chancel of the former Norman church. The one at Bray was a chantry chapel until the seventeenth century, when it became a school; and that at Bodmin is the ruin of the former chapel of St Thomas Becket, pre-dating the present church of St Petroc. This also was used as a school – a grammar school, in fact, which it only ceased to be in 1856.

In the days when the parish priest was the only literate member of a rural community, the church porch often doubled as a village school, and as the demand for education increased, and porches were no longer adequate, schools were built by the Church, often in close physical contact with the church buildings. The pride of a village in acquiring its own school is shown by the fact that schools were the only buildings which medieval villagers allowed to encroach on the communal preserve of the village green. Some parishes went further subsequently and built them in the churchyards.

Old village buildings such as cottages, almshouses and schools are commonly found adjacent to churchyards, but small church-school buildings occur *inside* churchyards at Wraxall and Old Cleeve, Somerset; Wythall, Hereford & Worcester; Felkirk, West Yorkshire, and Leyland, Lancashire, this latter being a seventeenth-century grammar school. The school at Felkirk is a sixteenth-century building and is believed to be the oldest church school in England. The one at Old Cleeve, opened in April 1911, was built of rubble stone with brick dressings at the expense of a long-time vicar, the Reverend William Newton.

In the churchyard at Brent Eleigh, Suffolk, is an even more unusual building – a former parish library. It was built in 1859 to house around 1,500 books which had been given to the village by Dr Edward Colman, Fellow of Trinity College, Cambridge, who also built the village almshouses. The books had been kept in the church at first, in an extension of the chancel. Alas, this unique later building no longer serves its original purpose, Dr Colman's library having been dispersed, some of the books going to the libraries of Cambridge, whilst the Bodleian at Oxford acquired for £6 an illuminated copy of the Gospels, dating from around 1000, which had once belonged to Queen Margaret of Scotland.

Another curious intrusion into some churchyards was the funeral shelter. This was a little shed, like a sentry box, called a 'hudd', and was intended to keep the parson dry, so it is said, during burial services in the rain. But as those few remaining are nearly all in eastern England, they no doubt also served to prevent the wind playing havoc with the leaves of his prayer-book. Lincolnshire has four of these shelters, at Deeping St James, Donington, Friskney and Pinchbeck. At Walpole St Peter, Norfolk, the fine church preserves an eighteenth-century hudd shaped like a sedan chair. Another parson's shelter is preserved at Odiham, Hampshire.

There are a great many other oddities to be found in churchyards throughout the country, among the most numerous being sundials. For some reason these seem to have been especially popular in the north of England (or, at any rate, that is where most have been preserved). Cheshire, in particular, has more than most counties. Sundials are often eighteenth-century relics, mounted either horizontally on pedestals in the churchyards or vertically on the wall of the church, usually above a doorway. Their use was more decorative and symbolic than practical by this time. Clocks were common, and you could tell the time by a sundial

The sundial on the church
wall at Eyam, Derbyshire

Sundial at Elmley Castle
village churchyard,
Hereford & Worcester

only during the day and when the sun was shining. The ubiquitous church
clock was soon to take over the sundial's function entirely, but they
remain as curious and sometimes very attractive churchyard ornaments.

A very ancient and simple 'scratch dial' at Stanton-by-Dale,
Derbyshire, was devised to tell villagers when it was time to attend church
for Mass and so on, but at Eyam in the same county there is a highly
complicated sundial, said to have been made by local people in 1775,
which shows the (approximate) time in various parts of the world as well
as giving assorted astronomical information. The scratch dial type is most
common in Gloucestershire and Somerset.

The sundial at Kirkdale, North Yorkshire, is justly famous because,
although it is by no means the only Saxon sundial remaining, it is the only
one whose date and origin are known fairly precisely (which dates the
church as well). An inscription on this dial, which is above the south door,
tells us that St Gregory's Minster was built anew from the ruins of the old
in the time of Edward the king (the Confessor) and Tostig the earl
(brother of King Harold). The date is thus around 1060. The names of two
priests, Haward and Brand, who made the sundial, are also recorded.

Most of the pillar sundials are relatively modern, and several of them
came to the churchyards from the gardens of country houses, where they

were fashionable ornaments in the eighteenth century. The one at Elmley Castle, Hereford & Worcester, is a case in point, though this is older and more elaborate than most of those in the north, such as at Ormskirk, Lancashire; Knutsford and Great Budworth, Cheshire, and Long Preston, North Yorkshire. At Bolton Percy, however, there is an interesting Elizabethan sundial, and at Edstone another, of ancient origin, made by one Othan, as the inscription records, again set over the south door of the church. Corhampton, Hampshire, and Daglingworth, Gloucestershire, are other places where the churchyards still have the passing hours shown by Saxon sundials, whilst that at Marsh Baldon, Oxfordshire, is a Norman job. Occasionally one also finds a sundial built onto an individual grave, as at Old Cleeve, Somerset.

The churchyard at Darrington, West Yorkshire, contains a former dovecote. As this dates only from the eighteenth century, it cannot have been meant to provide the parson with meat and eggs, as medieval dovecotes often were, so presumably it was thought a fitting accompaniment for the dead buried there. A beerhouse, on the other hand, was unequivocal in its purpose, and one was built in the churchyard at Datchworth, Hertfordshire, and was known as the Tilbury until it was demolished. It was the property of the parish, which paid ground rent to the Church – and even more convenient, for those who praise the Lord and drink to the Devil, than Westmill in this beery county, where the pub is right next door to the church.

Morwenstow, Cornwall. The ship's figurehead

The churchyard at Morwenstow, Cornwall, contains a ship's figurehead, on a slope overlooking the graves of many seamen. The Reverend R.S. Hawker was a poet as well as a clergyman – author of the famous poem with the refrain:

> And shall Trelawny die?
> Here's twenty thousand Cornish men
> Will know the reason why!

But he became locally more celebrated for his efforts to save the lives of sailors shipwrecked on this coastline, and the figurehead is that of the *Caledonia*, wrecked on the homeward voyage from Odessa in 1843.

Wells are to be found in a few churchyards, such as Whitstone, Cornwall, (where a notice tells you that you are at the entrance to God's Acre); Binsey, Oxfordshire; and East Dereham, Norfolk. The last-named contains the well of St Withburga, the daughter of a Saxon king, who founded a convent at the site and whose body, according to the Anglo-Saxon Chronicle, was found 'quite sound and free from corruption … fifty-five years after she departed this life'. The well, which George Borrow described as 'a mouldering edifice', is said to have begun as a spring on the spot where the saint's grave was rifled by the abbot and

The holy well in the
churchyard at Whitstone
Cornwall

monks of Ely in 984, and miracles were subsequently claimed for the water.

The well at Binsey is St Margaret's, and it used to be a place of pilgrimage on account of the spring having arisen in answer to the prayers of St Frideswide, the comely daughter of another Saxon king, and a performer of alleged miracles. Holy wells are two a penny in Cornwall, but St Anne's Well at Whitstone is in the churchyard there, shaded by a thorn bush which cannot be old enough to have been itself regarded as sacred like the famous Glastonbury Thorn. Hawthorn was regarded as an unlucky tree in Celtic quarters, oddly enough, though frequently associated with holy wells.

Medieval stone steps lead to St Hilda's Well in the churchyard at Hinderwell, near the North Yorkshire coast, while at Boldre, near the Hampshire coast, the hilltop churchyard has, by contrast, a modern memorial fountain.

In the churchyard at Bisley, Gloucestershire, is the only exterior example of a 'poor souls' light' in England. The thirteenth-century stone structure, twelve feet high, was built as a well-covering and was called 'the bonehouse' locally because a priest's body had been found in the well, causing the cover to be built. But later on, lighted candles were stood on it as Masses were said for the poor.

The churchyard at Dunwich, Suffolk, has the ruins of a Norman leper hospital, only the apse of the hospital chapel remaining. And in the churchyard at Great Chart, Kent, there is a pesthouse. This is a timber-framed building of the sixteenth-century and is single-storeyed, long and narrow. Pesthouses were medieval hospitals for victims of 'pestilence' – plague and other contagious or infectious diseases, and a churchyard seems a curious place to build one, notwithstanding that care of the sick was largely left to the Church in those days. As the pesthouses were places of last resort, however, the situation of this one saved transport problems when the dead were to be buried.

The very soil of the churchyard has been credited with magical properties. One Richard Foster was presented to an ecclesiastical court in London in 1497 for taking from the churchyard 'sanctified earth, that is turffes, otherwise called flagges'. We are not told what he claimed, in his own defence, they were required for, but oddly the case was dismissed. In Devon it was believed at one time that if you took three tufts of grass from a grave on the south side of a churchyard on St Mark's Eve at midnight, you might see your future in a dream, though if you dreamed of thunder and lightning you would have a life of misery, and if you failed to dream at all, the end result would be the same.

The Lollards, on the other hand – those heretical fourteenth- and fifteenth-century disciples of John Wycliffe – had strongly opposed the very idea of consecrated ground, and a Portsmouth man was presented

St Mary's, Bow, London

even in the seventeenth century for declaring that the churchyard was no holier than the common field. This heresy was roughly in line with the views of the Puritan iconoclasts, who were given licence at that time to smash all relics and idols, and zealously destroyed churchyard crosses and monuments as well as statues and other objects inside the churches.

Some churchyards were defiled by actual fighting during the Civil War, quite apart from the destruction wrought by fanatics. Cromwell's officers were apt to lock their Royalist prisoners in churches, or billet their own troops in them and tether their horses in the churchyards. Royalists were executed in the churchyard at Burford, Oxfordshire, in 1649, three men being put up against a wall and shot. Alton, Hampshire, saw a battle take place in and around the churchyard when in 1643 Colonel Boles and eighty men took refuge in the church from Parliamentary troops and fought to the last man. At Chapel-en-le-Frith, Derbyshire, in 1648, over a thousand Scottish prisoners were herded like cattle into the church and locked up there for more than a fortnight. When the church was opened, forty-four of the men were already dead, and more died soon after, and were buried in the churchyard.

Bisley, Gloucestershire. The Poor Souls' Light

We must not blame Cromwell and his men alone for such misuse of churches and graveyards, however. The church at Elmesthorpe, Leicestershire, had been used to billet Richard III's soldiers before the Battle of Bosworth in 1485, and Westonzoyland church in Somerset was used as a prison for captured rebels at the Battle of Sedgemoor in 1685.

Every region has its own folklore about Cromwellian damage to churches and other buildings – some true, some false, some merely exaggerated for dramatic effect – but at Alton you can still see the marks where bullets ricocheted off the church walls.

At Tunstall, Norfolk, villagers believed once that, if you put your ear to the ground in the churchyard at Christmas, you could hear the bells of an older church that had been swallowed up centuries ago in an earthquake. The present church is itself partly in ruins now, and in this region of so many lost villages it is hardly surprising that such legends have grown up to account for lingering folklore about earlier communities.

During the religious persecutions of the sixteenth century churchyards were often the scenes of spying and turmoil, as at Bow in east London, where the Protestant minister and his congregation of thirty were arrested in 1555 for holding a communion service. The minister, one Rose, was sent to the Tower. And Nonconformists caused scenes in churchyards later, as when the Countess of Huntingdon and a large assembly of her Methodist followers held an emotional service, conducted by George Whitefield standing on a tombstone, in the churchyard at Cheltenham in 1768, after they had been refused access to the church. John Wesley himself preached more than once in the churchyard at Epworth, Humberside, standing on his father's tomb, when he was refused permission to preach in the church. On one occasion in 1742 he spoke there for nearly three hours to what he called 'a vast multitude'.

Churchyards can be the repositories of all sorts of more or less predictable paraphernalia. Old stone coffins may lie about in areas where stone was more plentiful than timber, such as in Cornwall (e.g. at Crantock) and at Compton Pauncefoot, Somerset. At Adel, West Yorkshire, two of the three stone coffins in the churchyard were in use at one time as water-troughs for cattle.

Fonts and bits of stone and statuary, often removed from the church during restoration, may lie in a corner of the churchyard half covered with vegetation. There is a discarded font in the churchyard at Iffley, Oxfordshire, and at Sandringham, Norfolk, a ninth-century font of marble brought from the island of Rhodes – a royal present. At Pattingham, Staffordshire, a bust of an angel in the churchyard came from London, where it was discarded during rebuilding of the Houses of Parliament. At Newtown Linford, Leicestershire, there is a ledger stone with numbers and the letters of the alphabet inscribed on it. It may have been a practice piece for a mason's apprentice. At Ashford, Surrey, there is a slab in the churchyard marking the site where the chancel of the Norman church stood before the present Victorian building replaced it.

A block of stone which used to serve as a doorstep at Braunston, Leicestershire, was discovered to have a carving on the underside – the figure of a woman, possibly of Saxon origin, but probably even older. It now stands near the wall of the church and may be a primitive earth goddess worshipped long before Christianity came to these islands. A stone in the outside wall of the church at Copgrove, North Yorkshire, has a primitive figure carving on it, believed to be of Celtic origin, though this implies that the stone came from some earlier building, as the church itself is Norman.

Wedmore's churchyard in Somerset contained buried treasure for nearly a thousand years. In the nineteenth century a hoard of Danish coins was found underneath the base of the churchyard cross, hidden by someone for safety in the troubled period of conflict between Danes and Saxons. The coins are now in the British Museum.

In the churchyard of St Peter at Sandwich, Kent, there is a stone window, complete with tracery, dating from the fourteenth century, and originally part of the chapel of some local almshouses. At Ivinghoe, Buckinghamshire, the village firehook is still kept hanging on the churchyard wall. This is a long wooden pole with a massive iron hook at the end, used to pull burning thatch from cottage roofs before the days of fire-engines, to save as much of the buildings as possible and prevent fire spreading in the wind to other houses.

The churchyard toolshed at Collingham, West Yorkshire, has a Norman arch built into it, while at Kirk Ella, Humberside, there are bits of a Norman doorway in the churchyard. At Naseby, Northamptonshire, there used to be a large copper ball in the churchyard (kept inside the church since 1980, when it fell off its base). It apparently came from Boulogne in the sixteenth century and was put on the spire which was added to the church around 1780. This curious object has given rise to such useless information as that it holds sixty gallons of ale.

Weddings, at least, brought more than a little gaiety to the usual sombreness of the churchyard, and of course the Puritans objected to this too. The musicians accompanying the bride and groom to the church, and the grain which the guests threw over them after the ceremony, were alike objectionable to the Protestant fanatics of Cromwell's time. Long custom prevailed, however. Wheat grain was eventually replaced by rice and paper confetti, but the thought remained – an old fertility rite like strewing the path with flowers and producing a chimneysweep for luck. Of course, the happy bride and groom avoided entering or leaving the churchyard by the lychgate, unless it was the only way, because of its association with death.

Confetti, of course, presents problems to those responsible for churchyard maintenance, particularly where there are gravel paths. People throwing ordinary litter and rubbish into churchyards can be dealt with under the same laws that seek to protect *all* public places from 'litter louts', but only the incumbent and the parochial church council can decide whether they will allow confetti to be thrown at weddings. Most do, in spite of the pagan origins of the custom, because the Church is necessarily wary of alienating its flock in trying to stamp out time-honoured customs.

Female fertility figure in the churchyard at Braunston, Leicestershire

The day-to-day upkeep of churchyards is often done by parish volunteers these days, but churchwardens keep contingency funds for necessary specialist work, such as drainage and tree-surgery. Local authorities often take on a share of the responsibility for financing churchyard upkeep, if not actually carrying out the work themselves.

Before photographers came along, painters provided views of churchyards which are, on the whole, more reliably descriptive than the fanciful reveries of the poets. Gainsborough's 1748 painting of St Mary's Church at Hadleigh, Suffolk, shows a churchyard with few monuments and two donkeys in it, and a sundial over the porch, which is not there now. Constable did several designs in the 1830s purporting to show 'Stoke Pogis' church for an edition of Gray's 'Elegy', but they are not accurate, and he probably took them from earlier engravings without visiting the scene. His studies of East Bergholt Church, on the other hand, are numerous and reliable, and one drawing shows the churchyard with the grave of his parents in the foreground, a low chest tomb surrounded by iron railings.

Churchyards both real and imaginary appear in the pictures of the

Pre-Raphaelites. Perhaps the best known is the painting in the Ashmolean Museum at Oxford called *Home from the Sea* by Arthur Hughes, showing a sailor-boy with his sister at their mother's graveside. This was based on the old churchyard (All Saints) at Chingford, Essex, before it fell into ruin.

Rather different – in fact, sensationally so – is the representation of the churchyard at Cookham, Berkshire, in Stanley Spencer's *Resurrection, Cookham* in the Tate Gallery, in which the dead are seen coming out of their graves and Christ stands in the church doorway. 'Places in Cookham seem to be possessed of a sacred presence of which the inhabitants are not aware,' Spencer once said. They were not aware of the erotic presence, either. The dead rise in a macabre orgy here, and the artist's wife Hilda puts in more than one appearance.

3

Ghosts, Graves and Robbers

The melancholy associations of churchyards were the inspiration of many poets of the romantic period, Thomas Gray's 'Elegy Written in a Country Churchyard' being merely the most famous and enduring:

> Beneath those rugged elms, that yew-tree's shade
>   Where heaves the turf in many a mouldering heap,
> Each in his narrow cell for ever laid,
>   The rude Forefathers of the hamlet sleep.

Whether it was Stoke Poges in Buckinghamshire where Gray thus mused among the headstones has been disputed, but most believe it to have been, and the churchyard has consequently become perhaps the most visited in England.

Robert Blair's 'The Grave' and Edward Young's 'Night Thoughts' were the precursors of the 'graveyard school' of poetry to which Gray made his contribution and which continued through the nineteenth century with works such as Warren de Tabley's 'The Churchyard on the Sands' and some of the verse of A.E. Housman and Rupert Brooke.

Poets were sometimes carried away by their imagination into absurd errors, as when Housman wrote of Hughley steeple (there is none), and when Matthew Arnold wrote his poem 'Haworth Churchyard' as a lament for the early death of Charlotte Brontë, saying that the grass 'blows from their graves to thy own', when in fact Charlotte was buried inside the church. But the genuineness of the feelings of poets for churchyards and their associations with man's mortality is evidenced by the number of

Stoke Poges, Buckinghamshire. A view from the lychgate

81

poets who have chosen to be buried in them (see the Appendix). Churchyards, like ruins, fuel the dreams of poets, being a source of the Sublime as defined by Edmund Burke: '... whatever is in any sort terrible, or is conversant with terrible objects, or operates in a manner analogous to terror ... is productive of the strongest emotion which the mind is capable of feeling.'

Shakespeare rather anticipated this in the last scene of *Romeo and Juliet*, which he set in a churchyard:

> *Paris:* Give me thy torch, boy: hence, and stand aloof:
> Yet put it out, for I would not be seen.
> Under yond' yew trees lay thee all along,
> Holding thine ear close to the hollow ground;
> So shall no foot upon the churchyard tread,
> Being loose, unfirm, with digging up of graves,
> But thou shalt hear it: whistle then to me,
> As signal that thou hear'st something approach.

Romeo, intent on joining Juliet in her tomb, addresses it as:

> Thou detestable maw, thou womb of death,
> Gorged with the dearest morsel of the earth,
> Thus I enforce thy rotten jaws to open,
> And, in despite, I'll cram thee with more food!

But the tragedy descends into final absurdity when the senior Montagues and Capulets hold an impromptu inquest into the deaths of their respective offspring and, with dead bodies strewn about all over the place, shake hands to end their long and destructive enmity – an extreme case, if ever there was one, of shutting the stable door after the horse has bolted.

Romantic prose made one or two churchyards famous, such as the one at Oare in Somerset, which features in R.D. Blackmore's *Lorna Doone* and rivals Stoke Poges as a tourist attraction, but the majority of churchyards in fiction exist only in the imagination of authors intent on conjuring up intimidating settings for ghost stories or such-like, as in Sheridan le Fanu's *The House by the Churchyard* or the opening paragraphs of Dickens' *Great Expectations*, when young Pip comes face-to-face with the convict Magwitch:

'Hold your noise!' cried a terrible voice, as a man started up from among the graves at the side of the church porch. 'Keep still, you little devil, or I'll cut your throat!'

A fearful man, all in coarse grey, with a great iron on his leg. A man with no hat, and with broken shoes, and with an old rag tied round his head. A man who had been soaked in water, and smothered in mud, and lamed by stones, and cut by flints, and stung by nettles, and torn by briars; who limped, and shivered, and glared and growled; and whose teeth chattered in his head as he seized me by the chin.

'O! Don't cut my throat, sir,' I pleaded in terror. 'Pray don't do it, sir.'

And Pip watches the fiend departing through the churchyard after their deal, 'as if he were eluding the hands of the dead people, stretching up cautiously out of their graves, to get a twist upon his ankle and pull him in.'

Wilkie Collins made effective use of an imaginary churchyard in *The Woman in White* – clearly churchyards rather preyed on people's minds in the middle of the nineteenth century.

Towards its end Jerome K. Jerome was able to poke a little gentle fun at the morbidly-inclined in *Three Men in a Boat*:

Harris wanted to get out at Hampton Church, to go and see Mrs Thomas's tomb.

'Who is Mrs Thomas?' I asked.

'How should I know?' replied Harris. 'She's a lady that's got a funny tomb, and I want to see it.'

I objected. I don't know whether it is that I am built wrong, but I never did seem to hanker after tombstones myself. I know that the proper thing to do, when you get to a village or town, is to rush off to the churchyard, and enjoy the graves; but it is a recreation that I always deny myself. I take no interest in creeping round dim and chilly churches behind wheezy old men, and reading epitaphs. Not even the sight of a bit of cracked brass let into a stone affords me what I call real happiness ...

Harris, however, revels in tombs, and graves, and epitaphs, and monumental inscriptions, and the thought of not seeing Mrs Thomas's grave made him crazy. He said he had looked forward to seeing Mrs Thomas's grave from the first moment that the trip was proposed – said he wouldn't have joined if it hadn't been for the idea of seeing Mrs Thomas's tomb.

By 1922, James Joyce could write his splendidly unromantic, unsentimental passage on a Dublin funeral in *Ulysses*, recalling the irrelevant and irreverent thoughts of the mourners on their journey to Glasnevin cemetery, reflecting on arrival that the deceased 'Got here before us, dead as he is.' All the clichés and superstitions about death are introduced into this riotous episode paralleling Homer's Hades. It includes a story about two drunks who wander about the place in the fog looking for the grave of their friend Mulcahy. When they find it one of them gazes at the statue of the Saviour put up by the widow and exclaims: 'Not a bloody bit like the man. That's not Mulcahy, whoever done it.'

The church and part of the churchyard at Combe Florey, Somerset, showing the difference in ground level between one and the other

And among Bloom's macabre musings is the reflection that it would save space if they buried them standing (as indeed pagan Ireland did in fact bury its monarchs and warriors), but the heads 'might come up some day above ground in a landslip ...'

By the beginning of the nineteenth century, the state of English churchyards, especially in the towns and cities, had begun to cause much concern. The rise in population, combined with the effects of the Industrial Revolution, increased the pressure on urban churchyards to a level of genuine alarm among health authorities.

Not that the nineteenth century crisis was the first time some church authorities had had to face problems of overcrowding. The number of fatalities from the Black Death in 1348-9 is generally reckoned to have been of the order of $1\frac{1}{2}$ million in England and Wales. These people were not all buried in churchyards: mass graves were sometimes dug in the common fields. But the churchyards must have received most of them, and at Worcester, for instance, further burials had to be forbidden in the cathedral graveyard because of congestion. The bishop was considering the dangers to the health of the living from 'the corruption of the bodies' when he arranged for a new graveyard to be opened some distance away, to serve the local parish churches as well as the cathedral.

The Victorian crisis was of a different order, however – not the overwhelming short-term problem caused by an unprecedented disaster but the mounting pressure of a rapidly rising population, which would continue to increase without any foreseeable let-up.

The population of England and Wales, which was about nine million in 1800, increased fourfold during the course of the century, and there was at the same time a huge migration from the country to the towns. The spread of industrial slums, combined with gin-drinking and inadequate sanitation, among other things, outweighed advances in medical knowledge. Hence the urban death-rate soon became more than the town churchyards could reasonably cope with.

The unwieldy title alone of one publication is enough to convey the tone of medical opinion: George Walker, a surgeon, published in 1839 *Gatherings from Graveyards, Particularly those of London, with a concise History of the Modes of Interment among different Nations, from the earliest Periods, and a Detail of dangerous and fatal Results produced by the Unwise and revolting custom of inhuming the Dead in the midst of the Living.* Walker founded a Society for the Abolition of Burial in Towns, but he was far from the first to be aware of the problem. As far back as the early eighteenth century a Church of England vicar had published pamphlets on the 'Indecent and Dangerous Custom' of burial in churches and churchyards and its 'Pernicious Consequences to the Living'.

Charles Dickens skilfully sketched the condition of a mid-century churchyard in *Bleak House*: ' "There!" says Jo, pointing, "Over yinder,

among them pile of bones, and close to that there kitchin winder! They put him very nigh the top. They was obliged to stamp upon it to git it in. I could unkiver it for you with my broom, if the gate was open. That's why they locks it I s'pose," giving it a shake. "It's always locked. Look at the rat!" cries Jo, excited. "Hi! Look! There he goes! Ho! Into the ground!" '

As drunken gravediggers buried coffins in shallow soil, cholera epidemics swept through London four times between 1832 and 1866, and many feared that churchyards were the chief cause. Open sewers and the absence of piped water permitted matter from decomposing bodies under the ground to seep into streams and wells. George Walker referred to black flies emerging from coffins in vast numbers in warm weather and infesting a chapel where children attending Sunday School soon christened them 'body bugs'. Dickens wrote in *The Uncommercial Traveller* that 'rot and mildew and dead citizens' formed the uppermost scent in London's churches, where the 'decay of dead citizens in the vaults below' produces 'a strong kind of invisible snuff', so that when 'we stamp our feet to warm them ... dead citizens arise in heavy clouds'. Sir Edwin Chadwick concluded from his influential investigation into the country's sanitation that, 'All interments in towns, where bodies decompose, contribute to the mass of atmospheric impurity which is injurious to the public health.'

France had long before forbidden further burials in its city churchyards, but in England in 1843 the journal *The Builder* could still refer to '50,000 desecrated corpses ... stacked in some 150 limited pits of churchyards' every year in London, 'and one talks of decent and Christian burial ...'

The problem was by no means confined to the large cities. The Reverend Patrick Brontë's churchyard at Haworth, in the West Riding of Yorkshire, was overloaded with decomposing corpses which gave much concern to health inspectors investigating the village's alarming death-rate. Brontë himself read the burial service over many Haworth children who had died before they were six years old, and the condition of the churchyard came in for criticism along with the insanitary conditions the villagers lived in. The local habit of covering graves with flat stone slabs inhibited the process of decomposition, which is aided by air in contact with the soil, and Charlotte Brontë wrote that the churchyard was 'so filled with graves that the rank weeds and coarse grass scarce had room to shoot up between the monuments'.

Heptonstall, another hilltop weaving village not far away, had an overcrowded churchyard with re-used headstones, engraved on both sides. Gravestones pave the floor of the old ruined church, and coffin lids are said to have formed the stairs of a former charnel-house uncovered there in 1960. (Paving with old headstones is a local custom also to be seen at St John's churchyard in Leeds and at other places on either side of the

nsecrated Ground. An
astration by Phiz for
eak House

87

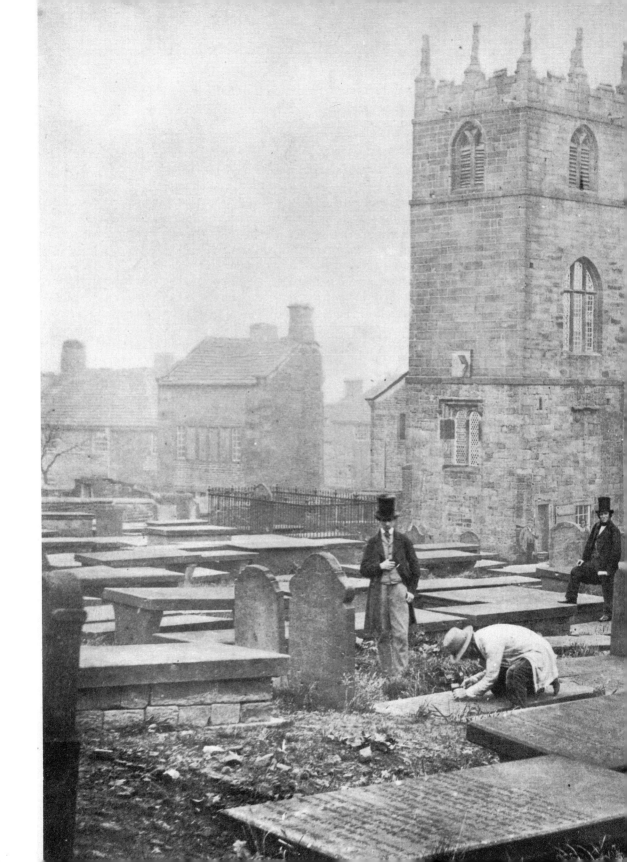

Haworth churchyard,
c. 1875

Pennines.) The damp and cold of northern England may have occasioned the grim metaphor of the 'churchyard cough' for the bronchial spluttering which hinted at the sufferer already having one foot in the grave.

The situation was not wholly different even in small rural churches at the end of the nineteenth century. As Flora Thompson remarked in her book *Lark Rise*: 'The cold, damp, earthy odour common to old and unheated churches pervaded the atmosphere, with occasional whiffs of a more unpleasant nature said to proceed from the stacks of mouldering bones in the vault beneath.'

The charnel-house, a building or vault in which bodies or unearthed bones were piled up, was an even greater cause of worry to health inspectors than the overcrowded churchyard. Often it was a part of the church crypt, but sometimes it was a special building situated in the churchyard. A medieval charnel-house with a chapel above it remains, covered in ivy, in the churchyard at Mildenhall, Suffolk, on the south side of the church. Another, more recent, can be seen in the parish churchyard of St Nicholas at Deptford, London.

Croyland, Lincolnshire, and Stratford-on-Avon had separate charnel-houses at one time, whilst at Hythe and Folkestone in Kent the church crypts for centuries contained bones said to be those of Saxons and Britons killed in battle in the fifth century. The charnel-house at Stratford, demolished in 1799, was reached from inside the church by a door in the north wall of the chancel, near the tomb of William Shakespeare, on which is the famous verse:

> Good frend for Jesus sake forbeare,
> To digg the dust encleased heare;
> Bleste be ye man y spares these stones,
> And curst be he yt moves my bones.

The lines are commonly supposed to have been written by Shakespeare himself (on an off day, presumably) as a plea that his bones should not be thrown into the charnel-house when subsequent burials uncovered them, as was the custom; but the curse prevented his widow being buried in the same grave, as she had wished, because no one dared to disturb it.

John Aubrey tells us that Sir John Birkenhead, the seventeenth-century poet, journalist and Member of Parliament, stated in his will that he wished to be buried in the churchyard of St Martin-in-the-Fields, not inside the church, for much the same reason – that 'they removed the bodies out of the church'.

Perhaps fear of disturbance was the reason for Samuel Butler's request that his grave should be six feet deep. The poet and satirist, author of *Hudibras*, died in poverty in 1680, but his wishes were observed when he was buried in the churchyard of St Paul's, Covent Garden, and his bones lay in peace at least until the churchyard was eventually levelled.

Aubrey says that the largest charnel-house he ever saw was at Hereford Cathedral and that a poor old woman lived in it, using bones as part-fuel for her fire. Alewives were said to mix bone-ash into their ale to make it intoxicating.

Not all writers who went into print about churchyards were intent on condemning their condition. Some turned them to distinct advantage, even in Victorian times, and the churchyard came to loom large in the Gothick novel, which succeeded the graveyard poetry of the earlier period. Mary Shelley's Dr Frankenstein pursues his studies in churchyards, dabbling among the 'unhallowed damps of the grave', and obtains his materials from charnel-houses. In *Dracula*, Bram Stoker accurately describes St Mary's churchyard at Whitby, where the bloodthirsty Transylvanian Count makes his first appearance in England:

> Between [the abbey] and the town there is another church, the parish one, round which is a big graveyard, all full of tombstones. This is, to my mind, the nicest spot in Whitby, for it lies right over the town, and has a full view of the harbour ... It descends so steeply over the harbour that part of the bank has fallen away, and some of the graves have been destroyed. In one place part of the stonework of the graves stretches out over the sandy pathway far below ... The steps are a great feature of the place. They lead from the town up to the church; there are hundreds of them – I do not know how many – and they wind up in a delicate curve; the slope is so gentle that a horse could easily walk up and down them.

Mary Shelley's story reminds us of the gruesome realities of body-snatching, Bram Stoker's of the absurd superstitions about suicide, which die hard, so to speak. St Augustine condemned it as a crime, and in the Middle Ages the Church regarded suicide as murder, yet despite Hamlet's lament that the Almighty had 'fix'd His canon 'gainst self-slaughter', there is nothing in the scriptures specifically forbidding suicide. The self-sacrifice of Samson in the Old Testament and Jesus in the New are in no way condemned, and the suicide of Judas Iscariot is not reported as compounding his crime but as a measure of the degree of his guilt.

Nevertheless, suicides were refused Christian burial from the sixth century onwards and were buried instead at crossroads with stones on their faces, to prevent evil spirits rising from them, or with stakes driven through their hearts, to prevent their turning into vampires. The idea of the crossroads location was to confuse the evil spirit's sense of direction! The so-called Ratcliffe Highway murderer, John Williams, was buried with a stake through his heart at Whitechapel on the last day of 1811, having hanged himself in his prison cell, and this method of burying a suicide was used as late as 1823 at Chelsea, when a man named Griffiths was buried thus within a stone's throw of Buckingham Palace; for it was only in the following year that England felt safe enough from vampirism and evil spirits to remove the necessity of burying suicides in this way from the statute book.

Grave robbery was a different matter entirely – a nightmarish reality in some areas, more especially in the vicinity of cities which could boast medical schools needing fresh corpses for dissection. No hair-raising tales of the dead dreamed up by imaginative writers could be as ghastly as the real horrors that occurred in the period of the 'sack-'em-up men'. Burke and Hare became notorious in Edinburgh because they actually murdered people in order to sell their bodies to the agents of Dr Knox, but elsewhere in Britain there were those ready to do the harder work of digging up freshly buried coffins at midnight and delivering the corpses to the anatomists for a suitable consideration.

A man at Whitwell in Hertfordshire stole and sold the body of his grandmother, on the grounds that it was more fitting that he, rather than some complete stranger, should have the money.

Such exhumation was not always that much of a labour, especially in city churchyards so overcrowded that there was a permanent stench of decomposition and gravediggers *had* to be drunk, like hangmen, to do their job at all, penetrating the foul soil to a depth of only a couple of feet. 'How long will a man lie i' the' earth ere he rot?' asks Hamlet, and the gravedigger replies, 'I' faith, if a' be not rotten before a' die ... a' will last you some eight year or nine year ...' But the town graveyards were too full to wait that long before one body was buried on top of another, and so many more corpses were 'knock'd about the mazard with a sexton's spade' in Victorian times than in Shakespeare's. Sextons were frequently bribed by the 'resurrection men'. Shallow burials provided other materials, too, for robbers other than the suppliers of anatomists' subjects, for bones were regularly stolen for grinding down to be sold as manure, and coffins were dug up to be used as firewood. Dogs could unearth human bones and drag them into the streets to gnaw away the flesh.

Gravediggers themselves were not beyond stealing the metal fittings from coffins before the graves were filled in. Not that grave-robbery was an invention of modern Britain, of course. The crime had been a by-product of inhumation since the ancient Egyptians had buried their dead pharaohs with all sorts of desirable riches, and in the time of the Emperor Constantine one of the grounds on which a woman could obtain a divorce was if her husband was a grave-robber.

In England, the desecration of graves was done on some occasions by both Church and State, as an act of religious or political symbolism. John Wycliffe, for instance, was buried in consecrated ground at Lutterworth in 1384 and dug up as a heretic forty-three years later, his remains being

arblington, Hampshire.
One of the watch huts
ected in the churchyard
to guard against
grave-robbers

burnt and his ashes thrown into the River Swift. And at the dissolution of the monasteries the remains of Richard III were exhumed from the church of Leicester's Grey Friars and thrown into the Soar. The body of Robert Shalder was dug up from the churchyard at Croft, Lincolnshire, in the seventeenth century: he had been imprisoned for his Nonconformism and died not long after his release, but his Christian enemies were not content to let him rest in peace. Modern criminals set no precedents in dishonouring the dead.

Even in 1817 strong feelings could lead to equally strong action, for in that year a farmer of Mockham, in Devon, was buried in the parish churchyard after lengthy soul-searching by the curate and his bishop as to whether it was proper, for the farmer, Joseph Gould, had been a Baptist. All might have passed without much comment if a friend of his had not put up a headstone, without the curate's permission, proclaiming Gould's membership of the Baptist denomination. Soon afterwards the smashed headstone was found lying in the road. Local folk immediately suspected it was the Devil's work, but it was more probably the sexton's. At any rate, a loyal old employee of the late Mr Gould was so incensed that he said, 'If they won't have master's stone in the churchyard, be damned if they shall have his body, either!' He and another man went to the churchyard one night and dug up the coffin, carrying it away by horse and cart to a Baptist chapel a mile or so distant, and re-burying it beneath the chapel floor, where it was allowed to remain.

Church authorities tried to combat the modern menace by erecting sheds or huts in their churchyards where volunteers could keep watch at night to protect graves from desecration, for a freshly buried corpse was likely to turn up on a dissecting table within twenty-four hours in some places if not guarded. Something of the sort seems to have happened to the Reverend Laurence Sterne, author of *Tristram Shandy*, who was buried at Bayswater, London, in 1768 and made a dramatic reappearance a few days later on the table of the Professor of Anatomy at Cambridge, who had acquired the corpse from body-snatchers and begun to dissect it when somebody recognized the face of the celebrated novelist.

In Hertfordshire in 1824 the corpse of a farmer, John Gootheridge, was found lying in the churchyard at Codicote where he had been buried a few days before. Grave-robbers had been disturbed at their work before they could stuff the body in a sack and make their getaway. The late Mr Gootheridge was buried again.

A few churchyard watch-huts survive. In London one remains at St John Horselydown in Bermondsey, beside Tower Bridge Road, built in the late eighteenth century but altered since. Another remains at Wanstead, Essex. There is a set of two watch-huts at Warblington, Hampshire – one small hut built of flint and brick at each end of the churchyard. This locality must have been a favourite haunt for the gruesome traders, to warrant such elaborate measures. Did the resurrection men in this vicinity supply subjects for teaching naval surgeons at Portsmouth?

In the north, Doddington and Morpeth churchyards in Northumberland have early nineteenth-century watch-huts. Where on earth did bodies stolen from here go to? From Morpeth to Newcastle, perhaps; but did Doddington corpses travel fifty miles across the border to Dr Knox's school in Edinburgh? Surely the price the robbers got would scarcely justify the labour cost of carting their conspicuous loot such a distance? It must be added, however, that there was also an export trade in corpses between towns linked by regular sea routes.

Other measures were employed occasionally to foil churchyard robbers. Some graves had iron railings erected round them as deterrents, and *mort-safes* – locked iron coffin covers – became fashionable, especially in Scotland, for a time. These contraptions were hired out until corpses were too old to be dug up for anatomical research, and then withdrawn from the graves for use elsewhere. Another device was to place a massive stone on the grave until it was safe from robbers. A 'body-snatchers' stone' survives in the graveyard of the Unitarian church at Frenchay, Avon, and there is another, called the 'resurrection stone', at Pannal, North Yorkshire.

Some people left bequests to pay for their protection from the fiends and the anatomists. Thus the tomb of a lady who was buried in 1773 at

Henham, Essex. The 'body-snatchers' cage'

Sutton, London, is still formally inspected once a year to satisfy public conscience that it has not been robbed! But the poor were at the mercy of others. In 1784 the master of a workhouse, a surgeon and another person were convicted of conspiracy when they were found to have arranged for the body of an inmate to be dissected.

95

It was only when the methods of Burke and Hare showed signs of appearing in London, with the murder in 1831 of a thirteen-year-old boy by two resurrectionists named Bishop and Williams, that the law took steps to place the study of anatomy on a respectable footing. Four years earlier a Select Committee of the House of Commons had been set up to enquire into the problem of teaching anatomy when only the corpses of executed criminals could be dissected legally, and the supply fell far short of the demand – hence the trade in grave-robbing. Sir Astley Cooper, President of the Royal College of Surgeons, told the committee that hospital patients were in danger of being operated on by surgeons ignorant of anatomy because of the shortage of subjects.

In 1829 Henry Warburton, MP, who had headed the Select Committee, introduced a Bill to Parliament aimed at preventing the unlawful disinterment of human bodies and regulating the study of anatomy. But the Commons debate produced a great deal of antagonism to the idea of dissecting human subjects at all. Some Members thought the dissection of animals was adequate, and one proposed that suicides should be added to the supply of victims of the death penalty.

The Bill was withdrawn and a new one presented in 1831, which became law early in the following year. It licensed qualified anatomists and appointed inspectors, and provided for executors, keepers of workhouses and such-like to assign bodies of which they had lawful possession for anatomical dissection, at the same time abolishing the practice of using the bodies of criminals for demonstration. The Act put an end to grave-robbing by providing surgeons with legitimate means of learning their science.

The grave-robbing trade provided Robert Louis Stevenson with the subject for one of his earliest stories, *The Body-Snatchers*, published fifty years after the new Act and set in the old churchyard (kirkyard) at Glencorse, a few miles south of Edinburgh.

Increase in medical knowledge helped to relieve the pressure on town churchyards by gradually reducing the death-rate, especially the high rate of infant mortality. But the greatest release came in the second half of the nineteenth century with the creation of public cemeteries and the growing taste for cremation.

Not that the desecration of graves ended entirely. In 1869 there was the famous occasion when Dante Gabriel Rossetti exhumed the coffin of his wife Elizabeth Siddal in Highgate Cemetery, in order to recover the manuscript of some poems he had rashly buried with her seven years before. The deed was done at night with the permission of the Home Secretary, by the light of a bonfire. The book had to be soaked in disinfectant and then dried page by page.

One of the famous cases of legal exhumation was that of Annie and Walter Palmer, the wife and brother of Dr William Palmer, from the churchyard of St Augustine at Rugeley, Staffordshire, in 1855. Walter Palmer had been buried in a lead coffin because of the rapidity of decomposition after his death, and no conclusive evidence of foul play was found, but Annie Palmer's body contained antimony and helped to convict her husband of wilful murder, for which he was duly hanged.

It was believed once that a corpse exhumed in connection with a suspicion of murder would itself incriminate the guilty by signs of life. Four defendants in a murder trial at Hertford in the seventeenth century were required to go to the churchyard where their alleged victim, a woman, had been dug up, a month after her death, and laid on the grass. Each of the men had to touch the corpse, 'whereupon the Brow of the dead, which before was of a livid and carrion colour, began to have a dew or gentle sweat arise on it, which increased by degrees, till the sweat ran down in drops on the face; the brow turned to a lively and fresh colour; and the deceased opened one of her Eyes, and shut it again three several times: she likewise thrust out the Ring or Marriage Finger three times, and pulled it in again, and the Finger dropt blood upon the Grass.' In days when more outrageous stories than this were taken seriously by the gullible public, there was no reason why the wink of a ghost should not be enough to condemn a man to death.

Nowadays the Home Office or the local coroner may order exhumation by the police when foul play is suspected, but otherwise bodies can be disturbed only with the granting of a 'faculty' (see p.65) by the church authorities for some valid reason, such as that a body has been buried by mistake in the wrong grave space.

The Towns Improvement Clauses Act of 1847 specified that there must be at least thirty inches of soil between the lid of a coffin and the surface of the ground, and this is always the legal minimum, but local regulations dictate varying depths, such as three, four or five feet. This gives gravediggers quite a job, especially in hot, dry summers when the soil is hard, but they are rarely glimpsed working in the nude these days, as depicted on Richard Shelley's sixteenth-century monument in the church at Patcham, East Sussex!

A widespread fear at one time was of being buried alive, and when gravediggers dug up skeletons which they said were lying in unusual positions, this only confirmed people's dread of being buried before they were really dead. 'All I desire for my own burial,' said Lord Chesterfield, 'is not to be buried alive.' Even a vicar, Richard Orme, succumbed to this fear, being buried in a chest tomb, in the churchyard at Essendon, Hertfordshire, with a door in it, the key being deposited inside the coffin with the body.

That the fear was not entirely without foundation was observed by those shocked gargoyles at Braughing (p.56), which saw the body of Matthew Wall, sixteenth-century farmer and ancestor of his afore-mentioned namesake, being brought for burial. When the bearers dropped the coffin, the 'corpse' woke up and banged on the coffin lid. Released by the startled, not to say thunderstruck, bearers, he lived on for many more years.

Satanism and witchcraft have naturally been much associated with churchyards, as well as the more common ghost tales. James I's Witchcraft Act made it a crime to 'take any dead man or child out of his or her grave ... to be employed or used in any manner of Witchcrafts, Sorcerie, Charm or Enchantment', but witchcraft has surfaced from time to time, even up to the present day. People with inverted crosses and all the trappings of the Black Mass are reported every so often in the popular Press, as in a Bedfordshire churchyard in 1963, when graves were rifled, bones arranged in the ruined church and a cock sacrificed. When a churchyard in Sussex was desecrated in the following year with magical signs scrawled on the walls of the church, the rector pronounced a formal curse on the desecrators but removed it when the damage was secretly repaired during the following night. Journalists and TV cameramen swarmed to the catacombs in Highgate Cemetery in 1970 when there were reports of black magic, satanic rites and even vampirism having occurred there. It was because of sensational media publicity that this part of the famous cemetery was closed.

Early in 1986 graves were smashed in the churchyard of St Mary at Totnes, Devon, with signs of black magic rituals; and residents at Barnstaple have petitioned the council recently to have a cemetery better protected after damage to monuments by vandals.

People all over the country have added their own sense of shock and outrage to that of the folk of Merthyr Tydfil revealed by a BBC documentary film *No Place to Rest* on the recent goings-on at Cefn Coed cemetery. Staff and council officials were sacked after human bones

Fourteenth-century ches
tomb at Loversall, South
Yorkshire

turned up on the surface and led to the discovery of a number of distressing violations of the law of the land, including graves that were much too shallow.

Damage to churches by vandals, rather than dabblers in the occult, has led to a great many churches being locked nowadays, but there is little that can be done to protect the churchyards. Vandalism in a churchyard at Hinckley, Leicestershire, many years ago, elicited some very un-Christian sentiments from the incumbent.

Damage due to natural causes is always seen as an Act of God by some, and associated with sinfulness or a feeling of guilt on the part of individuals or the whole parish. Imagine the horror at Husbands Bosworth, Leicestershire, when lightning struck the church steeple one evening in 1755, splitting it open for thirty feet of its length and hurling shattered masonry into the churchyard, one block falling on a grave which had only just been filled in after a burial.

When the church tower of St Chad at Shrewsbury suddenly collapsed in a thunderous roar and a cloud of dust early one morning in 1788, to the astonishment of two passing chimneysweepers, it was undoubtedly an omen to the superstitious, but the disaster had been forecast only a few days before by the young civil engineer Thomas Telford, who had advised the church wardens that the danger of subsidence due to shallow foundations had been aggravated by ill-advised grave-digging too close to the church walls.

In the Welsh borderland, an omen connected with the churchyard was known as the 'corpse candles', when ghostly lights were seen moving from a house where a death was soon to occur, to a spot in the churchyard where the grave of the doomed person was to be dug. George Borrow reported in *Wild Wales* a conversation near Llangollen with a woman who had seen a corpse candle:

'When a person is to die his candle is seen a few nights before the time of his death.'

'Have you ever seen a corpse candle?'

'I have, sir; and as you seem to be a respectable gentleman, I will tell you all about it. When I was a girl I lived with my parents, a little way from here. I had a cousin, a very good young man, who lived with his parents in the neighbourhood of our house. He was an exemplary young man, sir, and having a considerable gift of prayer, was intended for the ministry; but he fell sick, and shortly became very ill indeed. One evening when he was lying in this state, as I was returning home from milking, I saw a candle proceeding from my cousin's house. I stood still and looked at it. It moved slowly forward a little way, and then mounted high in the air above the wood, which stood not far in front of the house, and disappeared. Just three nights after that my cousin died.'

'And you think that what you saw was his corpse candle?'
'I do, sir! what else should it be?'

The eve of St Mark (24 April) was associated, as we noticed in the
previous chapter, with ghosts and magic, one belief being that the ghosts
of those due to die during the succeeding twelve months would walk in the
churchyard at midnight. In parts of northern England, you were supposed
to keep vigil in the church porch at midnight for three years running and
saw the ghosts only in the third year (though presumably those who had
started their watch two years before you would see the doomed in your
first year, and could thus save you the trouble). James Montgomery
described how

> ... when the midnight signal tolls,
>   Along the churchyard green,
> A mournful train of sentenced souls
>   In winding sheets are seen.
> The ghosts of all whom death shall doom
>   Within the coming year,
> In pale procession walk the gloom,
>   Amid the silence drear.

This belief survived until the nineteenth century. That it was vaguely
associated with witchcraft is shown by the record of the presentment of
Katherine Foxgale, of Walesby, Nottinghamshire, before the ecclesiastical court in 1608, charged with 'watching upon St Mark's Eve at night
last in the church porch to presage by devilish demonstration the death of
some neighbours within the year'. The local witch expected to be invited
to funerals, and it was her right as a parishioner to be included in the
share-out at graveside doles. If she was left out, she would be inclined to
cast spells against those whose responsibility it was to invite her.

Some said the ghosts came into the churchyards to look at the sites of
their as-yet-undug graves. If the sexton kept watch as well, he could no
doubt buy his wife a new spring outfit on the strength of his financial
expectations from grave-digging.

These beliefs were pagan in origin and bear some relation to the
superstitions about All Souls' Eve (1 November), when the spirits of the
dead were said to leave their graves and return to this world for a brief
reunion with the living. Country folk were so terrified of this annual event
that they used to leave food and drink to pacify the ghosts, and burning
candles to light their way. In some parts they cooked special 'soul cakes'
for the occasion. It was the beginning of the Celtic new year and of the
winter season, and a time of many supernatural occurrences. Belief in the
rising of the dead on All Souls lingered on in some parts until the Second

Elizabethan magician Dr
John Dee and Edward
Kelly raising a ghost in
Walton-le-Dale,
Lancashire, 1581

'He ... beheld a crouchin[g] object beside a newly made grave.'
An illustration from Wilkie Collins' book *The Woman in White*

World War, a survival of a widespread tradition that souls in Purgatory were released for forty-eight hours on All Hallows Eve, but this was only a Christian interpretation of the much older pagan festival of the dead.

No one expected the placatory drink to have disappeared by morning, as children expect the refreshment left for Santa Claus to have been consumed. For as W.B. Yeats explained:

> ... it is a ghost's right,
> His element is so fine
> Being sharpened by his death,
> To drink from the wine breath
> While our gross palates drink from the whole wine.

There have been widespread superstitions, eventually passed down to children as feats of daring, that to run three times, or seven, or twelve, round a certain grave, cross or tree will raise the Devil or make the ghost of a dead person appear, and other ghost stories connected with churchyards are legion, of course, mostly surviving from the days when ghosts, like witches, were implicitly believed in by the population at large.

Witchcraft, magic and science were almost inextricably linked in the Tudor period, and nowhere was superstition more deeply embedded than in Lancashire. The churchyard at Walton-le-Dale is associated with the attempt of the charlatan Edward Kelly to raise the dead, necromancy being only one of the sorcerer's arts he and his associate, the mathematician and astrologer Dr John Dee, were credited with. Dee himself was frequently consulted by Queen Elizabeth and chose the date of her coronation, as the most auspicious according to the stars. Magic formulae of the time often involved human bones and soil from churchyards, and the raising of spirits – eventually made a capital offence, if you please – was taken seriously by some, and mocked by others:

> Shall I make spirits fetch me what I please,
> Resolve me of all ambiguities,
> Perform what desperate enterprise I will?
> Marlowe, *Dr Faustus*

> 'I can call spirits from the vasty deep.'
> 'Why, so can I, and so can any man;
> But will they come when you do call for them?'
> Shakespeare, *Henry IV*, Part I

The churchyard might generally be regarded as a sacred and peaceful place during daylight hours, but it took on a whole new meaning at night, as Hamlet remarks:

> 'Tis now the very witching time of night,
> When churchyards yawn, and hell itself breathes out
> Contagion to this world.

The former churchyard of the Franciscan Greyfriars in London's Newgate Street was said to be haunted by Edward II's queen, Isabella, 'the She-Wolf of France', who was buried there. Greyfriars Passage and King Edward Street still flank the site where Wren built his Christ Church later, but both church and graveyard have gone since the Second World War, when presumably the ghost was bombed out too. The ghost of Mary Fitton, the lady-in-waiting to Queen Elizabeth I, whom many believe to have been the 'dark lady' of Shakespeare's sonnets, is said to have been seen in and around the churchyard at Gawsworth in Cheshire, near her former home.

Some graveyards are traditionally believed to have secret passages beneath them, usually passing from the church crypt to some other ancient building. One such is reputed to run underground from the ruined Ivychurch Priory near Alderbury, Wiltshire, to the Green Dragon inn, and to be haunted by monks. Some of these legends are no doubt connected with the Elizabethan persecution of Catholic priests, when hiding-places and escape routes were made in many buildings both religious and secular.

Another subterranean passage was believed to run from St Mary's Church at Bow in London, which occupies an island site in the middle of the High Street, to Bromley Palace, a hunting lodge built for James I some distance from the church. Bromley Palace was demolished at the end of the nineteenth century, but the passage of so much local legend was proved to exist. It did not go to the church but did pass close to the north side of the churchyard, and a stone coffin was found in the part that was excavated. Furthermore, a part of it collapsed near the north-west corner of the churchyard beneath a van passing on the road above it.

Body-snatchers and black magicians were not the only ones to brave the haunted darkness of churchyards at night. In coastal villages, smugglers often used the church as a safe and convenient place to hide their contraband after bringing it ashore. It is hardly surprising that gravediggers should be among the retailers of churchyard ghost stories, but it is said that resurrection men were also fond of recounting horrific tales to deter people from going near churchyards at night, though probably grave-robbers themselves were scared off by ghosts occasionally.

Knowlton, Devon. The ruined church showing the ancient circular site surrounded by a ditch

Bridell church, Gwynedd, with its large and dramatic Dark Age grave slab

Home from the Sea:
Arthur Hughes's
painting of an orphaned
sailor boy in Chingford
churchyard, Surrey

Churchyard yews at
Painswick,
Gloucestershire

Cross and churchyard
at Snowshill,
Gloucestershire

At Radwinter, Essex, a gang tried to frighten away the unpopular parson by faking ghosts in his churchyard. Sightings of phantom funerals were commonplace, feared as omens of real deaths to come. Dorset, for instance, has tales of phantom funerals associated with Milborne St Andrew, Marnhull, Powerstock and Broadwindsor, to mention only a few, the mourners and pall-bearers usually appearing headless. Stratton St. Margaret in Wiltshire has an old legend about a phantom coach and horses which are said to hurtle past the churchyard wall, though one might think even the Four Horsemen of the Apocalypse would hesitate about galloping in the vicinity of Swindon.

Alexander Pope's ghost is said to haunt the church at Twickenham as a result of his skull having been exhumed for examination by a phrenologist. (The skull of Robert Burns was also removed from his grave in St Michael's churchyard at Dumfries, when it was opened for the burial of his wife, so that a cast of it could be taken.)

Dickens described a City churchyard which he called 'St Ghastly Grim' in *The Uncommercial Traveller*. The spiked iron gate had skulls and crossbones on it, in stone, with spikes projecting above the skulls as if they were impaled, and seeing the gates in a thunderstorm, Dickens said they had 'the air of a public execution', the skulls seeming to 'wink and grin with the pain of the spikes' as the lightning flashed.

The laying of a churchyard ghost was best done by the incumbent and several of his neighbouring colleagues standing on the spirit's grave holding Bibles and lighted candles and praying like mad. This was the method adopted at Northenden, Greater Manchester, where the wailing ghost of a crooked shopkeeper was apt to come out of his grave in the churchyard when there was a full moon. The *modus operandi* was a variation of the ceremony of excommunication by bell, book and candle in the Catholic Church.

Many dark deeds have been done under cover of respect for the dead. In the reign of William and Mary the French are said to have captured and plundered Lundy Island by the simple ruse of bringing a coffin full of arms and ammunition to the churchyard on the pretext of desiring to bury a dead naval officer in consecrated ground.

Certain graves have attracted notoriety, superstition or morbid veneration, like the tombstone to Richard Smith in the churchyard at Hinckley, Leicestershire. Smith was a young saddler who was killed by a recruiting sergeant in 1727, and local people were quick to notice that 'tears of blood' appeared on his monument. The phenomenon was actually due to the friable sandstone used, for it appeared only in wet weather!

Lore about death, funerals and churchyards finally passed down to children as ghoulish jokes and skipping-rope rhymes, chanted with youthful bravado, in the modern climate of emancipation from benighted

verleaf: Romsey
hurchyard, Hampshire

terrors when, in any case, death seems very remote to youngsters of school age:

> There was a woman all skin and bone
> Who lived in a cottage all on her own.
> She thought she'd go to church one day
> To hear the parson preach and pray.
> When she got to the wooden stile,
> She thought she'd stay and rest awhile.
> When she reached the old church door,
> A ghastly ghost lay on the floor.
> The grubs crawled in, the grubs crawled out
> Of its ears, eyes, nose and mouth.
> Oh you ghastly ghost, she said,
> Shall I be like you when I am dead?

And in popular song, too, the subject has escaped taboo as music-hall entertainment:

> In the corner of the churchyard where the myrtle boughs entwine,
> Grow the roses in their posies fertilized by Clementine.

Though not in BBC circles, where the song 'Ain't it Grand to be Blooming Well Dead', among others, has been banned from the airwaves.

How different all this is from the tear-jerking efforts of adults like Wordsworth and Dickens in relation to children and death. From the false premise that 'origin and tendency are notions inseparably co-relative', Wordsworth deduced that, because children are inquisitive about where they came from, they also 'meditate freely upon Death and Immortality'.

Oscar Wilde said, 'One must have a heart of stone to read the death of Little Nell without laughing', and the same goes for Wordsworth's lines about a little girl whose brothers and sisters are buried in the churchyard close to her home:

> And often after sunset, sir,
>   When it is light and fair,
> I take my little porringer,
>   And eat my supper there.
> My stockings there I often knit,
>   My kerchief there I hem:
> And there upon their graves I sit –
>   I sit and sing to them.

Charles and Mary Lamb also exploited the churchyard in like vein, as a scene of repellent sentimentality in their children's story *Mrs Leicester's School*. It is a wonder Hollywood has never bought the film rights!

How refreshing after such mawkish sentiment to turn to the macabre satire of that poetic nineteenth-century doctor Thomas Lovell Beddoes, who proposed in his *Death's Jest Book* that:

After all being dead's not so uncomfortable when one's got the knack of it. There's nothing to do, no taxes to pay, nor any quarrelling about the score for ale. And yet I begin shrewdly to suspect that death's all a take-in: as soon as gentlemen have gained some 70 years of experience they begin to be weary of the common drudgery of the world, lay themselves down, hold their breath, close their eyes and are announced as having entered into the fictitious condition by means of epitaphs and effigies. But, good living people, don't you be deceived any more: It is only a cunning invention to avoid paying poor's rates and the reviewers. They all live jollily underground, and sneak about a little in the night air to hear the news and laugh at their poor innocent great-grandchildren, who take them for goblins ... which is at best only a ridiculous game of hide-and-seek.

The superstitions and vague apprehensions felt by many people in churchyards are remnants of the collective unconscious of 10,000 years of human bemusement about death. The incomprehension of primitive peoples gave rise to all sorts of dreads and rituals which have gradually been built up into a system of half-belief that lets fragments rise to consciousness like bubbles when we loiter in churchyards. And we have only to enter these 'cities of the silent' (as the Moslems of Afghanistan called their burial grounds) by moonlight, for repressed thoughts to come surging to the fore. Are the dead merely lying there quietly, listening for our footsteps to pass? We see the cold, dark gravestones lined up almost like living things themselves; the shadows casting strange shapes around them; devoid of all sound except perhaps the wind murmuring softly and causing the trees to stir and sigh a little; and it is enough to make our hair stand on end and our flesh creep, not because anything is happening or is going to happen, but because the situation taps that well of unconscious lore from which we cannot escape, since it is part of our being, and our imagination responds to it so predictably that story-tellers have been exploiting it for centuries.

4

The Business of Burial

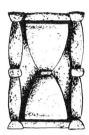

Those who profit financially from burial of the dead include timber merchants, quarry-owners, carpenters, monumental masons, funeral directors and gravediggers. But it is chiefly the quarrymen and masons who have made the churchyard what it is – a repository of memorials to the dead of the last two or three hundred years, full of absorbing interest to local historians, connoisseurs of stone-carving, collectors of epitaphs, and seekers of the last resting-places of the famous.

When it became customary for almost everyone to have a memorial in the churchyard, during the course of the eighteenth century, local quarries provided the material where stone was readily available, and where it was not, it had to be transported by sea, road or canal and was a laborious and costly business. Later on, with the coming of the railways and the popularity of certain types of more easily available stone, churchyards became jungles of monuments of assorted shapes and various colours, but in the earliest decades of personal memorials the English churchyard was a place of considerable restraint and good taste, with headstones and monuments in materials that matched the walls of the church itself, more often than not, and in which the dead, their monuments and the sentiments expressed on them, were all local products.

A good place to see the effect of this local uniformity is the churchyard of Stoke-sub-Hamdon in Somerset, where church, tombs, cross and headstones, as well as the churchyard wall and gate, are all of the local buff-coloured limestone from the quarries of Ham Hill, with very little in the way of alien intrusions. For a startling contrast in colour, see the dark

elaborate cast-iron
b of the Baldwin
ily at Madeley,
opshire

111

An unusual mosaic headstone in the churchyard at Madeley, Shropshire

brown ironstone chest tombs in the churchyard at Banbury, Oxfordshire.

This kind of matching stonework is far from common today. Churchyards will contain bodies that were buried far from home, with monuments of Welsh slate or Italian marble above them, inscribed with memorial lines that are not original. As Thomas Hood observed in 'Our Village':

And close by the church-yard, there's a stone-mason's yard, that when the time is seasonable
Will furnish with afflictions sore and marble urns and cherubims very low and reasonable.

112

The first individual monuments with inscriptions on them, as opposed to prehistoric grave mounds over unidentified dead, were introduced by the Romans and are known as *stelae*, and although none remains in Christian churchyards, several can be seen in museums; for instance at Carlisle, Colchester and the British Museum. The stones are usually decorated with ornamental borders and sometimes have crude images of the deceased carved in relief. The Latin inscription on a Roman tombstone at Chester translates as follows: 'To the spirits of the departed, Atilianus and Antiatilianus, aged 10, Protus, aged 12; their master, Pompeius Optatus, had this set up.' The three children were slaves and almost certainly British. About 1,500 years later, in 1720, a British master erected a monument to his Negro servant in the churchyard at Henbury, Bristol. The inscription to Scipio Africanus, who was eighteen when he died, reads: 'I who was born a pagan and a slave, Now sweetly sleep a Christian in my grave.' The look of the modern English churchyard owes almost as much to pagan Rome as to Christianity.

Some Anglo-Saxon, Danish and Norman headstones are also preserved in museums and occasionally inside churches, as at Whitchurch, Hampshire, and Wensley, North Yorkshire; but in the north of England Viking tombstones known as 'hogbacks' can still be found in some churchyards, dating from the ninth century. These are long stones which covered the graves, with curved tops, and are carved with ornamental patterns and serpents significant in Norse mythology. The churchyards at Penrith and Crosscanonby in Cumbria have examples, while another of later date, perhaps early eleventh century, is in the church at Brompton-in-Allerton, North Yorkshire; other fine specimens of ninth- and tenth-century grave slabs are in the churches of Levisham and Melsonby.

Celtic crosses were also set up as individual memorials and can be seen, for instance, at Llantwit Major, South Glamorgan, and in Cornwall along with the local variants of hogback stones.

Medieval graves often had stones at both head and foot with coffin-slabs or 'ledgers' between them. These covered the stone coffin which was let into the ground only to a depth where its top edges were flush with the level of the soil. But only the better-off could afford stone coffins, which were hewn out of solid blocks. Some people were buried in wooden coffins, but most were buried directly in the soil in shrouds of cloth or perhaps leather, tied at head and foot.

Only ecclesiastics were buried inside churches in the early medieval period, but the rich and important were buried inside during the later Middle Ages, in alabaster or Purbeck 'marble' tombs. The taste for well-designed and lasting monuments gradually spread to other classes of society, buried outside, however, and from the thirteenth and fourteenth centuries the quarries that were supplying stone for the great rebuilding of churches were also providing material for tombs and headstones in their own localities, while the styles of monuments were becoming increasingly diverse, from simple grave-markers with circular heads on tapered shafts, which were probably just rammed into the soil, to elaborate chest-tombs like the one at Loversall, South Yorkshire, dating from the fourteenth century, which resembles a flat-roofed church building in miniature, with traceried windows of various design, as if copied by the mason from a pattern-book of the period. There were also the first signs of identification of the dead person's trade or profession, with a sword and shield carved on the gravestone of a knight, or the implements of a weaver.

Coped stones and chest-tombs of pre-Reformation date are relatively rare, but examples of the type can be seen in the churchyards of Sutton Courtenay, Oxfordshire, and Buckden, Cambridgeshire. By the end of the

The type of grave known a 'body stone'. This one at Westerham, Kent

fourteenth century, in any case, until the revival of 300 years later, there seems to have been a decline in the desire for individual monuments, perhaps reflecting disillusionment with the prospect of life hereafter, in a period of religious turmoil, but also to a lesser extent a result of the Black Death, which produced a shortage of masons and led gradually to a shift of emphasis from the work of local masons operating independently to the workshop products of trade guilds. The Black Death also, of course, reduced the population of the country by a third, and so cut the demand for burial space for the following generations.

During the seventeenth century, churchyard monuments blossomed anew. Rich and poor alike desired to be perpetuated in memory by those visible proofs that they had lived and died. The poorest, if they were not buried in unmarked paupers' graves, might have the simplest of headstones, small and engraved on both sides in the medieval fashion, with perhaps a cross on one side and merely the year of death and the initials of the deceased on the other. At the opposite end of the social scale, one who was not *quite* wealthy or eminent enough to merit a space inside the church might aspire to an extravagant pedestal tomb which might make him seem a lot more important, and certainly a lot more wealthy, than some of those who *were* buried inside.

The epitaph of Robert Phillip at Kingsbridge, Devon, is a well-known comment on the wish of many to rest in peace indoors:

> Here lie I at the Chancel door
> Here lie I because I'm poor
> The farther in the more you'll pay
> Here lie I as warm as they.

But not without a monument, we may note, for why should not the poor, as well as the rich, suffer from the delusion that a monument conferred some kind of immortality and deserved the respect of posterity? In a speech on funeral reform at Rochdale in 1879, a Mr Greenwood remarked that Lancashire folk liked their headstones to be three times the size of those in the south of England. This outward show is characteristic of the neighbouring corner of Derbyshire, too.

George Fox's Society of Friends, the 'Quakers', saw *all* monuments to the dead, whether inside or out, as marks of pride or arrogance, and Quakers were generally buried in unmarked graves in their own burial grounds, though they subsequently relaxed this rule a little when Fox's famous disciple William Penn and others were buried with simple headstones at Jordans in Buckinghamshire.

At one time there were a great many graveboards or monuments of wood, and in areas where there was no readily available stone this type of memorial persisted well into the nineteenth century, passing the trade in

William Penn's grave in
the Quaker burial groun
at Jordans,
Buckinghamshire

churchyard furnishings from the stone-mason to the carpenter or maybe
the local wheelwright. They occur mostly in the Home Counties,
particularly Sussex, Surrey, Essex and Hertfordshire, and generally take
the form of a horizontal board over the length of the grave, supported by a
short post at each end. They were called 'bed-heads' in some parts and
often had spikes inserted along the top edge to prevent people sitting on
them. They were often painted white with black lettering, but sometimes
had inscriptions carved in the wood. Even with the latter method, which
lasted longer, such memorials were short-lived compared with stone, of
course, and the examples which remain are mostly rotting and
indecipherable. They can be seen at such places as Sidlesham, West
Sussex; Mickleham, Surrey; Baldock, Hertfordshire, and High Easter,
Essex. One at Ditchling, East Sussex, commemorates George Howell, who
died in 1855 at the age of '100 years and 336 days'.

Another material that came into use in regions where little natural
stone occurs was iron. The iron industry of the Weald produced iron grave
slabs on a large scale, varying from simple slabs recording only the initials
and year of death of the deceased to ornately decorated memorials used
inside churches as well as outside. The churchyards at Wadhurst, East
Sussex; East Grinstead, West Sussex, and Cowden, Kent, are rewarding
places in this respect.

Whilst on the subject of iron, it was the discovery in Shropshire of the
method of smelting iron with coke that weakened the iron industry of the
Weald in the eighteenth century, and the new centre of mass-production
in the Severn valley around Coalbrookdale also went in for cast-iron
tombs and gravestones to some extent. The churchyards of Broseley and

Madeley – now parts of Telford – have good examples, the finest being a nineteenth-century monument to the ironmaster William Baldwin at Madeley.

Iron monuments did not disappear from the south-east. Bepton, West Sussex, has some iron headstones of the late nineteenth century, no doubt imported from another part of the country to continue a local tradition, and they are occasionally found in other areas which are without suitable stone, for instance at Amersham, Buckinghamshire.

Other departures from the engraved stone slab include plates of brass or copper sometimes fixed to flat gravestones in the Cotswolds, such as at King's Stanley, Sapperton and Bisley, in Gloucestershire. They were used from the seventeenth right up to the present century, and some bear the names of their engravers. The elements have turned these small metal plates green, but they remain legible for much longer than would have

One of the wooden grave-boards in the rchyard at Mickleham, Surrey

117

Cast-iron memorial, L
Melford, Suffolk

been the case if the graves' occupants had been commemorated by incised lettering directly on the soft local limestone.

Wood and metal apart, however, it is natural stone that overwhelmingly populates our churchyards with the tottering ranks of tombs and headstones rising up from the grass to proclaim the former existence of parish inhabitants of the last 200 years. By the eighteenth century upright headstones were becoming uniform in shape and size, if not in design and material. Dictated partly by the amount of information that people wanted the masons to inscribe on them, they became larger than the squat medieval type of stone that stood only two feet above the ground, and instead of the thick block inscribed on both sides, thin slabs came into favour, lettered on one side only.

The stone came from local quarries, so that in many Cornish, Cumbrian and Welsh churchyards we find the earlier headstones of slate; limestone in central southern England, the Cotswolds and parts of the Midlands; sandstone farther north; granite in the south-west, and again in Cumbria. In addition to the various colours of the stone, which always weathered to match the church when supplied from the local quarry, some stones gathered lichens over a period of time, and gave churchyards a mellow aesthetic appeal which was soon lost when stone began to be transported to other than its native regions, and particularly when foreign marbles began to be imported – from Italy especially – to provide the shining white angels and crosses which the Church now rightly frowns upon.

Mass-produced white marble angel on a grave at Awliscombe, Devon

Angels in the standard pose – gazing down at the grave and pointing heavenwards – are to be found everywhere, sometimes in native stone but more often in Italian marble. They are usually singular, but occasionally a company of angels is found, like a garden full of plastic gnomes. At Ringsfield, Suffolk, one standing and two kneeling angels adorn the grave of Caroline Murat, the grand-daughter of Napoleon's sister.

The trade in alien stones was due partly to questions of durability. A thin slab of softish limestone standing out in all weathers will not take many years to lose the legibility of its shallowly incised lettering. Stone is subject to decay by all sorts of natural and man-made agents, including frost, salts absorbed from the soil or from sea spray in coastal districts, atmospheric pollutants, such as sulphur acids and smoke in industrial areas, and so on. Thus in the course of time it came to be realized that the harder the stone the better. Not only would it wear better than the softer and younger rocks, but it took lettering better and remained legible for much longer. In due course, therefore, slate took precedence for headstones over limestone, sandstone and other natural rocks, and it remains the predominant material in churchyards in most parts of the country, being obtained from the Lake District, Cornwall and, above all, Wales.

There was one area of slate production which brought a new art form to churchyards before slate began its nationwide monopoly. This was Swithland in the Charnwood Forest area of Leicestershire, where slate deposits had been worked as far back as Roman times and were used for roofing and other purposes from the Middle Ages to the late nineteenth century, when the quarries were abandoned in the face of overwhelming competition from the Welsh product. Water-filled pits in Swithland Wood are the only remaining signs of this centuries-old industry, except for the

Headstones of the local slate at Swithland, Leicestershire

roofs of many houses in the district, and headstones in the churchyards of Leicestershire and some of the neighbouring counties.

In the eighteenth century Swithland slate was considered ideal material for headstones. Not only was it far more attractive than Welsh slate, coming in blue-grey, greenish-grey and purplish tones, but it was also hard enough to obtain a polished surface and took finer engraving than could be achieved with softer stones. Moreover, it was lighter in weight than other stones, and thus easier and cheaper to transport. So as monumental masons gradually discovered its potential, their delight in using it grew, and they became more and more ambitious with their designs and styles of lettering.

Leicestershire churchyards are models of sophistication in headstone engraving of the period. Before the demand for memorials created the profession of monumental mason, writing-masters, clerks and other literate people with a talent for lettering were able to supplement their incomes by supplying the village churchyard with its headstones in their spare time. Usually the calligraphic inscriptions and elaborate decorative motifs were incised in the slate, but sometimes ambitious and skilful craftsmen would painstakingly reduce the surface of the slate to leave their designs and lettering in relief. In the end, the stone-cutters exceeded themselves, and ostentatious design and flamboyant rococo flourishes degraded the more restrained stylishness of the earlier work, but in the churchyards of Leicestershire and southern Derbyshire and Nottinghamshire we can see the work of such local craftsmen as Henry Castledine, a schoolmaster of Syston; Robert Waddington, the parish clerk of Clipstone; John Hind, who was a part-owner of the Swithland quarries at one time; members of the Kirk family of Leicester, and many others, all of whom had their individual styles and trade marks.

The best churchyards for their wealth of Swithland slate headstones are perhaps those of St Margaret and St Mary de Castro in Leicester, and at Loughborough and Narborough, but there is hardly a town or village in Leicestershire that does not have at least one or two examples of the local speciality in its churchyard. The oldest surviving example is believed to be that of 1641 to one Elias Travers in the churchyard at Thurcaston. A headstone to John Phipps in St Margaret's churchyard at Leicester complains that 'Life is but a fleeting shadow', though Mr Phipps was 119 when he died.

Other masons in other areas achieved minor fame, too. The Strong family in the Cotswolds were quarry-owners as well as masons, and Valentine Strong left money at his death for a way to be made between the two bridges at Barrington, 'that two men may go a front to carry a corpse in safety'. The way is still known as 'Strong's Causeway'. In Cornwall, Daniel Gumb, who carved some of the gravestones in the churchyards at Linkinhorne and elsewhere in the eighteenth century, was a noted local eccentric, living with his family in a home-made rock house, with beds, table and benches of granite, near the Cheesewring quarry on Bodmin Moor. A Buckinghamshire mason, James Andrews, became a friend of the poet William Cowper when the latter was living at Olney, and gave him lessons in drawing. Some of his headstones can be seen in the churchyard at Olney, which convince us that Cowper was a little extravagant in calling his friend 'my Michelangelo'.

As well as the assorted types of stone, epitaph and lettering, a lot of solemn symbolism began to appear in the ornamentation of headstones as the art developed. The Christian cross has always remained by far the most popular, not least because it is the easiest to cut, and therefore cheaper. Some of the more obvious symbols of mortality were generally popular and widespread, like the hour-glass, scythe, skulls and crossed bones, and clasped hands. But others became the favourite specialities of certain localities or even of particular masons, who often used images as their trade marks. John Pearce, a mason of Frampton-on-Severn, 'signed' his work with drooping sheaves of foliage above oval tablets bearing the lettering; and James Sparrow of Radcliff-on-Trent, Nottinghamshire, was partial to acorns. Jonathan Harmer, of Heathfield, East Sussex, specialized in making terracotta plaques for fixing to tombs and headstones in the early nineteenth century, and these can best be seen in the churchyards at Mayfield and Herstmonceux.

The butterfly, as a symbol of the soul, is hardly found except around Evesham, Hereford & Worcester, while Cotswold churchyards are specially devoted to the figure holding a book as a symbol of knowledge. I was puzzled to find a little sculpted pelican on a grave at Hope Bowdler, Shropshire, until I discovered that this bird is a symbol of piety and can also be found at Wolverton, Buckinghamshire, Spalding, Lincolnshire, and Hendon, London, among other places.

The anchor as a symbol of hope is found everywhere, but more especially in the churchyards of coastal towns and villages where it is understandably popular on the graves of sailors. Anchors form a kind of fence round a monument to the Crawshay family in the churchyard at Brasted, Kent.

Other trades and occupations attracted appropriate emblems or representations of their tools, like the hammer and anvil for a blacksmith; square and compasses for a builder or carpenter; plough and sickle for a farmer; brushes and palette for an artist; mallet and chisel for a stonemason. The well-known headstone to John Peel in the churchyard at Caldbeck, Cumbria, has a hunting horn among its ornaments, and at Bromsgrove, Hereford & Worcester, the adjacent graves of the railwaymen Thomas Scaife and Joseph Rutherford carry accurate representations of contemporary steam locomotives; while at Wetton, Staffordshire, a gravestone with fossils carved on it marks the burial place of Samuel Carrington, a nineteenth-century archaeologist who excavated several prehistoric barrows in the region.

The majority of headstones of the last 200 years are around four or five feet high, with about one foot buried below the soil – enough to keep most of them more or less stable except when exposed to extreme weather conditions, as in the large, bleak and treeless churchyard at Tintagel, Cornwall, where some headstones are buttressed against the force of Atlantic gales. It is the monumental mason's responsibility in law to ensure that gravestones are securely erected. In 1934 a firm was held liable for injuries a little girl suffered when she was putting fresh flowers on her

Mayfield, East Sussex. A nineteenth-century headstone with terracotta plaque made by Jonathan Harmer

grandmother's grave and the headstone toppled over and fell on her.

Interesting headstones occur all over the country, but one or two places that might be picked out as containing collections of a local style or material are Potton, Bedfordshire, where there are many interestingly carved headstones; Little Dean, Gloucestershire, which has characteristic Forest of Dean tombstones with some local specialities of carving; Borden, Kent, where there are splendid eighteenth-century headstones carved with allegorical scenes in relief; Cley-next-the-Sea and Walsoken, Norfolk, both rich in headstones with symbolic imagery; and Cropredy, Oxfordshire, particularly good for the quality of lettering on its memorials. In industrial areas, the headstones are often as heavy and depressing as the buildings, as at Amblecote, West Midlands, and blackened by pollution, as at Haworth, West Yorkshire. At Alveley, Shropshire, where the old churchyard and its extension are linked by a pretty lychgate, all the red sandstone headstones are leaning backwards. In Wales and Cornwall many headstones are to be found with their heads carved in the shape of a Celtic cross.

The upright headstone has remained the cheapest and most common form of outdoor memorial for a couple of centuries, but most churchyards have at least a few examples of different types, and some localities are noted for their accumulation of certain styles of monument. One kind of slightly better memorial is the 'table tomb'. This consists of a flat slab raised above ground level either on four legs at the corners or on stone supports at head and foot. The type is practically confined to the north of England, and examples can be seen almost anywhere north of the Humber, Haworth and Keighley in West Yorkshire having characteristic specimens.

Top to bottom: 'Chest',
'Table' and 'Pedestal'
tombs

The 'chest tomb' was a medieval type which persisted into modern times as something rather superior to the simple headstone or flat grave slab. Some medieval examples survive, mostly in the southern half of England, though the afore-mentioned exception at Loversall, South Yorkshire, is reckoned to be possibly the oldest surviving individual churchyard monument in England. (There is a rival claimant at Chapel-en-le-Frith, Derbyshire, however – a headstone with the letters PL and an engraved axe, said to be the grave of a forester and dating from the thirteenth century.)

It was in the Cotswolds that the chest tomb received its greatest approval, and Stroud, Painswick and Burford, among other places, display masons' achievements in this type of monument, basically a hollow oblong box with a flat lid, or 'ledger'. It derived from the 'altar tomb' inside churches, which was designed to support an effigy of the deceased. Effigies were only rarely placed on outside chest tombs. There are examples here and there, but one must be cautious when coming across outdoor effigies, since some churchyards contain tombs which have at some time, for reasons of space, been moved outside from their original positions inside the churches, like the one at Astbury, Cheshire.

One of the most spectacular chest tombs is at Elmore, Gloucestershire, a monument of 1707 to Arthur Knowles, lavishly carved with scrolls and figures, including angels and a skeleton representing Death. Another interesting one is at Cley-next-the-Sea, Norfolk, where the inscription describes the deceased, James Greeve, as Sir Cloudesley Shovel's assistant 'in burning ye Ships in ye Port of Tripoly in Barbary' in 1676.

Because chest tombs are hollow, they are often found to have collapsed through soil erosion or root damage, and gaping holes in the tombs, half covered with weeds and ivy, often seem somewhat macabre to many people, who expect to glimpse grinning skulls inside, but there never were bodies in chest tombs. The burials were below the ground, just like those with a headstone.

The wealthy wool towns of the Cotswolds developed a variation on the chest tomb known as a 'bale tomb'. It was basically the same thing, but instead of the flat ledger stone it has a curved top, like a baker's 'tin' loaf. The curved lids have grooves carved into them, sometimes running across the stone and sometimes diagonally. Popular tradition has associated the idea with representations of bales of wool, but the occasional appearance of carved skulls at the ends of the capping stones has also led to the belief that the shape represents the corpse wrapped in a woollen shroud – a compromise between the simple, inexpensive memorial of the relatively poor and the elaborately carved effigy of the wealthy inside the church.

It could be that this idea became fashionable as a result of the law requiring burial of everyone in woollen shrouds in the seventeenth century. The Act was passed in the reign of Charles II and was intended to

Overleaf: A typical 'bale tomb' at Burford, Oxfordshire

125

help the wool trade at a time of serious decline. It was not repealed until early in the nineteenth century, but it found little favour among the rich (except perhaps the wool merchants themselves), since they often expected to be buried in their finest silks and satins.

Cotswold village churchyards such as Swinbrook, Asthall, Bibury and, especially, Burford are good places to see bale tombs, while Painswick, surely among the two or three most enjoyable of all English churchyards, also has examples of the so-called 'tea-caddy tomb', in which the chest type seems to be set up on its end with a ball finial or an urn on top.

This is the simplest form of a type known as the 'pedestal tomb', in which the monument is given height as opposed to length and is thus inclined to impart a degree of elegance and sophistication not often present in flatter memorials. Painswick can claim some of the best examples of the pedestal tomb, mostly dating from the eighteenth century and having various shapes and often lavish carving with classical motifs. But although the pedestal tomb found most favour in the churchyards of the Cotswolds and the Severn valley, examples are to be found here and there in other parts of southern England and the Midlands. The plan of the pedestal may be circular, square or even hexagonal, and it is often finished at the top with a sort of outsize teapot lid, whose 'handle' is a finial in the shape of an urn, ball or pineapple.

A pedestal tomb in the churchyard of St Mary at Handsworth, Birmingham, has a recessed arch on the rectangular base, with sculptured cut or broken flowers in it, another of the popular themes on Victorian monuments, like the broken column, though that is more common on monuments inside churches.

A further refinement of the pedestal tomb was to make it support a sarcophagus. One of the most extraordinary monuments of this type is in the churchyard at Burton Lazars, Leicestershire. It is twenty feet high and was built for the Squire family out of money left by William Squire, a local weaver, who died in the eighteenth century. He directed in his will that the money remaining after his monument had been built should go towards the education of poor children, but by the time this preposterous memorial was finished there was little money left. Vanity preceded philanthropy, as it so often does, and if Mr Squire's intention was to make sure that his name lived long after his own death, he succeeded. There is a touch of megalomania in this enormous tomb with its sarcophagus on volutes, surmounted by an obelisk resting on cannon-balls, and with an urn and carvings of figures, globes, skulls and cross-bones, and formerly an eagle and serpents on top of the whole thing, which was originally painted to look like marble, with parts gilded. Who did weaver Squire think he was? The answer is, however, that this tomb and other isolated examples look so out of place only in churchyards mostly populated with more humble headstones. The taste for ostentatious pedestal tombs grew when cemeteries like Kensal Green and Highgate were being established in the nineteenth century, and in the typical Victorian necropolis they are in good company. (One cannot mention the well-known London cemeteries in this connection without drawing the reader's attention to Lawnswood at Leeds, the nearest thing in England to the famous Père Lachaise cemetery in Paris.)

There are several heavy Victorian sarcophagi in the parish churchyards of Clapham and Fulham, and at Shirley, near Croydon, is a small classical temple and sarcophagus erected as a monument to the parents of John Ruskin. The monument to Rebecca Waterlow in St Mary's churchyard at Reigate, Surrey, is a Victorian mass of white Portland limestone, with two angels seated on a sarcophagus which is in turn perched on a huge base with copper urns at the corners.

In the churchyard at Sheepstor, Devon, is a huge sarcophagus of red Aberdeen granite erected as a memorial to Sir James Brooke, the first Rajah of Sarawak, though why the stone should have been brought from Scotland when there is plenty of the stuff on Dartmoor is a mystery. His nephew, Sir Charles, who succeeded him as Rajah, is buried beside him under a massive boulder of the local granite. Sir James was once left for dead in his youth, after a battle in India, and came close to being buried alive.

Further overtones of megalomania in the churchyard came with the mausoleum, the tomb-house built by an important family when it could not fit impressive vaults and tombs in the church itself. Mausoleums erected in the grounds of stately homes like Castle Howard and Brocklesby Park can be imposing architectural achievements, but in churchyards they are always overwhelming and usually pompous. Such structures need space to succeed as architecture, and churchyards do not have it.

Yorkshiremen seem fond of mausoleums. The Turner mausoleum at Kirkleatham is actually an extension of the church, attached to the chancel in the form of an octagon with a pyramid roof. It was built for the Turners by James Gibbs in 1740. At Little Ousburn is the Thompson mausoleum, a domed rotunda with Tuscan columns; and at Rotherham, in the graveyard of the Independent Chapel, the Walker mausoleum, a brick job of the late eighteenth century. At Ombersley, Hereford & Worcester, the Sandys mausoleum is the rebuilt chancel of the old church in the same churchyard as the new. Other interesting churchyard mausoleums can be seen at Shotleyfield, Northumberland; Buckminster, Leicestershire; Wroxham, Norfolk; Southwold, Suffolk; Claverton, Avon; Turvey, Bedfordshire; Chilton Foliat, Wiltshire; Fawley (where there are two) and Hambleden, Buckinghamshire; St Pancras, London (old parish church); Cobham, Surrey; and Chiddingstone and Farningham, Kent. Every single one of them looks out of scale and character with the churchyard it dominates, but we have still to see yet more startling eccentricities in churchyard memorials.

Considering that no personal monument of any sort can be erected in a churchyard without the authority of a faculty, except for a straight-forward grave-slab or headstone for which the incumbent's permission is sufficient, one wonders how some of the monstrosities have got by, especially as so many of them are self-evidently pagan in concept, such as miniature Egyptian pyramids. One of the best known of these is at Brightling, East Sussex – the grave of the eccentric MP John Fuller, known as 'Mad Jack', whose corpse is reputed to have been interred seated inside it wearing a silk top-hat and holding a bottle of claret. Well might the builder of this have been named Smirke!

There is a low pyramid monument to Benjamin Wyatt and his family in the churchyard at Llandegai, Gwynedd, made of local slate, for Wyatt was the agent of Lord Penrhyn, the owner of the local quarries. Another pyramid occurs at Wootton St Lawrence, Hampshire, this one built of granite and stepped like the Pharaoh Zoser's. Did Mary Poynder, whose nineteenth-century memorial this is, have delusions of grandeur? And who put up the pyramid at St Anne's, Limehouse, in Stepney, London? It stands to the west of the church, and no one seems to know when or why it

Pyramid at Painswick, Gloucestershire. This one is over the grave of John Bryan

130

was built, though we may safely assume it resulted from the rise in popularity of Egyptian styles after Napoleon's archaeological conquests. A pyramid modelled like the Great Pyramid at Gizeh marks the grave at Sharrow, North Yorkshire, of Charles Piazzi Smith, who spent much of his life studying this famous tomb in Egypt.

From Egypt to Arabia, and from pagan images to Islam, is no farther than from Stepney to Mortlake, as far as the English churchyard is concerned, for in the Catholic churchyard of St Mary Magdalen at Mortlake is a massive stone tent, erected as a monument to Sir Richard Burton, the explorer and translator of *The Arabian Nights*. Where the entrance to the tent would be, if it were real, are two tablets, one in the form of an open book with the names of Burton and his wife Isabel, who was responsible for this monstrosity at a cost of £688; and above them is a crucifix – a sort of nod in the direction of Christianity added almost as an afterthought, it seems. The entrance *was* real originally, and Lady Burton conducted séances in the tent before her own death. It was blocked up after vandals damaged the monument in 1951.

Vulgarity may have entered the English churchyard when the working classes aspired to the same monumental distinction as their peers, but as always the rich have exceeded them in it.

In the parish churchyard at Pinner is the monument J.C. Loudon put up to his parents – an obelisk with the ends of a sarcophagus protruding from it in the air like some surrealist image. This is said to have been a gesture to his father who had wanted to be buried above ground, but there is no body in the sarcophagus – it was merely a symbol. And at Otley, West Yorkshire, in a part of the churchyard separated from the main area by a narrow lane, is a huge monument to the men who were killed during construction of the Bramhope railway tunnel in 1845-9 – a scale model of the tunnel's northern portal.

Another 'industrial' monument is at Lindale, Cumbria, where St Paul's churchyard has near, but not *in* it, a tall cast-iron obelisk to the ironmaster John Wilkinson, with an image of his head in profile. The thing is rusty and cracked and held together with iron bands, and it was not, in any case, intended for the churchyard, having been moved here from Wilkinson's former home, Castlehead. The man was so obsessed with the material that he had himself buried in an iron coffin.

Many such monuments are sombre as well as pagan, but the Christian churchyard has not been condemned totally to the erection of gloom-laden memorials inducing deathly solemnity. As with humorous inscriptions, the Church has, to its credit, allowed a little broad-minded escape from puritanical head-hanging on occasion. The naked bronze boy sitting on the grave of thirteen-year-old Vincent Corbet in the churchyard at Moreton Corbet, Shropshire, might be slightly unusual, but what of the splendidly pagan memorial to David Ricardo at Hardenhuish, Wiltshire?

Splendid pagan figures on the tomb of David Ricardo at Hardenhuish, Wiltshire

This is a classical monument of 1823 by William Pitts, consisting of a stone canopy, supported on four Doric columns and, beneath it, an abbreviated Corinthian column with three nude Greek maidens leaning against it, mournful but gorgeously life-asserting as well, as if to say 'We're no angels!'

There are, of course, more modest eccentricities, too, as well as smaller outrages, like the occasional monuments to animals which the Church ought to have forbidden absolutely and without question if it wished to be taken seriously, instead of pandering to the absurd sentimentality of the English. An example is the ludicrous monument to the 'Church Cat' at St Mary Redcliffe, Bristol. (Surely Evelyn Waugh knocked this nonsense on the head once and for all in *The Loved One*: 'Aimee sobbed in the corner and presently said: "That awful funeral." "The Joyboy parrot? Yes, I think I can explain that. Mr Joyboy would have an open casket. I advised against it and, after all, I knew. I'd studied the business. An open casket is all right for dogs and cats who lie down and curl up naturally. But parrots don't. They look absurd with the head on a pillow." ')

John Buchan, Lord Tweedsmuir, the novelist and Governor-General of Canada, is buried in the churchyard at Elsfield, Oxfordshire, beneath a flat circular gravestone that can only be described as a man-hole cover. Nancy Mitford's grave at Swinbrook, in the same county, is marked by a

Nancy Mitford's gravestone with mole, Swinbrook, Oxfordshire

thick block of stone with the mason's chisel marks on it and a mole in relief. She, like Bernard Shaw, had said she did not want a cross and had always been fond of moles. Perhaps they keep her company still.

A four-foot model of an organ forms the monument to John Laycock, an organ-builder, in the churchyard at Kildwick, North Yorkshire; whilst at Jevington, East Sussex, there is a model of a fully rigged sailing ship on a grave believed to be that of a merchant who traded between Britain and China, though he is unnamed. Newton Harcourt, Leicestershire, has a miniature church, complete with spire and battlements, over the grave of an eight-year-old boy.

A bell is carved on a tombstone in the churchyard at Closworth, Somerset, to Thomas Purdue, who died in 1911 at the age of ninety. He was a bell-founder who made bells for the church here as well as for many others in the region.

The gravestone of Edward Capern at Heanton Punchardon, Devon, has a real bell hanging on it. Mr Capern was a postman and part-time poet, who delivered letters to farmsteads outside Bideford, walking thirteen miles a day with his postman's bell. His poems were admired by Lord Palmerston and Walter Savage Landor, among others, the latter calling him 'the Burns of Devon' in a moment of mental aberration. When his first poems were published, the Post Office increased his wages from 10s

Heanton Punchardon, Devon. The headstone of Edward Capern with his postman's bell hanging on it

6d a week to 13 shillings. His patriotic verses boosted the morale of troops in the Crimea.

Occasionally those who might have aspired to great and famous memorials have had to settle for rather less. At Scrayingham, North Yorkshire, for instance, is the unprepossessing grave of George Hudson, the former draper who built up a railway empire and became MP for Sunderland and thrice Lord Mayor of York but whose financial wizardry was fraudulent. He spent his last years living on the charity of friends and died a broken man.

In the present century, large-scale monuments have gone out of fashion, even for the famous and deserving. Sir Winston Churchill is buried beneath a simple ledger stone in the churchyard at Bladon, Oxfordshire, like Viscount Nuffield at the village from which William Morris took his title. Another William Morris, the Pre-Raphaelite poet and artist, is buried in the churchyard at Kelmscot, Oxfordshire, beneath a long gravestone resembling the wooden graveboards once used in the Home Counties.

At Wylye, Wiltshire, a monument surrounded by iron railings is of uncertain origin and intent. Local legend has it that a fellow named Popjay had it erected but disappeared without paying for it.

The fashionable and well-paid sculptors of the eighteenth and nineteenth centuries – Nollekens, Flaxman, Chantrey, Westmacott – did not see fit to devote their energies and talents to perishable outdoor monuments, but in our own time Sir Edwin Lutyens, Eric Gill and John Skelton have been prominent among modern artists who have influenced the type and style of monument and lettering which are now regarded as tasteful and appropriate. Several tombs by Lutyens for members of the Jekyll family are in the churchyard at Busbridge, Surrey, linked by a stone balustrade. At Godalming, nearby, there is a monument to the wireless operator of the *Titanic* in the form of a small brick-built cloister, a distinctly twentieth-century idea by Thackeray Turner. A modern memorial to Arthur and Betty Asquith in the form of a headstone with a parabolic niche, at Clovelly, Devon, was designed by Laurence Whistler, and at Kingston near Lewes, East Sussex, is a fine headstone to Kathleen Coleridge-Taylor by John Skelton, made of Blue Hornton limestone. Henry Moore designed the headstone on Dame Edith Sitwell's grave in the churchyard extension at Weedon Lois, Northamptonshire.

Eric Gill's stylish and deceptively simple work is widespread. There is a tall war memorial by him in the churchyard at Harting, West Sussex, and in the Catholic churchyard of St Mary and St Edmund at Abingdon, Oxfordshire, a fine monument to the seventh Earl of Abingdon. But simple headstones are the marks of Gill's influence, substituting finely engraved Roman lettering for the flamboyant script and typographical hotchpotch with which monumental masons got carried away in showing

Weedon Lois,
Northamptonshire. Edith
Sitwell's headstone was
designed by Henry Moore

off their skills in the eighteenth and nineteenth centuries. Eric Gill is himself buried beneath a short rounded headstone of simple dignity in the graveyard of the little Baptist chapel at Speen, Buckinghamshire.

To undertakers it makes relatively little difference whether the deceased they are dealing with is to be buried or cremated, but a large share of the market is still taken by the Co-operative Funeral Societies, especially in the north. People who could not afford costly funerals went to the Co-op to get their 'divvy' on the job. A gravestone in the churchyard at Elsham, near Scunthorpe, Humberside, bears the legend 'Scun. Co-op.' which one might think an inappropriate advertisement, though it seems inoffensive enough when compared with the high-pressure salesmanship that goes on in the United States, making profit out of grief. It is very difficult today, in bustling towns especially, to maintain the traditional solemnity of the occasion right through the funeral process. I recall travelling to a churchyard for one funeral when the hearse was brought to an abrupt halt by traffic lights and a sign saying 'Do not enter the box

Eric Gill's grave at Speen,
Buckinghamshire

until your exit is clear.' There are, however, clear signs that such hypocritical capitalism is, like so many bad things in the American way of life, crossing the Atlantic, practitioners here tumbling to the realization that there is more money to be made out of the bereavement business than meets the eye.

The penny a week insurance that people used to pay out for each of their children from birth, to provide for their funerals when the expectation of life was not high in working class circles, has been largely replaced, if hardly equalled, by the National Insurance Death Grant. Thirty pounds will scarcely nowadays pay for the wreaths of flowers which mourners place on coffins. A very simple cremation funeral I arranged recently cost over five hundred pounds. How can people, especially in these days of high unemployment, afford 'decent' funerals for their loved ones when undertakers' charges are so unrealistic? Economy will undoubtedly have long-term effects on social attitudes to disposal of the dead, especially if suspicions of dishonest as well as money-grabbing undertakers arise. In one recently reported case, an unearthed coffin believed by the relatives of the deceased to be oak, and paid for as such, turned out to be chipboard.

'How long hast thou been a gravemaker?' Hamlet asks one of the men digging Ophelia's grave and, after some circumlocution, gets the answer: thirty years. Nowadays, few if any sextons do the job for so long, although the epitaph to Edward Barradell, a sexton of Sileby, Leicestershire, claimed that

> For fifty-two revolving years
> Devoutly he attended prayers,
> With mellow voice and solemn knell,
> He sang the psalms and tolled the bell.

He must have dug a good many tons of earth in his time, too. Hezekiah Briggs, buried at Bingley, West Yorkshire, was a sexton for forty-three years and is said to have buried 7,000 corpses, indicating an average death rate of one every two days in the parish at the beginning of the nineteenth century.

Digging a hole six feet deep is not an easy task in any soil, and particularly in the heavy clay soils of some parts of England, yet grave-digging seems to be a job for old men. Richard West, writing in the *New Statesman* in 1963, remarked that, 'The average age of grave-diggers is over 50 and the cramped, damp work makes them vulnerable to sickness.' A coal-miner at Barnsley was told in 1962, by the vicar who was to bury his dead son, that he, the father, would have to dig the grave himself, as the grave-digger was away. Already mechanical diggers were being tried out here and there. It is, however, against the law to use a mechanical digger on re-used grave sites; only on virgin soil may machines be used for digging. The swing towards disposing of the dead by cremation has eased the burden on most sextons, but there are still a few hundred thousand six-foot holes to be dug around the country each year – a lot of collective earth-moving.

Assorted superstitions attached themselves to open graves. If a grave had been dug in a churchyard and a wedding was to take place before the grave was occupied and filled in, the hole would be screened off from view, for it was tempting fate for a newly married couple to see an open grave. In some parts care was taken to avoid having an open grave in the churchyard on a Sunday, as this was believed to portend another death in the parish during the coming week.

Rural grave-diggers were often village builders and carpenters, too, and I recall one such, featured in a TV documentary, guiding us round the churchyard at Bromfield, Shropshire, identifying many villagers he had known and for whom he had dug graves, almost as if he were introducing us to living people. The Reverend Francis Kilvert wrote some 200 years ago in similar terms of those buried in his churchyard at Bredwardine: 'When all the people had left the Church ... I walked alone round the silent, sunny peaceful Churchyard and visited the graves of my sleeping friends ... There they lay, the squire and the peasant, the landlord and the labourer ... There they lay sleeping well and peacefully after life's fitful fevers and waiting for the great Spring morning and the General Resurrection of the dead.'

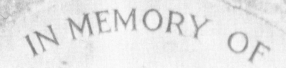

IN MEMORY OF

HANNAH TWYNNOY
Who died October 23rd 1703
Aged 33 Years.

In bloom of Life
She's snatchd from hence,
She had not room
To make defence;
For Tyger fierce
Took Life away.
And here she lies
In a bed of Clay,
Until the Resurrection Day.

Here Lies Buried …

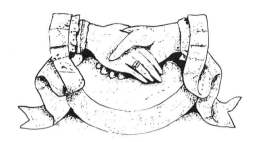

The county historians who proliferated in the eighteenth and nineteenth centuries were inclined towards minute detail rather than the broad sweep of events and often felt it their duty to record the unvarying epitaphs of every Tom, Dick and Harry who had 'departed this life' or 'fallen asleep' with enough money for the purchase of a headstone in the local churchyard.

Wearying of this monotonous antiquarianism, the attention of local historians and the compilers of guide-books has been largely transferred to the grand monuments inside churches, and the contents of churchyards have been ignored altogether. But not every great and famous person has wished to be buried indoors, and English churchyards are the 'final resting-places' of many celebrated people who did not share the whimsical reservations of the photographer Norman Parkinson about being buried among folk to whom they had not been introduced.

The chief population of churchyards, however, consists of the countless legions of the forgotten and obscure local people whose monuments were seen as their little shares of immortality. This is a sentimental error. The human beings who lived in the shapes of the bodies buried beneath the soil are remembered by their friends and relations for a certain time, which is rarely extended by the erection of a headstone in the churchyard; and rarely does the monument earn them a passing thought from anyone who did not know them. The value of a permanent grave is an illusion, whether marked by a grand monument inside or a humble one outside. It is only by a man's deeds that he is remembered, and the vast majority of us must resign ourselves to oblivion, content that we have made our little marks on humanity while we lived, however insignificant, and cannot expect to be thanked for it for ever after we are dead. Of course, it can be argued that monuments are intended to benefit the living, not the dead, but surviving friends and relations do not need monuments to help them remember, and that this realization is now fairly general is shown by the enormous increase in cremation and the scattering of ashes, as we shall see.

There are, however, unknown people whose graves have attracted attention for some reason other than memory of the individuals. It may be that unusual memorials have distinguished them in death more than in life, or that curious epitaphs have singled them out for notice, like the famous one at Winchester to Thomas Thetcher, a twenty-six-year-old Grenadier who died in 1764 from drinking 'cold small Beer'. Some churchyards have their local specialities, like the coastal villages with their graves of seamen. Others have interesting collections through accidents of history, like Ashby-de-la-Zouch, Leicestershire, where Swithland slate headstones bear such names at Etienne Lenon, as a result of French prisoners being taken there during the Napoleonic wars. Some stayed to marry local girls and settled there.

Foreign names occur also at Wasdale Head, Cumbria, where climbers killed on the Lake District fells have been buried. And names such as Serafino Turchich and Nils Pettrson occur at Northam, Devon; sailors wrecked along the coast or washed up after being lost at sea – Serafino Turchich was the mate of an Austrian barque wrecked on Northam Sands in 1868. Gravestones in such coastal churchyards bear the names of foreign seamen and exotic places like Valparaiso and Quebec, where the dead had come from when they came to grief on British shores.

In the churchyards at Bideford and Appledore – the latter a steeply sloping churchyard overlooking the estuary of the rivers Taw and Torridge – native men who made their living from the sea are lined up, master-mariners, captains and mates, pilots and shipbuilders. The churchyard at Mawgan-in-Pydar, Cornwall, contains a timber memorial shaped like the stern of a boat, to ten men who were frozen to death at sea in a boat that eventually floated ashore.

At Cardington Bedfordshire, there is a monument to the victims of the R101 airship disaster in France in October 1930, and at Little Rissington, Gloucestershire, are the graves of young men who lost their lives during service with the Royal Air Force at the Central Flying School.

The churchyard at Linby, Nottinghamshire, has 163 graves of children who died as a result of labour conditions in the factory system before the law forbade the employment of children under ten and put limits on the hours worked by those under eighteen. And at Kirkheaton, West Yorkshire, is a column to seventeen children who were killed in a fire at a wool mill at Colne Bridge in 1818.

Some corner of a foreign
ld'. A climber's grave at
Vasdale Head, Cumbria

Devizes, Wiltshire (St John's), has a monument to five people drowned whilst out enjoying themselves on 30 June 1751. It was a Sunday, and the obelisk bears the admonition, 'Remember the Sabbath Day to keep it holy.' As if to say, 'Serve 'em right'.

Unmarked communal graves at the east end of Bramham churchyard in West Yorkshire received the bodies of soldiers killed in local battles during the Wars of the Roses and the Civil War – one example among many of churchyards containing the mass graves of war dead.

Four youthful victims of a mining disaster were buried at Little Dean, Gloucestershire, in 1819, after a chain had broken, by means of which they were being lowered into Bilston Pit. One of them was only twelve, another sixteen. Many a Nonconformist chapel graveyard in Wales contains the graves of men killed in mining disasters, and at Silkstone, South Yorkshire, the churchyard of All Saints has a monument to twenty-six miners killed in 1838, all between the ages of seven and seventeen, and many of them girls.

Multiple burials like some of those above are not altogether unexpected when one is aware of the history or industry of the localities they are found in. It is when we look at individual graves that we get occasional surprises and sometimes a little amusement.

Haworth, West Yorkshire, has the grave of Lily Cove, an adventurous lady who went up in a balloon in order to make a parachute jump but came down more quickly than she intended when the parachute failed to open. At Malmesbury, Wiltshire, is the grave of Hannah Twynnoy, who was killed by an escaped circus animal in 1703 – a 'Tyger fierce' as her monument in the abbey graveyard records. Then there is Phoebe Hessel at Brighton (St Nicholas) who 'served for many years as a private Soldier in the 5th Regt of Foot' and lived to be 108. She became a soldier to be near the lover whom she duly married. There is no sex discrimination in churchyards and men and women alike are recalled in the pages of Death's curious diary.

St Mary's churchyard at Shrewsbury has a plaque on the church wall recording the death of Robert Cadnam, who in 1739 attempted to cross by rope from the spire of the church to the opposite bank of the Severn but fell to his death when the rope broke.

At Whitby is the grave of a man who fell into Sunderland dock, and at Mylor, Cornwall, that of a man who fell over the edge of a cliff – his rude slate headstone reads:

> In memory of mr Joseph Crapp shipwright
> who died y 26th Nov^br 1770. Aged 43 years.
> Alass Frend Joseph.

His End was All most Sudden
As thou the mandate came Express from heaven –
his foot it slip And he did fall
help help he cries & that was all

Morwenstow, Cornwall, has a very old granite tomb recording the deaths in 1601 of John Manning and his wife Christina: they had been married only five months, and Christina was pregnant when she saw her husband gored to death by a bull, and died of a miscarriage. At Minster-in-Sheppey, Kent, the headstone of Simon Gilker refers to his death 'by means of a Rockett' on 5 November 1696.

Legend says that grass will never grow on the so-called Robber's Grave at Montgomery, Powys, because John Newton Davies, who was buried there after being hanged for robbery in 1821, was innocent of the crime.

Several gravestones around the country tell tales of murder, none more shocking than the headstone under the yew tree at Monksilver, Somerset, where Elizabeth Shillibeer, eighty-eight, and her daughters Sarah and Anne were buried after being murdered in their home in 1775.

A 1792 headstone at East Portlemouth, Devon, reads:

> By poison stung he was cut off,
> And brought to death at last.
> It was by his apprentice girl
> On whom there's sentence passed.
> All who read fair warning take
> For she was burnèd to a stake.

Hunstanton, Norfolk, has the graves of two revenue men murdered by smugglers in 1784.

In Duffield churchyard in Derbyshire, the slate headstone of Elizabeth Sowter has a hole in it, reputedly caused by a shot from a blunderbuss. The story goes that when Mrs Sowter's husband Joseph married again he went on so much about his first wife's virtues that the second lost her temper and marched off to the churchyard to relieve her feelings, putting the shot through the half of the double gravestone reserved for her husband's name – whether by design or inaccurate aim we shall never know, but better there than through the old man himself.

At Bowes, Durham, is recorded the more touching story of the lovers Rodger Wrighton and Martha Railton, buried in the same grave after 'He died in a fever, and upon tolling his passing bell, she cry'd out, my heart is broke, and in a few hours expired ...'

The grave of Sarah, Lady Cowper, wife of the unpopular Lord Chancellor Sir William Cowper, is in the churchyard at Hertingfordbury, Hertfordshire. So is that of his mistress, Elizabeth Cullen, identified only

Overleaf: 'The whole district seemed to be there at the grave of their dear one.' A village funeral, 1868

145

as E.C., who preceded the wife to the grave by sixteen years, in 1703.

A few gravestones record deaths caused by lightning and bring us to a consideration of epitaphs, for death by an 'Act of God' seems to have roused a curious assortment of sentiments in rural communities. A betrothed young couple at Stanton Harcourt, Oxfordshire, were victims of lightning while working in the fields at the harvest in 1718, and earned a verse inscription from Alexander Pope, no less; but Lady Mary Wortley Montagu held up to ridicule what she saw as Pope's false sentiment:

> Who knows if 'twas not kindly done?
> For had they seen the next year's sun,
> A beaten wife and cuckold swain
> Had jointly curs'd the marriage chain.
> Now they are happy in their doom,
> For P hath wrote upon their tomb.

One feels that Wordsworth ought to have taken this to heart, for his solemn and rather pedestrian essay 'Upon Epitaphs' is overflowing with lofty idealism, subscribing to the view that the purpose of epitaphs is to 'preserve the memory of the dead, as a tribute to his individual worth, for a satisfaction to the sorrowing hearts of the Survivors, and for the common benefit of the living'. But Pope himself had written, in a more characteristic moment, of epitaph writers in general:

> Friend! for your epitaphs I'm griev'd,
>   Where still so much is said,
> One half will never be believ'd,
>   The other never read.

To 'lie like an epitaph' became a common saying at one time, the verbose effusions of the obsequious to the memory of the powerful, in particular, being seen for what they were by the more cynical, or realistic.

No maudlin verse commemorates the young man killed by lightning at Great Torrington, Devon:

> Here lies a man who was killed by lightning;
> He died when his prospects seemed to be brightening.
> He might have cut a flash in this world of trouble,
> But the flash cut him, and he lies in the stubble.

The famous, much-quoted epitaph on the grave of an engine-driver at Bromsgrove, Hereford & Worcester, who died in 1840, was utilized as a memorial to another railwayman at Newton-le-Willows, Lancashire (now Merseyside), who died two years later:

148

> My engine now is cold and still,
> No water does my boiler fill;
> My coke affords its flame no more,
> My days of usefulness are o'er …

and so on, *ad nauseam*.

It is remarkable that survivors could sometimes be so insensitive to the levity of epitaph writers at the expense of their dear departed, but the English sense of humour is irrepressible, even in the context of death and burial, and it is a better antidote to the morbid contemplation of death than all the comforting sermons preached from pulpits through all the ages of Christendom, and certainly preferable to those fulsome epitaphs to local dignitaries which make them seem too good to have remained in this wicked world for as long as they did. As someone remarked of Lord Grimthorpe, the sooner he was called to his heavenly reward for his good works, the better.

Humour can sometimes remind us that it is not Death we should be afraid of, only the process of dying. Who could be offended by the inscription on an infant's grave recorded at Lynton, Devon?

> Opened my eyes, took a peep,
> Didn't like it, went to sleep.

Or the headstone at Eyam, Derbyshire, of the county and England cricketer Harry Bagshaw, which shows the raised finger of the almighty umpire giving him *Out*?

Many a joke appeared in the churchyard before it found its way into the music hall or the pub, and several tombstones caution the visitor against treading too heavily near the grave of a woman lest he set her tongue wagging again, as at Troutbeck, Cumbria:

> Here lies a woman,
> No man can deny it,
> She died in peace, although she lived unquiet,
> Her husband prays, if e'er you this way walk,
> You would tread softly – if she wake she'll talk.

These, like a great many verse epitaphs to ordinary people, were debased versions of more elegant or economical lines, in this case the poet Dryden's neat epitaph to his wife:

> Here lies my wife: here let her lie!
> Now she's at rest, and so am I.

We smile at these witticisms, but more often than not, perhaps, they were meant in earnest. Grief and mourning are not the universal rule at death. R.D. Laing mentions the man who remarked to a minister after the burial of his wife, 'You know, I've lived with that woman fifty years, and I never liked her.' Death can come as a relief, but the 'rules' of society, especially in the more sensitive times of the nineteenth and twentieth centuries, dictate that we should be hypocritical, and at least put on the appearance of sadness and a sense of loss, even if we do not feel it.

At Birdbrook, Essex, is the 1681 gravestone of Martha Blewitt, who buried eight husbands and was married to a ninth before she died herself. Perhaps we could learn something from her if we knew her full story.

The superstitious objection to speaking ill of the dead was no deterrent to the wicked humour of epitaph-composers in days when libellous allegations were made more freely than they are now. James Pady, a brickmaker, was buried at Awliscombe, Devon, with the inscription neatly carved for all to see for generations afterwards: '... in hopes that his clay will be remoulded in a workmanlike manner far superior to his former perishable materials.' A side-swiping epitaph recorded at Bideford, Devon, says:

> Here lies the body of Mary Sexton,
> Who pleased many a man, but never vex'd one;
> Not like the woman who lies under the next stone.

To say nothing of an apparently unlamented physician:

> Here lies the corpse of Doctor Chard,
> Who fill'd half of this churchyard.

Mere epitaphs could scarcely do sufficient injustice to certain notorious characters. In Devon, for instance, there is the grave of Richard Cabell at Buckfastleigh, protected by an iron grille, intended not to keep others out but to keep him in. Legend has it that he lived so evil a life that the fiends and hell-hounds of Dartmoor rejoiced at his death in 1677.

A strange tale is told of the occupant of an eighteenth-century chest tomb at Swinford, Leicestershire, the village parson, William Staresmore, a noted eccentric. He was so strict that he used to lock his servants in the house at night to prevent their getting into mischief. Worse still, he used to chain one of his many bulldogs to each of his apple trees to prevent scrumping by local children after dark. One morning he went out early – so the story goes – to release his dogs, leaving the servants still locked up, but the excitement of his fifty-eight dogs caused him to fall into his pond, and as no one could get out to help him, he drowned.

Few of the more famous epitaphs are entirely original. The defamatory reflection on a deceased wife quoted above is recorded in Somerset as well as Cumbria. Just as the individuality of gravestones made by independent rural craftsmen gave way to the pattern-book designs employed by firms of monumental masons, so epitaphs likewise took on a conveyor-belt range of similarity. A few literate versifiers seem to have made a living out of syndicating rhyming epitaphs as some do today by composing verses for greetings cards. You were given a few popular phrases or sayings to choose from, but you could have one of your own if you preferred, as long as it was approved by the incumbent.

By far the most common verse on the gravestones of those whose survivors could not restrain themselves with a simple record of the dead person's name and dates is that old *memento mori*

> As I am now, so you must be:
> Therefore prepare to follow me.

There are many variations on this theme, such as at Hickling, Nottinghamshire:

> You readers all both old and young
> Your time on earth will not be long
> For death will come and die you must
> And like to me return to dust.

One is always slightly surprised that so many eighteenth – and nineteenth-century bereaved were prepared to pay for the laborious engraving of such statements of the obvious, which have no reference to the life or faith of the deceased and which have un-Christian undertones of a desire for revenge on the living for surviving them. There is even occasionally a slightly threatening tone, as on the grave of a twenty-two-year-old at Heanton Punchardon, Devon: 'Reader – Boast not thyself of tomorrow; for thou knowest not what a day may bring forth.'

In Aubrey's time, many people believed in werewolves, and Webster has a doctor in *The Duchess of Malfi* explaining lycanthropy:

> In those that are possess'd with't there o'erflows
> Such melancholy humour they imagine
> Themselves to be transformed into wolves;
> Steal forth to churchyards in the dead of night,
> And dig dead bodies up: as two nights since
> One met the duke 'bout midnight in a lane
> Behind Saint Mark's Church, with the leg of a man
> Upon his shoulder; and he howl'd fearfully ...

151

Country parsons were the most frequent composers of suitable individual epitaphs, however, when they were the most (and sometimes the only) literate members of their communities; and they jumped at the chance, when the opportunity presented itself, of a little moralizing. Who can doubt the sanctimonious and self-righteous mind of a churchman behind the unpitying inscription on the grave of Sarah Lloyd, who died in her twenty-second year, at Bury St Edmunds, Suffolk in 1800? 'Suffer'd a Just but Ignominious Death for admitting her abandoned seducer into the Dwelling House of her Mistress ... and becoming the Instrument in his Hands of the crimes of Robbery and House-burning. These were her last Words: May my example be a Warning to Thousands.'

The age of mass-production affected our words just as much as our merchandise, and nowhere is this seen more clearly than in the groan-making epitaphs to tradesmen and professional entertainers, which can be found repeated verbatim or with slight variations all over the country. We get the one to the village blacksmith ('My fire's extinct, my forge decay'd'); and the village wheelwright ('My horses have done running, my waggon is decay'd'); as well as the afore-mentioned railwayman ('My engine now is cold and still'); and even the butcher ('His knife is laid, his work is done.')

Too often inscriptions are hideously facetious, like that to the watchmaker ('In hopes of being taken in hand by his Maker, And of being thoroughly cleaned and repaired, And set a-going in the world to come'); and the angler ('Death threw out his line, hook'd him, and landed him here ...'); and the dentist ('filling his last cavity'); and the printer ('No more shall type's small face my eye-balls strain'). There is the wrestler ('Time has thrown whom none e'er threw before'); the cricketer ('Bowled at last'); and the sailor ('At anchor now in Death's dark road'), and so on.

One of the worst examples of this kind of sepulchral facetiousness surely occurs at Ramsgate, Kent (St Lawrence), where a grave bears these words: 'This marks the wreck of Robert Woolward, who sailed the sea for fifty-five years. When Resurrection gun fires, the wreck will be raised by the Angelic Salvage Co; surveyed and if found worthy, refitted and started on the voyage to Eternity.'

Such working-class commemoration, which fills many books devoted to epitaphs, is quite as bad as the overblown sentiment that one finds on the tombs of the minor nobility and persons of 'quality'. But such effusions are the result of mass education in the eighteenth century and after. Before that, the churchyard must have been a source of learning to many illiterate country folk. Dr Robert Hall, the famous Baptist minister whom Pitt compared with Demosthenes, taught himself the alphabet from the gravestones in his father's churchyard at Arnesby, Leicestershire, and was writing hymns when he was eight years old.

The parsons and schoolmasters instructed the masons, whose errors in

Good Prince Albert's folly, Whippingham church on the Isle of Wight

The loveliest churchyard in England. St Just-in-Roseland in Cornwall, overlooking Falmouth Bay

Constable's painting of
East Bergholt
churchyard in Suffolk
where his parents lie
buried

John Peel's gravestone
with hunting horns at
Caldbeck, Cumbria

IN MEMORY OF
JOHN PEEL OF
RUTHWAITE, who died
Nov.13th 1854 aged 78 Years.
Also MARY, his wife, who
died Aug. 9th 1859 aged 82
Also JONATHAN their Son
who died Jan. 21st 1806.
aged 2 Years.
Also PETER their Son, who
died Nov.15th 1840.
aged 27 Years.
Also MARY DAVIDSON their
DAUGHTER who died Nov 30th
1865. aged 48 Years.
Also JOHN their Son who died
Nov.22nd 1887 aged 60 Years

Northern austerity at
Arncliffe, North
Yorkshire

No names, no pack-drill. The sentiment on this headstone at Sheepstor, Devon, is common enough – but whose is it?

spacing, as well as quaint spelling, can be seen in country churchyards everywhere. The 'forkner' to three Stuart kings, who was buried at Great Livermore, Suffolk, turns out to have been the royal falconer. There is some delightful originality to be found, of course. An epitaph appears on a tablet on the outside wall of St Mary's at Wirksworth, Derbyshire, describing Philip Shallcross, who died in 1787, as 'once an eminent quill-driver to the attorneys of the town'. But against this wit there is the atrocious example of (presumably unintentional) ambiguity recorded at Woolwich: 'Sacred to the memory of Major James Brush who was killed by the accidental discharge of a pistol by his orderly, 14th April 1831. "Well done good and faithful servant." '

It is interesting to note how frequently masons were unsure about the use of punctuation and how often their spelling and grammar reflect local pronunciation and dialect. An epitaph recorded in Cornwall, for example:

> In this grave ye see before ye,
> Lies buried up a dismal story;
> A young maiden she wor crossed in love,
> And tooken to the realms above.
> But he that crossed her I should say
> Deserves to go t'other way.

A nice example of local dialect is recorded at Dymock, Gloucestershire:

> Too sweeter babes youm nare did see
> Than God amity give to wee,
> But they were ortaken wee ague fits,
> and yur they lies as dead as nits.

Characteristic confusion of verbs is found at Masham, North Yorkshire (1809):

> My friends, read this and shed no tears
> I must lay here till Christ appears ...

And dialect as well as medical history distinguished the grave of Martha Snell at Bangor, Gwynedd:

> Poor Marth Snell, her's gone away,
> Her would if her could, but her couldn't stay.
> Her had two bad legs and a baddish cough,
> But her legs it was that carried her off.

In the cemetery at Bath, Avon, Jane Pitman is described as the wife of

Isaac, 'Fonetik Printer of this Siti'. (He was also the inventor of Pitman's shorthand.)

Latin tags are often to be found on headstones, the favourite of course being *'Sic transit gloria mundi'* ('So passeth away earthly glory'), but there are rarer languages, too. At Llanfair Waterdine, Shropshire, the headstone of a young gypsy, Herbert Lock, has a long inscription in Romany on it, and at Stowford, Devon, there is an ancient stone near the churchyard gate with an inscription in Ogham to one Gunglei. The monument to Dolly Pentreath at Paul, Cornwall, incorrectly credits her with being the last person to speak the ancient Cornish language, and bears a text in it from Exodus. Her monument – a rather ugly obelisk – was erected at the expense of Prince Louis Napoleon, who had a keen interest in languages.

Language apart, one may find here and there an inscription which passeth all understanding, like the one on a headstone at St Peter's, Oxford, where Sarah Hounslow is recorded as having died on 31 February 1835. Or the one at Great Yarmouth, Norfolk, which tells us that

> Here lies the body of Nicholas Round
> Who was lost in the sea and never was found.

Of all the figurative expression to be found in churchyards, euphemism is the most common. 'Fell asleep' is a ubiquitous substitute for 'died'; others include 'called away', 'passed on', 'gone to join Jesus', 'promoted to higher service', 'at rest', 'safely gathered in' and so on. The grave is also alluded to by a picturesque assortment of phrases, such as 'bed of clay' or 'last lodging', a 'last cosy tenement' or a 'final port of call', or even as 'The Wardrobe of my dusty clothes', as on the grave of Elizabeth Oldfield at Chipping Sodbury, Avon.

Puns and other word-play rose in popularity with the increase in literacy in the eighteenth century and were clearly thought by many to be, as it were, the last word in sophistication, though perhaps one of the most original of such inscriptions is also one of the oldest, an acrostic recorded in Gunwallow churchyard in Cornwall, and also to be found on a brass of 1708 to Hannibal Basset in the church at Mawgan:

Shall	weee	all	die?
Weee	shall	die	all.
All	die	shall	weee?
Die	all	weee	shall.

Metaphor is employed fairly often, one of the best examples coming from Heanor, Derbyshire, on the 1815 tombstone of William Brough:

What is life? a Breath; a Dream;
A Bubble in a rapid Stream;
A lurid Shade, with scarce a ray;
A short and Stormy Winter's day;
A falling Star; a morning Flower;
A passing Cloud, an Autumn Shower.
A flying Shuttle, nay a Span;
So short and frail's the Life of Man.

This theme is adapted from Sir Francis Bacon, but it would have reduced the mason's bill, and been equally effective, to have quoted one of Shakespeare's neater epigrams on life.

Graves are generally fairly uniform in size, except for the tiny graves of infants, but at the other end of the scale there is the long one at Hale, Cheshire, where John Middleton, the so-called 'Childe of Hale', was buried in 1623, he being reputedly over nine feet tall; and the wide one at Stamford, Lincolnshire, where Daniel Lambert was buried in 1809, after a wall had been demolished to remove his body, weighing over fifty-two stone, from the inn where he died.

Occasionally monuments can be found in churchyards to people who are not actually buried there. There is one at Kirkby Mallory, Leicestershire, to Augusta Ada, Countess of Lovelace, the daughter of Lord Byron. She had lived there, after her parents' separation, on the estate of her grandfather Sir Ralph Milbanke, but she was buried beside her father in the church at Hucknall Torkard, Nottinghamshire. At Eastwood in that county there is a stone to D.H. Lawrence, who was born there but died and was buried in New Mexico.

Also, of course, many epitaphs have been composed which have never been inscribed on stones in churchyards, though in some cases people believed, and were meant to believe, that they had been, like Swift's epitaph to John Partridge, in 1708. Partridge was an astrologer and compiler of almanacs, who wrote badly and attacked the Church, so Swift conducted an elaborate debunking of Partridge and his preposterous predictions by himself forecasting that Partridge would die on 29th March 1708. On the day after this date, or possibly on April 1st, Swift duly published an account of Partridge's death and his death-bed confession that his astrological predictions were all deceits, together with the following epitaph:

Here, five feet deep, lies on his back
A cobbler, star-monger, and quack;
Who, to the stars in pure good will,
Does to his best look upward still.
Weep, all you customers, that use

His pills, his almanacs, or shoes:
And you, that did your fortunes seek,
Step to his grave but once a week:
This earth, which bears his body's print,
You'll find has so much virtue in't,
That I durst pawn my ears, 'twill tell
Whate'er concerns you full as well,
In physic, stolen goods, or love,
As he himself could, when above.

Of course, the ever-gullible public swallowed the story hook, line and sinker, the Stationer's Company deleted Partridge's name from its roll, and he was faced with the embarrassing and far-from-easy task of proving himself to be still alive, which he signally failed to do on one occasion even in a court of law.

Other writers jumped gleefully on Swift's farcical bandwagon and one, possibly Congreve, reported a visit by a sexton to Partridge's house:

'I am Ned, the sexton ... and come to know whether the doctor left any orders for a funeral sermon; and where he is to be laid, and whether his grave is to be plain or bricked?'

'Why, sirrah,' says I, 'you know me well enough; you know I am not dead, and how dare you affront me after this manner?'

'Alack-a-day, Sir,' replies the fellow, 'why it is in print, and the whole town knows you are dead; why, there's Mr. White, the Joiner, is but fitting Screws to your Coffin ...'

One or two monuments present us with enduring mysteries. In the churchyard at Finsthwaite, Cumbria, is a tall white cross erected to the memory of Clementina Johannes Sobieski Douglass, who was buried there in May 1771, only in her twenties and whose identity is one of the unsolved riddles of British history. She is said to have been brought to the neighbourhood as an infant around 1746, to live with a family named Taylor at a house called Waterside, on the banks of the River Leven at Newby Bridge, and she was known locally to some as 'the Princess'.

The supposition is that the young lady was the daughter, legitimate or otherwise, of Bonnie Prince Charlie. His mother, the 'Old Pretender's' wife, was Maria Clementina Sobieski, the grand-daughter of John III, King of Poland. In 1726 she became godmother to the child of an officer in the Old Pretender's army, John Walkenshawe, who named his daughter Clementina after her. When Clementina Walkenshawe grew up, she happened to be staying with relatives in Scotland when Charles Edward Stuart fell ill after his victory over the English at Falkirk. She had known him since their childhood in Rome, and she nursed him back to health

and probably became his mistress then. When the Young Pretender fled
to the Continent after his crushing defeat at Culloden, Clementina joined
him, and in 1754 she bore him a daughter, Charlotte, who cared for him
later when he drifted aimlessly from court to court, sponging on the
Catholic princes of Europe, a shattered and dissolute drunkard, until his
death in 1788.

Mystery surrounds the
identity of Clementina
Douglass in the
churchyard at
Finsthwaite, Cumbria

The question is, was Charlotte the first and only child of Charlie and Clementina Walkenshawe? Bonnie Prince Charlie, a fugitive with a price of £30,000 on his head, travelled under the pseudonym Douglass after his escape to France. Clementina claimed that he had made her his wife, but there is no evidence of that, and in 1772 Charles married Princess Louise of Stolberg, who entered a convent after six childless years – though not for long. We shall probably never know the true identity of the young lady buried at Finsthwaite with the words 'Behold thy king cometh' carved on her memorial. But the fact that there is a mystery at all suggests that some secrecy attended the little girl who may well have been deposited with loyal Jacobites for her own safety after the failure of the '45 Rebellion. Furthermore, the monument was not put up until a century after her death, as she was buried in an unmarked grave.

What are we to make of the supposed graves of Robin Hood's lieutenants, Little John and Will Scarlett, at Hathersage, Derbyshire, and Blidworth, Nottinghamshire, respectively? The ancient grave of 'John Little' was opened in the eighteenth century and a large thigh-bone found, indicating a man about seven feet in height. The grave at Blidworth is reputed to be that of William Scathelock, identified as Will Scarlett by those who want to believe in Robin Hood and his merry men even though there is not a shred of real evidence that he ever existed.

Peter the Wild Boy certainly existed. His small and simple headstone is in the churchyard at Northchurch, Hertfordshire, with only his given name and the date of his death, 1785. He was found at a farm near Hanover in 1724 – a boy of about thirteen who could not speak, walked on all fours and was seen sucking at a cow's teats. He was brought to England and kept like a pet animal at the court of George I, with whom he shared a taste for music, an ignorance of English and a degree of imbecility. He became known as Peter the Wild Boy and excited the curiosity of Jonathan Swift, among others. But the court lost interest in him when it failed to teach him any human language, and he was farmed out to a man named Fenn at Northchurch, where he spent the rest of his long life with a leather collar round his neck, in case he wandered off, with the inscription: 'Peter the Wild Man from Hanover, whoever will bring him to Mr Fenn, at Berkhamsted, Hertfordshire, shall be paid for their trouble.'

The appendix lists some of the people who were famous, nationally or world-wide, buried in churchyards throughout England and Wales, but of course this can only be a personal selection, limited in equal proportions no doubt by ignorance and lack of space. There are around 12,000 parish churches in England and Wales, most with their own churchyards, and every one contains something of interest. There may be the grave of someone who was famous locally, if not nationally, and even if there is not, every churchyard can provide a glimpse of local history from its tombstones.

Eyam, Derbyshire. The plague epidemic broke c in 1665 in the cottages b the churchyard

I have pointed out a few churchyards which contain interesting groups of graves, like those of sea-faring men at Appledore, Devon, but most churchyards tell us something about the towns or villages they are in if we look carefully enough. The names recorded are interesting even when they are not strange or foreign ones. You could be lowered by helicopter, in which you had travelled blindfolded, into almost any churchyard in Britain and tell roughly what part of the country you were in, not only from the style and materials the church and monuments were in but also from the names on the headstones. If there were several Foxons, for example, you would almost certainly be in Leicestershire; if Slees, in Devon; Brookers, in Kent. It will often be found that the local telephone directory perpetuates the most common names in any churchyard.

Similarly with trades and professions. No one is surprised to find the graves of sea-faring men in coastal churchyards, but it might be more puzzling to find that the churchyard at Corby, Northamptonshire, for instance, is populated with farmers rather than steel-workers. The reason is that Corby is a twentieth-century industrial creation. Before the railway came in 1879, it was a little village of stone cottages in farming country.

If there is a churchyard in which one finds a disproportionately high number of deaths in the same year, it may have been the result of a local epidemic. The graves of plague victims at Eyam, Derbyshire, include that of Katharine Mompesson, the wife of the vicar who persuaded his parishioners to isolate themselves in an heroic determination to prevent the spread of the disease. Paulton, Avon, has two memorials to mass victims of what is described as 'the dreadful scourge of Asiatic cholera' – seventy-two parishioners died within a fortnight in 1832, and another sixty-two at the end of 1849. At Landewednack, Cornwall, elm trees were planted on the mass grave of plague victims so that the spot could not be re-used and the infection released from the disturbed soil.

Many a churchyard provides testimony to the high rate of infant mortality in centuries earlier than ours. Those who die as children get no chance to make their marks on history, and it is natural that we should be especially touched by the evidence of so much waste, but we should also spare a thought for the mothers who often lived short enough lives ruined by child-bearing. Rebecca Town, of Keighley, West Yorkshire, bore thirty children by the time she herself died at forty-four in 1851, and all but one of her children died before they were three years old. In Leicester, Ann Chawner's first child died in 1789 while she was pregnant with her second, which also died, to be followed to the grave by two more infants within five years. The four of them are commemorated by a Swithland slate headstone in the churchyard of St Mary de Castro. The churchyard at Easton-in-Gordano, Avon, has the nineteenth-century graves of fifteen children of the Pains family who all died in their infancy except one sister who made it to ten.

One of my favourite epitaphs is said to have been on the coffin of a little girl washed ashore from a sunken ship at Lydd, Kent, early in the nineteenth century. It seems that someone asked the parish constable what name should be put on the coffin plate, to which that official replied 'God knows!' And that is exactly what *was* engraved – 'God knows' – all that any Christian should require, surely.

IN·LOVING·MEMORY·OF
MARY·AUGUSTA·WARD
WIFE·OF·THOMAS·HUMPHRY·WARD
DAUGHTER·OF·THOMAS·ARNOLD·OF
OXFORD·AND·DUBLIN·AND·GRAND-
DAUGHTER·OF·D⁰·ARNOLD·OF·RUGBY
BORN·IN·TASMANIA·JUNE·11ᵗʰ·1851
LIVED·AT·STOCKS·1892~1920
DIED·IN·LONDON·MARCH·24ᵗʰ·1920
"Others·I·doubt·not·if·not·we
The·issue·of·our·toils·shall·see
And·(they·forgotten·and·unknown)
Young·children·gather·as·their·own
The·harvest·that·the·dead·had·sown"

HERE·ALSO·RESTS
THOMAS·HUMPHRY·WARD
HUSBAND·OF·MARY·AUGUSTA·WARD
FORMERLY·FELLOW·AND·TUTOR·OF
BRASENOSE·COLLEGE·OXFORD
BORN·AT·HULL·NOVEMBER·10ᵗʰ·1845
LIVED·AT·STOCKS·1892~1922
DIED·IN·LONDON·MAY·9ᵗʰ·1920
"Blessed·are·the·pure

The English Way of Death

The establishment of the churchyard as a receptacle for dead bodies inevitably surrounded the church, both literally and metaphorically, with a great deal of belief and superstition that had nothing to do with Christian doctrine, since disposal of the dead is a matter which, in all ages and all societies, generates human responses quite independent of established religion. Religion may, indeed, be said to arise wholly to mitigate the fact of death, which is the only certainty every human being is born with.

The social custom of inhumation, which Christianity inherited, as it were, from its parents in the eastern Mediterranean and Asia Minor, was accompanied by emotional ritual long before the Church of Rome worked out its own approved form of funeral rite. Prehistoric, Roman, Anglo-Saxon and Danish burials are well known in Britain, and Christian burial grounds, as we have seen, are often on or near the same ground; as at Sancton, Humberside, for instance, where the churchyard is close to a large Anglo-Saxon burial ground; and Aylesford, Kent, where an Iron Age cemetery was discovered near the churchyard. It is certain that if England had never become Christian, the practices of burial and cremation would still be its customary methods of corpse-disposal, attended with some ritual ceremony by those close to the deceased, and with similar ideas of rebirth and continuation of the soul. The low mound of earth raised over many churchyard graves is reminiscent of the barrows marking the sites of prehistoric burials thousands of years before Christianity arrived on the scene.

The reason why we can be so certain is that methods of disposing of the dead are dictated largely by climate and social factors rather than by religion, which merely consents to what is practical. Thus, tribes in Africa left their dead in the jungle to be consumed by wild animals, and Parsees in India left their dead on rooftops in full confidence that their bones would be picked clean by vultures. These methods were probably – and cremation is certainly – more hygienic than inhumation.

The Christian tradition of burial, however, is for the corpse to be interred, lying flat out on its back, facing the east. This practice no doubt had its origins in pagan sun-worship and thus gave rise to the curious folklore about burial on the north side of the church. Widespread superstition about the sunless side of the churchyard meant that there were fewer graves there in most churchyards, and this therefore tended to be the area where most communal activities took place. It was believed that bastards, strangers, unbaptized infants and, in particular, suicides, were always buried on the north side of the churchyard if they were allowed in consecrated ground at all, and – especially in south-eastern England – suicides were laid on a north-south axis instead of east-west. This is referred to in *Hamlet* when the burial of the drowned Ophelia takes place:

1st gravedigger: Is she to be buried in Christian burial that wilfully seeks her own salvation?
2nd gravedigger: I tell thee she is; and therefore make her grave straight.

At any rate, the north sides of churchyards will usually be found to contain more modern headstones, because shortage of space has eventually demanded the fuller use of that area and there is not nowadays the same objection to a body being buried there. At least one client who was free from superstition caught on to the advantage of being buried on the north side, where he would lie undisturbed for longer, and had the fact recorded on his headstone at Epworth, Humberside in 1807, with the words:

And that I might longer undisturb'd abide,
I choos'd to be laid on this northern side.

There was also a superstition about being the first burial in a newly consecrated churchyard. It was believed that the spirit of that person was responsible for ever for protecting the churchyard from evil.

Pagan superstitions accounted also for other rituals that were not prescribed Christian practice, like the habit of carrying a coffin three times round the churchyard cross, always in clockwise direction, following the movement of the sun. At Formby, Merseyside, coffins were carried round a stone called the Godstone in the churchyard, in the belief that

164

lychgate at Sheepstor,
von, showing the stone
shelf for resting coffins

this would prevent the soul of the deceased from being snatched by the Devil. Although incumbents here and there preached against these pagan rituals, the beliefs were too strong to be easily stopped, and the practice continued. This ritual, or a variation of it, was common in the west of England at one time, Brilley, Hereford & Worcester, being one place where it was the local tradition. At Pembridge and elsewhere, they carried the coffin clockwise round the churchyard before taking it into the church, and similar rituals were observed in Devon. Perhaps the holes sometimes found in the shafts of churchyard crosses, such as the one mentioned at Bitterley, Shropshire, were actually bored for a wooden crosspiece to be inserted at the time of a funeral, for in the Tudor period the Church was at pains to forbid wooden crosses 'to be set upon the cross in the churchyard'.

The practice of setting up crosses for prayers wherever the coffin rested on its journey to the grave was widespread at one time, the most famous example being the crosses built at the order of Edward I at the resting-places of his wife Eleanor of Castile's body between Nottinghamshire and London.

In the north of England, especially in Durham and Northumberland, 'bidders' used to knock at the door of every house in the locality to announce a funeral and invite the occupants to attend. It was unthinkable *not* to attend the funeral of a neighbour, but it was necessary to follow the procession for only a few yards. This was deemed sufficient to pay one's proper respects to the departed.

In some parts, such as the Haworth district of West Yorkshire, the sexton would announce the funeral feast beside the open grave, naming the pub in which it was to be held.

Another one-time belief, said by Sir James Frazer to have been prevalent down the east coast of England, was that most deaths occurred at ebb tide. Shakespeare has Falstaff die 'e'en at the turning o' the tide'; and in *David Copperfield* Dickens makes Mr Peggotty say: 'People can't die, along the coast, except when the tide's pretty nigh out.'

The 'passing bell' tolled before funerals in many places according to the identity of the deceased – perhaps four chimes for a child, eight for a woman, and twelve for a man, though each parish had its own procedure, just as some folk saw fit to throw a sprig of yew on to the coffin as it was lowered into the grave, and others a sprig of rosemary – 'That's for remembrance', as Ophelia says – or box: the important thing would seem to be that it was evergreen. In parts of East Anglia it was common to bury a handful of wool with the bodies of shepherds, as token of their honest occupation excusing them from attending church on Sundays.

As old superstitions fade from memory, fresh ones often grow to take their places. By the Victorian era there was a whole new set of beliefs concerning the flowers used to dress churchyard graves. Roses were unimpeachable, but marigolds and foxgloves were out of the question. Sweet-scented flowers were the only admissible kinds, and if they were species recognized as symbols of purity, such as snowdrops and lilies of the valley, so much the better.

All sorts of other curious rituals occurred at churchyard burials in different parts of the country, but most have disappeared in this materialistic age. One such custom was 'sin-eating'. This macabre routine, often performed at the graveside, involved a symbolic consuming of the departed spirit's sins, sometimes by the mourners, sometimes by a professional sin-eater who was hired for the occasion by the dead person's relatives.

John Aubrey described this practice in Herefordshire: 'In the County of Hereford was an old Custome at funeralls to have poor people, who were to take upon them all the sinnes of the party deceased. One of them I remember lived in a cottage on Rosse highway. He was a long leane, ugly, lamentable poor raskel. The Manner was that when the Corps was brought out of the house and layd on the Biere, a Loafe of bread was brought out and delivered to the Sinne-eater over the corps, as also a Mazer-bowle of maple full of beer, which he was to drinke up, and sixpence in money, in consideration whereof he took upon himself ipso facto all the Sinnes of the Defunct, and freed him (or her) from walking after they were dead ...'

By taking the burden of the departed soul's sins upon himself, the sin-eater supposedly prevented the dead walking again but brought upon himself the superstition that made others shun him. The ritual may well be a token survival of the primitive practice of eating dead relations in order that their strength or wisdom might be passed on to their descendants. The symbolic eating might involve only a lick of the salt placed on the chest of the corpse, or it might be the consuming of small cakes or biscuits handed out over the coffin, with ale to wash them down – this variation on the theme was a sort of graveside communion to assist the dead through the pains of Purgatory. The custom seems to have been especially common in Wales and the neighbouring counties of England. The idea of the scapegoat is, of course, not only pre-Christian but almost universal, so perhaps the only surprising thing is that the ritual has not been more widespread in Britain.

The habit of placing a small amount of salt in a dish on the dead person's chest was certainly more widespread, being done in Devon and East Anglia, at least. It seems to have been believed that this would ensure a 'good corpse' – one that would not start rising.

Mary Webb wrote an electrifying account of sin-eating in her Shropshire novel, *Precious Bane*:

Now it was still the custom at that time, in our part of the country, to give a fee to some poor man after a death, and then he would take bread and wine handed to him across the coffin, and eat and drink, saying –

I give easement and rest now to thee, dear man, that ye walk not over the fields nor down the by-ways. And for thy peace I pawn my own soul.

And with a calm and grievous look he would go to his own place. Mostly, my Grandad used to say, Sin Eaters were such as had been Wise Men or layers of spirits, and had fallen on evil days. Or they were poor folk that had come, through some dark deed, out of the kindly life of men, and with whom none would trade, whose only food might oftentimes be the bread and wine that had crossed the coffin. In our time there was none left around Sarn. They had nearly died out, and they had to be sent for to the mountains. It was a long way to send, and they asked a big price, instead of doing it for nothing as in the old days. So Gideon said –

'We'll save the money. What good would the man do?'

But Mother cried and moaned all night after. And when the Sexton said 'Be there a Sin Eater?' she cried again very pitifully, because Father had died in his wrath, with all his sins upon him, and besides, he had died in his boots, which is a very unket thing and bodes no good. So she thought he had great need of a Sin Eater, and she would not be comforted.

Then a strange, heart-shaking thing came to pass. Gideon stepped up to the coffin and said –

'There *is* a Sin Eater.'

'Who then? I see none,' said Sexton.

'I ool be the Sin Eater.'

He took up the little pewter measure full of darkness, and he looked at Mother.

'Oot turn over the farm and all to me if I be the Sin Eater, Mother?' he said.

'No, no! Sin Eaters be accurst!'

'What harm, to drink a sup of your own wine and chumble a crust of your own bread? But if you dunna care, let be. He can go with the sin on him.'

'No, no! Leave un go free, Gideon! Let un rest, poor soul! You be in life and young, but he'm cold and helpless, in the power of Satan. He went with all his sins upon him, in his boots, poor soul! If there's none else to help, let his own lad take pity.'

'And you'll give me the farm, Mother?'

'Yes, yes, my dear! What be the farm to me? You can take all, and welcome.'

Then Gideon drank the wine all of a gulp, and swallowed the crust.

There was no sound in all the place but the sound of his teeth biting it up.

Then he put his hand on the coffin, standing up tall in the high black hat, with a gleaming pale face, and he said –

'I give easement and rest now to thee, dear man. Come not down the lanes nor in our meadows. And for thy peace I pawn my own soul. Amen.'

The graveside rituals of burial have now largely given way to the post-burial rituals of outward show of which Dickens wrote in *The*

The Anglican bur
service. A solemn sce
that has hardly chang
since this engraving w
made around 18

Uncommercial Traveller: 'Real affliction, real grief and solemnity, have been outraged, and the funeral has been "performed". The waste for which the funeral customs of many tribes of savages are conspicuous, has attended these civilised obsequies; and once, and twice, have I wished in my soul that if the waste must be, they would let the undertaker bury the money, and let me bury the friend.'

The laws governing burial do not require that it should be in a churchyard, cemetery or any particular place. It need not be on consecrated ground nor be attended with any religious ceremony. Nor is any wish expressed in the will of the deceased as to the disposal of his or her remains binding on those left with the responsibility of disposal. Witness the case of Dickens himself, who was placed in Westminster Abbey, despite his wish to be buried at Gad's Hill, Kent, where he had lived. And Thomas Hardy, who had expressed a desire to be buried with his kinsfolk in the churchyard at Stinsford, Dorset, was in the event cut up and divided between Stinsford and London, the bulk of him going to Westminster Abbey, though he was an atheist, and only his heart being buried in the grave at Stinsford – and even that is uncertain, since it was rumoured that the extracted organ had been eaten by the surgeon's cat.

Every inhabitant of a parish, whether a member of the Church of England or not, has the right in Common Law to be buried in the parish churchyard, unless excommunicated, though there is no automatic right to have a monument of any kind erected over the grave, and no one has a right to specify in which part of the churchyard his body shall be buried, unless a faculty has granted permission for a space to be reserved for that person. A Church of England minister is duty-bound to conduct a burial service if required, over everyone entitled to Christian burial, but the representatives of the deceased may appoint someone other than the parish priest to conduct a service, such as a Nonconformist minister. No fee for burial in a churchyard is required by law but a fee is charged for the maintenance of the churchyard, and if a non-parishioner desires burial, permission is usually granted by the incumbent, provided there is space, and subject to the guidance of the parochial church council, on payment of a fee which is higher than for a parishioner, usually double.

These are the basic laws in relation to churchyard burial, but in practice and by long custom matters are rather more complicated than that. For instance, the container for the corpse is nearly always a wooden coffin, but it need not necessarily be so. Coffins came into use by all classes of society only at about the same time as personal monuments, i.e. in the eighteenth century, when the financial means of the lower classes enabled them to aspire to the same dignity in death as their 'betters'. Before then the custom was for the corpse to be wrapped in a shroud and carried to the graveside in the parish coffin, from which it was removed before being lowered into the ground. Wealthy people had themselves buried in lead coffins in medieval times, but an attempt to bring iron coffins into more general use in the nineteenth century was resisted on the obvious grounds that, if parishioners thus preserved their remains against decay, there would be less room for future burials.

A story is told of the churchyard at Rearsby, Leicestershire, that the lead coffin of one Andrew Sacheverell, buried in 1658, was dug up in the following century and sold for 28 shillings, the profit being used to buy a new coat for the parish clerk.

Incidentally, the churchyard at Great Wakering, Essex, is the driest in England; the wettest is at Wasdale Head, Cumbria. It seems likely that if you want your body to remain uncorrupted in the earth for the longest possible time, Essex is the best place to be.

People were not always as squeamish in earlier times as we are now about the realities of death and annihilation. When John Donne preached a memorial service for Lady Magdalen Herbert in the seventeenth century, he told his congregation that her body 'now, whilst I speake, is mouldring and crumbling into lesse, and lesse dust, and so hath some motion, though no life'. Possibly her relatives did not find this macabre sentiment especially comforting, but there was no call for the clergyman to be sacked. A minister in Essex *was* brought before a church court in 1593 for 'burieing the dead corps of one Father Cooke not saing servyce in manner and form as it is in the book of Common Prayer prescribed'. The reverend gentleman's excuse was that a great wind was blowing and he did not want to catch cold.

Gravediggers and undertakers used to be shunned as practitioners in the so-called 'dismal trade' – frequenters of the necropolis and handlers of dead bodies. Gravediggers still retire behind bushes with their shovels when a funeral takes place, waiting for the mourners to disperse before they get on with their task of filling in the grave. It would be unseemly to do otherwise. They are at those moments in a class apart from the folk who have often, in working-class society, spent much money on this ceremony, not least for the black costume still usually considered obligatory in giving the departed a 'decent' send-off to eternity.

Class distinctions prevail in England, of course, even in death. One is reminded of the 'quality vault' reserved by the parish church at Clifton, Avon, in the eighteenth century, for the reception of aristocrats who did not wish to be mixed up with plebeian dust when they 'shuffled off this mortal coil'. Their illustrious decomposing corpses smelled less, no doubt, than those of the ordinary folk outside.

Dorothy Wordsworth described a pauper's funeral at Grasmere in her journal of 1800:

About 10 men and 4 women. Bread, cheese and ale. They talked sensibly and cheerfully about common things. The dead person 56 years of age buried by the parish. The coffin was neatly lettered and painted black and covered with a decent cloth ... I thought she was going to a quiet spot and I could not help weeping very much. When we came to the bridge they began to sing again and stopped during 4 lines before they entered the churchyard. The priest met us – he did not look as a man ought to do on such an occasion – I had seen him half-drunk the day before in a pot-house.

Overleaf: The overgrown churchyard at Powerstock, Dorset

171

The 'pauper's grave' is a thing that still strikes horror into many people, as did fear of being sent to the workhouse. It is seen as the worst possible disgrace if one cannot be given a 'decent' burial. An eighteenth-century observer described how the parish buried paupers in Manchester: 'They dig in the churchyards, or other annexed burial places, large holes or pits in which they put many of the bodies of those whose friends are not able to pay for better graves; and then, those pits or holes (called the Poor's Holes), once opened, are not covered till filled with such dead bodies ... How noisome the stench is that arises from these holes so stowed with dead bodies, especially in sultry seasons and after rain, one may appeal to all who approach them.'

Mrs Pember Reeves drew attention to the public shame of burial by the parish in a Fabian Society tract in 1912, citing the unanimous view of poor people that to be buried in a common grave was without dignity and respect for the dead. A mother saw her three-year-old daughter 'buried in a common grave with twelve other coffins of all sizes. "We 'ad to keep a sharp eye out for Edie ... she were so little she were almost 'id." '

Curious rituals attended the burial of women who had died in childbirth in some areas, especially in the north. In parts of Yorkshire they were buried at midnight, with four female mourners holding a white sheet over the coffin as it was borne to the graveside. In Lancashire the baby was held over the grave of its mother during the burial service. In no aspect of modern humanity have pagan overtones been so pronounced as in burial of the dead. In the far north of England, it was for long a custom to sacrifice an animal or bird prior to a funeral as a propitiation; and the burial of a gypsy chief was accompanied by the sacrifice of his horse.

There have also, of course, always been the heretics and eccentrics who have chosen to evade the churchyards, or the dignity customarily accorded people of their position in society, altogether. Sir Joseph Danvers MP, who would in normal circumstances have been buried inside the church at Swithland, Leicestershire, is in fact buried in a tomb half in and half out of the churchyard, since he wished to be buried with his favourite dog, which could not be admitted in consecrated soil. John Baskerville, the printer and type-founder, was an atheist and had himself buried in a tomb in his garden, though his remains were subsequently dug up and deposited elsewhere. And at Botus Fleming, Cornwall, William Martyn was buried in a field on the grounds that, being a 'Catholic Christian, in the true, not depraved Popish sense of the word', he knew 'no superstitious veneration for church or churchyard'.

Although refusal to be buried in a churchyard was exceptional, it was common enough, even in the Tudor period, for those who were sympathetic to the new puritanism to avoid unnecessary ritual. John Willocke, a rector of Loughborough, Leicestershire, directed in his will in 1585 that he should be 'buried christenly in the grounde without any

Rynginge after my deathe, or any pompe, miche lesse without any Supersticon ...'. When John Underwood was buried in the churchyard at Whittlesey, Cambridgeshire, in 1733, he was followed to the grave, as requested in his will, only by six paid mourners who did not wear black, and he was buried fully clothed in a green coffin. It is said that the funeral

Old gravestones set in the retaining wall of the churchyard at South Molton, Devon

of Dolly Pentreath (see p.155), who died in 1777, was interrupted for a whisky break.

Generally speaking, though, good and evil men, as well as rich and poor, have bowed their heads in respect at a decent and 'proper' funeral. Blackmore described the winter funeral of one of the villainous Doones in an Exmoor churchyard, where old Sir Ensor 'was to lie upon his back,

175

awaiting the darkness of the Judgment-day': 'To see those dark and mighty men, inured to all of sin and crime, reckless both of man and God, yet now with heads devoutly bent, clasped hands, and downcast eyes, following the long black coffin of their common ancestor, to the place where they must join him, when their sum of ill was done; and to see the feeble priest chanting, over the dead form, words the living would have laughed at, sprinkling with his little broom drops that could not purify; while the children, robed in white, swung their smoking censors over the cold and twilight grave ...'

This or something like it is the English way of death still for those who prefer burial to cremation, and for a while their graves are attended at regular intervals by their relatives, until memory fades and protestations of everlasting memory on their headstones are belied by the neglected graves before them, overgrown with grass and weeds, and with an occasional milk bottle or jam jar holding a few wilting chrysanthemums or some other desperate glimpse of life in these extensive monuments to decay, where stone crosses and angels loom up like ghosts themselves out of the mist in winter.

The church may re-use grave spaces when it is known that there are no surviving or objecting relatives of the subjects buried there, or in a part of the churchyard which has not been in use for a suitably long period of time. And there are other occasional valid reasons for the disturbance of old graves. Thomas Hardy had an irreverent word to say on the subject:

'You see those mothers squabbling there?'
Remarks the man of the cemetery.
'One says in tears, '"Tis mine lies here!"'
Another, "Nay, mine, you Pharisee!"
Another, "How dare you move my flowers
And put your own on this grave of ours!"
But all their children were laid therein
At different times, like sprats in a tin.

'And then the main drain had to cross,
And we moved the lot some nights ago,
And packed them away in the general foss
With hundreds more. But their folks don't know.
And as well cry over a new-laid drain
As anything else, to ease your pain!'

The removal of graves and headstones is usually done with discretion, but some controversy has been aroused in recent years by the practice of tidying up churchyards and making them easier to maintain, by stacking

The first cemetery to be opened. Kensal Green, London

up old headstones along the churchyard perimeters, or using them to pave paths. This can sometimes go to such extreme lengths as to deprive churchyards of any semblance of historic or consecrated ground, and turn them into what look like public parks or gardens which happen to have churches in the middle. One may compare the photograph of St Wendreda's churchyard at March, Cambridgeshire, with the one in Pevsner's *Buildings of England* volume on that county, 1954, to see the dramatic effects of such overdone cosmetic treatment.

An old churchyard with relatively few graves in it (such as Morston, Norfolk) may imply that the church and its burial ground are too large for the population it serves, or that the place is a very healthy one to live in. But a churchyard which has been entirely cleared to permit an easily mowed lawn, with gravestones lined up in rows out of the way, can only imply an indifference to the past, which affects the visitor's reaction not only to the churchyard but to the whole community as well. The spirit of place has been exorcised along with the ghosts of the inhabitants. Sir John Betjeman went on record in characteristic fashion about this treatment:

I hate to see in old churchyards
Tombstones stacked round like playing cards
Along the wall which then encloses
A trim new lawn and standard roses ...

Undoubtedly the increase in the incidence of cremation has been partly responsible for this tidying-up operation, which is akin to the Department of the Environment's treatment of ruins in its care; all is clinically neat and well cared for, but the special atmosphere that should be conjured up has been irretrievably lost. Parts of churchyards have been turned into 'gardens of remembrance', where cremated remains can be buried or scattered, and the relative ease of maintenance of these areas compared with ground thick with old gravestones has impressed the church

A pavement of old gravestones in the churchyard at South Molton, Devon

wardens, particularly in urban areas, a little too much in some cases.

Around the middle of the nineteenth century, when cemeteries were being developed all over England to relieve the pressure on churchyards for the sake of public health, some churchyards began to be closed by Orders in Council, virtually banning further burials in them, with certain minor exceptions, such as the continued use of a family vault, and this practice has continued. Cremated remains may still be buried in a 'closed' churchyard and it must, of course, still be maintained as consecrated ground as before. But a 'disused' churchyard (that is, one in which no living relatives of the last burials in it are known to remain or object) may be turned over to the local authority for redevelopment as an open space amenity. The Church Commissioners can declare a churchyard 'redundant' and sell it off for redevelopment. Provided that no burial has taken place in it during the past fifty years, a redundant churchyard can be built on, and this obviously occurs most in urban areas. Thus the former churchyard at St Botolph Bishopsgate in London now has tennis courts on it, while streets cover the former churchyard of St Mary-le-Bow, Cheapside.

When a churchyard is declared redundant, however, no work can take place on it until the human remains have been removed and either re-interred elsewhere or incinerated, and tombstones and monuments removed. Where there are next of kin or personal representatives of the deceased, they have the right to order the disposal of both the remains and the monument as they see fit. Where there are not, the Church decides on the fate of the remains and may dispose of tombstones and monuments by breaking up and defacing them, or by other appropriate means, which sometimes means lining them up against walls, as at Paddington Green, for instance, and many other places.

This cosmetic treatment of churchyards would have been condemned at one time for other reasons than the mere loss of the traditional appearance. Disturbing the final resting places of the dead was believed, as we have already seen, to be playing with fire. If old headstones were laid out as paving, either inside or outside the church, the dead would be likely to walk. You were, so to speak, taking the lid off the underworld. One way of preventing this, which does not appeal to modern taste because the value of the paving is in seeing the inscriptions, would be to lay them face downwards. This derives from a belief that if bodies were buried face down they would only go deeper if they moved at all. As a sexton said in the nineteenth century when a church floor at Kington, Hereford & Worcester, had been so paved: '... the owd gravestones ... be quite se'af wi' their faces down'rts.'

Occasional threats of action, however discreetly and diplomatically carried out, are bound to be a cause of concern, if not actual distress, to some people. When Nuthampstead, Hertfordshire, was under threat as a site for the third London airport, one local farmer whose family had been working the land for generations said: 'Forty of my ancestors lie in that churchyard. If they are put under concrete, how will they get out on the Day of Judgment?'

When famous figures are involved, the remains will usually be buried in consecrated ground elsewhere. Thus Laurence Sterne (see p.94) was not left to rest in peace for long, his bones having once again been dug up in 1969 when the churchyard at Bayswater was redeveloped, and re-buried at Coxwold in North Yorkshire where he had been vicar for eight years. His original tombstone went with him. The Bayswater churchyard eventually became a nursery school playground, but among the old gravestones lined up round it is that of Ann Radcliffe, the novelist and author of *The Mysteries of Udolpho*, who was buried somewhere here in 1823.

The Burial Act of 1852 provided for cemeteries to be set up and maintained by local councils, to relieve the intolerable overcrowding of urban churchyards. Several cemeteries preceded the Act, especially in London, where Kensal Green Cemetery was founded in 1832 by the General Cemetery Company with the approval of Parliament. But privately owned burial grounds earned some notoriety by falling below the standards of decency that the Church and public considered proper, and the 1852 Act established public cemeteries on a proper footing.

The publicity given to the appalling condition and possible consequences of overcrowded churchyards created much public disquiet, and between 1852 and 1906 no fewer than fifteen Burial Acts were passed by Parliament in response to widespread concern. Cholera epidemics were only one of the evils blamed by some on the practice of inhumation in towns and cities, and it was inevitable that a new attitude to disposal of the dead would grow in an industrial and materialistic society. Scientific thought led to ideas of more hygienic disposal such as burial at sea (which would increase the supply of fish), or burial in the earth in more perishable containers, so that 'dust to dust' would come to pass the more easily and quickly. There is no law of God that says a dead body must be buried in a 'wooden jacket', as coffins are euphemistically called, and if bodies had always been buried simply in shrouds, as they are in modern Israel, churchyards would not have become heaped up to such an extent with materials designed to keep decomposition at bay. Straightforward earth burial was strongly advocated in the nineteenth century by many who could see the growing problems facing churchyards but were revolted by the idea of cremation. This alternative naturally had a strong appeal for Catholics for whom cremation was an unthinkable denial of their belief in resurrection of the body as opposed to immortality of the soul.

Nevertheless, 'ashes to ashes' came next. There had been little, if any, resort to the practice of disposing of the dead by means of fire in Britain for well over a thousand years, though it had often been advocated, especially by the nineteenth century, and indeed occasionally practised, at the risk of criminal prosecution. In Italy, in August 1822, the bodies of the drowned poet Shelley and his friend Edward Williams were burned on a funeral pyre on the beach at Viareggio, after some opposition from the Italian authorities. Shelley's heart was snatched from the flames by Edward Trelawney and eventually came to rest in St Peter's churchyard at Bournemouth, his ashes being buried in the Protestant Cemetery at Rome, which the poet had considered so beautiful that 'it might make one in love with death'. It was over thirty years before Trelawney's full description of the events became known in England, but it was regarded by some as a powerful argument against cremation.

In 1874 a Cremation Society was founded in London with several well-known public figures among its supporters, and headed by the Queen's physician, Sir Henry Thompson, but the first 'official' cremation did not take place until 1885, because the Home Office, under pressure from the Church, would not permit it. Then in 1884, at Cardiff assizes, Dr William Price, physician and self-styled Archdruid, was indicted for attempting to burn, in public, the corpse of his young son, Iesu Grist, instead of burying it. The judge, Mr Justice Stephens, declared that there was nothing in the law to prevent cremation unless it was a public nuisance, and the case was dismissed with a farthing costs.

There was, all the same, fierce public and ecclesiastical opposition to the very idea of cremation for a long time, and indeed there still is in some quarters, the Catholic Church being still theoretically hostile to it, as well as orthodox Judaism. Many Catholics ignore the official doctrine, however, as indeed do many Jews.

Attitudes vary not only according to class and religious persuasion, but also in different parts of the country, though it is difficult to be sure of the extent. Certainly the formal family gathering for a funeral is a stronger survival in the north than in the south, but attitudes to cremation are changing very rapidly. Richard Hoggart referred in 1957 to the northern (i.e. Leeds) working class emphasis on a 'proper' funeral, a 'decent burial', 'putting 'im away splendid'; and the dislike of cremation as 'unnatural'. Eleven years later, D. Elliston Allen could report that Yorkshire folk 'vehemently opt for cremation ... unlike the Scots, their neighbours spatially and emotionally, who candidly prefer to be buried.'

It was not until 1902 that the Cremation Act was passed which legalized and regulated the practice of cremation. Even then ministers of religion were exempted from any obligation to conduct a service when cremation was involved, and the strength of public feeling was such that police protection was sometimes called for when a cremation was arranged. Nevertheless, a great swing in the public's attitude was set under way, common sense prevailing in England, as it usually does in the end. In the

Beaconsfield,
Buckinghamshire.
Tree-shaded and peaceful
– a 'normal'
well-maintained
churchyard

hundred years since the first official cremation at Woking in March 1885 (two more took place in that year), Britain has become the leading practitioner of cremation among nominally Christian countries. The spread of crematoria was rapid. Manchester's, for instance, was launched in 1892 with the disposal of an eighty-four-year-old man named Brown. By 1946 there were more than forty crematoria in the United Kingdom, and around 50,000 cremations a year in England alone; by the early 1960s a quarter of a million, and the proportion of cremations to burials is still rising. Ironically, in 1946 there was but one crematorium in the whole of the materialistic Soviet Union!

All this has served to take much of the pressure off churchyards and cemeteries, but with hundreds of thousands of burials still taking place each year, there is as yet no end in sight to the vast acreage of land still necessarily reserved for disposal of the dead, and many of the old fears and superstitions remain deeply embedded in the human psyche. It will be a long time before cremation becomes once again the normal method of disposal for the whole population of Britain, as it was in prehistoric times, but it will happen. Hygiene, economy and the weakening of religious dogma are all on its side and, as Bernard Shaw wrote: 'Earth burial ... will some day be prohibited by law, not only because it is hideously unaesthetic, but because the dead would crowd the living off the earth if it could be carried out to its end of preserving our bodies for their resurrection on an imaginary day of judgement.'

The Church generally falls in line behind public opinion, rather than leading it, when it is struggling to establish or maintain its position. Much of the early history of Christianity in Britain was concerned with compromise with pagan beliefs and practices in order to win over the pagan people, and much the same has happened in regard to cremation. 'If you can't beat 'em, join 'em' has been the general approach of the Church of England, and although the *burial* of ashes is recommended by the Church (though not in polythene containers, as the *Churchyards Handbook* points out), scattering or 'strewing' has become the most popular method of disposal. It was formally approved by the Church of England in 1944.

The English churchyard is a doomed institution. The idea of consecrated ground will fall by the wayside as surely as other outdated superstitions, and land hitherto reserved for the dead will be released for the living. Monuments and other objects of historic or artistic value will quite properly be removed to museums. No one should mourn the gradual disappearance of the churchyard, except gravediggers and monumental masons, for whom its demise will be bad news economically. I suspect that few will mourn its passing when the time comes, but eventually churchyards (and, of course, cemeteries and gardens of remembrance) will be seen, if not as relics of barbarism, at least as aspects of civilization's immaturity.

A friend asked me, towards the end of my work on this book, if I was 'ever aware of some special presence' whilst researching around old churchyards. The plain answer is that I was not. I *did* have a feeling of slight discomfort, but not through fear or anticipation of seeing ghosts or supernatural occurrences. I can readily go along with Professor W.G. Hoskins in regarding a country churchyard as the best possible place on a summer's day to sit down for lunch with a bottle of wine after a long walk and lean against a tombstone for a quiet snooze. I was, however, and remain, disturbed by the realization that churchyards embrace ritual burial of the dead in a way that goes back, at the very least, over 6,000 years, and we have not yet shaken off this primitive habit of regarding corpses as holy relics.

It seems to me that despite mankind's slow and painful groping towards the light of civilization, he has an awfully long way still to go, when he can gather round a hole in the ground, dressed in black, and listen to the ritual incantations of a priest whilst the dead is solemnly lowered into it.

It is not our honouring of the dead that I find disturbing, but our public demonstration of it, as represented by religious rites and the erection of monuments. Men and women who have done public service will be remembered, and those who have not will be remembered by those who knew them, for as long as is necessary, which is all that matters. Mary Coleridge had the right idea:

> Some hang above the tombs,
> Some weep in empty rooms,
> I, when the iris blooms,
> > Remember.

> I, when the cyclamen
> Opens her buds again,
> Rejoice a moment – then
> > Remember.

It is a fallacy to suppose that a monument in a churchyard does anything to perpetuate the memory or enhance the reputation of anyone, whether great and famous or not. When Sir Winston Churchill was buried at Bladon, in 1965, many thousands of people visited his grave in the first few months afterwards, but already there is a grown-up generation for whom he is little more than a name in the history books.

The substitution of cremation for inhumation does not entirely dispose of the problem of ancestor-worship, but it is undoubtedly a move in the right direction – a quicker, cleaner and less morbid approach to a necessity that has to be faced in respect of every one of the billions of human beings who inhabit the earth.

Geoffrey Gorer maintained, twenty years ago, that the decline of ritual for dealing with death and grief had some ominous link with the growth of violence in society, and that the stress on sex, as reflected in modern literature, was an escapist response to the 'harsh facts of life'. I do not think this is so. The modern preoccupation with sex is a generally healthy life-asserting trend, compared with the morbid emphasis on death and burial in Victorian life and literature.

Disposal of the dead ought, in due time, to be a matter of state control rather than religious preference, and the churchyard a recorded symbol of a people's growth *towards* civilization, not a thriving sign of its assumed achievement. In the meantime, however, we can safely ignore the over-sensitive strictures of the Reverend Leigh Richmond against 'trifling, licentious, travellers, wandering about the churchyards of the different

Skull and crossbones on a gravestone at the Saxon church of Escomb, County Durham

Dry-stone-walling around Llangelynin churchyard, Gwynedd

The Church — Bettws y Coed — J.W.
15th July 1850.

Sir John Gilbert's
painting of the church
at Bettws-y-Coed

Neglected, illegible and
lichen-encrusted
headstones at Cerne
Abbas, Dorset

places through which they pass, in search of rude, ungrammatical, ill-spelt and absurd verses among the gravestones', and continue to enjoy churchyards for what they are – evocative and highly fascinating records of all sorts of conditions of men and women, local life, death and religious feeling during a particular stage of our country's history and evolution.

If we should seek to end with a fitting epitaph on churchyards themselves, I think we could hardly find a better one than the words of John Donne in one of his sermons:

'... when a whirle-winde hath blowne the dust of the Church-yard into the Church, and the man sweeps out the dust of the Church into the Church-yard, who will undertake to sift those dusts again, and to pronounce: This is the Patrician, this is the noble flowre, and this the yeomanly, this the Plebeian bran.'

vestones in the grass,
mbury St Mary, Surrey

185

Appendix: Some Notable Churchyard Graves in England and Wales

This catalogue of silent citizens, listed by county, makes no pretence at being comprehensive, even if that were possible (for everyone must decide for himself who is sufficiently worthy of note and who not). Only those graves are included which can still be identified. Churchyard extensions are included, these sometimes being detached from the ground immediately round the church in some villages. One or two Quaker and other Nonconformist burial grounds are also included, but not public cemeteries, as these are outside the scope of this book. Place-names refer to the parish churchyard unless otherwise stated.

ENGLAND

Avon

Wrington
HANNAH MORE, 1833. Religious writer and philanthropist, and friend of Garrick and Dr Johnson. She built a house called Barley Wood near the village and lived here for thirty years, turning her attention from drama, poetry and fiction to religious writing and founding Sunday Schools etc.

Richard Burton's great
ne 'tent' at Mortlake,
ndon

Bedfordshire

Campton

ROBERT BLOOMFIELD, 1823. Poet, who died at Shefford nearby. His chief work was 'The Farmer's Boy', which sold 26,000 copies within three years of its publication in 1800 but did not prevent its author dying in poverty.

Cockayne Hatley

W.E. HENLEY, 1903. Poet and journalist. A cripple from boyhood, due to tuberculosis. He was the editor of several newspapers and journals and collaborated with Robert Louis Stevenson in writing plays, but his claim to fame was as a poet, his best-known work being 'England, my England':

> What have I done for you,
>   England, my England?
> What is there I would not do,
>   England, my own?

Berkshire

Cookham

STANLEY SPENCER, 1959. Artist. Known chiefly for his religious subjects, frequently set in and around Cookham, where he was born and spent most of his life. The churchyard is featured in his work. Intermittently associated with the Royal Academy, he was knighted shortly before his death. See also p.79.

Swallowfield

MARY RUSSELL MITFORD, 1855. Author, whose *Our Village* remains famous as the precursor of a new form of literature, a series of sketches of rural life and character published originally in *The Lady's Magazine*. The village described in the book is Three Mile Cross, near Reading, where she lived for thirty years before moving to Swallowfield four years before her death.

Waltham St Lawrence

JOHN NEWBERY, 1767. Publisher and writer of children's books, possibly the author of *Goody Two Shoes*, though this is often attributed to Goldsmith, who refers to his friend in *The Vicar of Wakefield*. An epitaph written by the Reverend C. Hunter is on his imposing monument.

Yattendon

ROBERT BRIDGES, 1930. Poet, appointed Poet Laureate in 1913 on the death of Alfred Austin. Practised as a doctor at first but retired to devote himself to poetry, his finest work being perhaps 'The Testament of Beauty'. He married the daughter of the painter Alfred Waterhouse. One of the founders of the Society for Pure English, he was an early adviser to the BBC on correct pronunciation. Awarded the Order of Merit in 1929.

Buckinghamshire

Beaconsfield

LORD BURNHAM, 1916. Sir Edward Levy-Lawson was the owner of the *Daily Telegraph* which his father had bought. Edward helped to make it one of the great national newspapers and was raised to the peerage as the first Baron Burnham in 1903. He lived at Hall Barn, which had been the home of Edmund Waller (below). His monument is an elegant chest-tomb.

The chest tomb of Lord Burnham – Beaconsfield, Buckinghamshire

EDMUND WALLER, 1687. Poet and Member of Parliament. Wealthy lord of the manor and related to John Hampden, his loyalties were divided between Royalists and Parliamentarians. In 1643 he was banished and fined £10,000 for his involvement in a Royalist plot, but he returned to this country in 1652. When Charles II complained that a poem Waller had written to him was inferior to one he had written to Cromwell, Waller replied 'Poets, Sire, succeed better in fiction than in truth' – a remark that is likely to outlast his poetry. His monument is a carved chest-tomb with urns at the corners and an obelisk on top.

Chalfont St Giles
BERTRAM MILLS, 1938. Travelling circus proprietor. He came from a family of undertakers and coach-builders in London and served in the First World War with horses, becoming an expert. He made a bet with a friend that he could mount a better show than the circus they had seen together, and never looked back. By 1930 he was the undisputed leader in the business and survived after others had failed. His grave is marked by a white cross.

Chorleywood
SIR GEORGE ALEXANDER, 1918. Actor and theatre manager. Handsome and popular, he ran the St James's Theatre in London for the quarter of a century prior to his death and urged Oscar Wilde into writing much of his best work for the theatre. Although he fell into the hypocritical mood of the time after Wilde's conviction, removing the disgraced author's name from posters and programmes while continuing to make money out of the productions, he realized the importance of being honest later and made amends to Wilde. His grave is marked by a flat ledger stone.

Hughenden
BENJAMIN DISRAELI, 1881. Novelist and Tory Prime Minister, first Earl of Beaconsfield. Disraeli and his wife bought Hughenden Manor in 1847 and lived there until their deaths. He was a born cynic, Jewish in race but not in religion, and radical by inclination but not by party. 'Everyone likes flattery,' he said once, 'and when you come to royalty you should lay it on with a trowel.' Queen Victoria erected a monument to her 'kindest and most devoted' of ministers, inside the church.

Jordans (burial ground of Friends' meeting house)
WILLIAM PENN, 1718. The simple stones marking the graves of Penn and others here are a departure from the Quakers' customary eschewing of personal monuments. Penn was the most famous and influential of George Fox's disciples, and the founder of Pennsylvania.

Like Fox, he was frequently in trouble with the authorities and spent some time in prison, though his wealth saved him from the indignities Fox suffered. Penn furthered the cause of religious toleration but suffered from mental illness before his death.

Little Marlow

EDGAR WALLACE, 1932. Novelist. He began as a newspaper boy and ended as Chairman of the British Lion Film Corporation but is remembered as a prolific writer of 'thrillers', most famous of which were perhaps *The Four Just Men, The Green Arrow* and *The Mind of Mr J.G. Reeder*. He was an inveterate gambler and died in Hollywood with large debts, which his royalties soon paid off.

Medmenham

SIR BASIL LIDDELL HART, 1970. Military historian. A simple but elegant headstone marks the grave of the military tactician and historian of both world wars, who served as an infantry officer in the 1914-18 war and wrote the official Army manual on drill and tactics. He also wrote a study of T.E. Lawrence and edited the Rommel papers for publication. He lived at States House in the village and was knighted in 1966.

Speen (Chapel graveyard)

ERIC GILL, 1940. The beautifully carved headstone describes Gill simply as 'stone-carver' but he was also an influential modern sculptor and designer of postage stamps and the type-face known as Gill Sans. See p.135.

Stoke Poges

THOMAS GRAY, 1771. Poet. Remembered chiefly as the author of one of the most popular poems in the English language, the 'Elegy Written in a Country Churchyard', which was probably this one at Stoke Poges. His grave and that of his mother are marked by a brick chest tomb, and there is an imposing monument to him in an enclosure near the churchyard, with lines from the famous work and a sarcophagus above, designed by James Wyatt and in the care of the National Trust.

Cambridgeshire

Helpston

JOHN CLARE, 1864. Poet. Clare was born in this village and lived with his wife, known to his readers as 'Sweet Patty of the Vale', in the cottage next door to his birthplace. But he suffered from mental illness

Basil Liddell Hart's g
in the churchya
Medmenh
Buckingham

for much of his later life and died in Northampton asylum, where Patty could never bring herself to visit him. 'If life had a second edition,' he wrote, 'how I would correct the proofs.'

Swaffham Prior

EDWIN MUIR, 1959. Poet and critic. He and his wife were the first translators into English of Kafka's work, and Muir was also a biographer of John Knox. One of his earliest volumes of verse was *Chorus of the Newly Dead*. The house he lived in for three years prior to his death was Priory Cottage, which he said 'looks out on two ruined church towers' (see p.40). CBE 1953.

Cheshire

Knutsford (Unitarian Church)

ELIZABETH GASKELL, 1865. Novelist. Elizabeth Gaskell's father and her husband were both Unitarian ministers. She was a friend and biographer of Charlotte Brontë, and her own most famous novel *Cranford*, was written as a serial for *Household Words* when Dickens was its editor. The 'Cranford' of the title was Knutsford.

Cornwall

Launcells

SIR GOLDSWORTHY GURNEY, 1875. Inventor. Now almost forgotten, he invented a steam carriage in 1826 which came to nothing due to public opposition, but his discovery of high-pressure steam jets was important in the progress of locomotion. He devised the lighting and ventilation of the Houses of Parliament, and his lectures influenced Faraday.

Mylor

HOWARD SPRING, 1965. Novelist. Born in Cardiff, he became a journalist with the *Manchester Guardian*. His third novel, *My Son, My Son*, published in 1938, became an international best-seller. *Fame is the Spur* followed in 1940, when he had come to live in Mylor. He moved to Falmouth later, and died there, but his ashes were buried in the churchyard here.

Cumbria

Caldbeck

JOHN PEEL, 1854. Farmer and huntsman. The famous ballad 'D'ye ken John Peel?' written by his friend John Woodcock Graves, made Peel immortal, and the tune became the official march of the Border Regiment. The son of a horse-dealer, Peel rode off to Gretna Green to marry Mary White after their parents had protested that they were too young. Their long and happy marriage produced seven sons and six daughters. Peel was a hunting fanatic, always off at dawn in his 'coat so grey', woven from the local wool in its natural colour. See also p.122.

MARY HARRISON, 1837. As Mary Robinson, the modest daughter of the innkeeper of 'The Char' (now the Fish Hotel) at Buttermere, she won unwonted fame as 'the Beauty of Buttermere' and was duly admired by Wordsworth, Coleridge and Southey. But she accepted a proposal of marriage from a visitor who called himself the Hon. Alexander Augustus Hope, and it was not until after their wedding that he was exposed as an impostor, John Hatfield, who left Mary pregnant and was later hanged for forgery. She married a farmer, Richard Harrison, later, and was able to escape from the attention of the national Press and lead a normal family life at Caldbeck until her death.

Carlisle (Cathedral yard)

ROBERT ANDERSON, 1833. Poet. Born here, his *Cumbrian Ballads* are dialect poems giving vivid and humorous impressions of country life. His monument was erected by public subscription.

Coniston

JOHN RUSKIN, 1900. Author and art critic. By the time Ruskin bought Brantwood, on the east bank of Coniston Water, he was the most famous and influential author of his time in England and drew men such as Tolstoy and Gandhi to his cause. But the 'divine rage against iniquity, falsehood and baseness' that Carlyle credited him with gradually led him into manic-depressive illness. He remains one of the supreme stylists of English literature. The tall and elaborately decorated cross marking his grave was carved from a single block of green stone brought from Mossrigg Quarry at Tilberthwaite.

Crosthwaite

ROBERT SOUTHEY, 1843. Poet Laureate. One of the so-called Lake Poets, he married Coleridge's sister-in-law and settled at Greta Hall, Keswick. His best-known poems are short works such as 'My days among the dead are past' and 'The Inchcape Rock', but he also wrote

The monument to John
Ruskin at Coniston,
Cumbria

many prose works, including the fairy story 'The Three Bears', the classic biography of Nelson, and a history of Brazil. He became Poet Laureate in 1813 when Sir Walter Scott turned the honour down in Southey's favour, and he was subsequently offered a baronetcy, which he declined. The Brazilian Government paid for the restoration of his monument, which was erected by public subscription and bears a white marble effigy with a book, and an inscription by Wordsworth, who succeeded him as Poet Laureate.

Dalton-in-Furness
GEORGE ROMNEY, 1802. Artist. He was born here, the son of a cabinet-maker, and was apprenticed to a portrait painter in Kendal, eventually going to London and becoming a fashionable rival to Reynolds, abandoning his wife on the grounds that married life could not be reconciled with his ambition. His most famous portraits, though not his finest works, are of Emma Hart, subsequently Lady Hamilton and Nelson's mistress, whom he idolized and painted many times in assorted allegorical poses and various states of *déshabille*. He returned to his wife in the north for his last years, having become senile, and she, notwithstanding his forty years desertion of her, nursed him until his death.

Finsthwaite
CLEMENTINA DOUGLASS, 1771. See p.157.

Grasmere
WILLIAM WORDSWORTH, 1850; DOROTHY WORDSWORTH, 1855.
The simple slate gravestones of the poet and his sister are here, together with those of William's wife, Mary Hutchinson, her sister Sara and other members of the family, as well as Hartley Coleridge, the son of William's great friend. The Wordsworths lived at Dove Cottage for nine years, during which Dorothy wrote her Journal recording every detail of their lives together, and they moved out only because William's growing family needed more space. Wordsworth freed English poetry from classical models and used the language of ordinary speech in much of his best work. He succeeded his friend Southey as Poet Laureate in 1843. Dorothy suffered a nervous breakdown in 1829 and was an invalid for the rest of her life.

Keswick
SIR HUGH WALPOLE, 1941. Novelist, born in New Zealand. He made his fortune with the so-called Herries Chronicle, a sequence of historical novels, of which *Rogue Herries*, published in 1930, was the

first. Among his earlier work, he is best known for *Mr Perrin and Mr Traill*, a fine novel about a schoolmaster's life. He was knighted in 1937.

Derbyshire

Edensor

SIR JOSEPH PAXTON, 1865. Architect and gardener. He wrote horticultural works and was Member of Parliament for Coventry for eleven years but is remembered chiefly as the builder of the Crystal Palace in 1851. His presence here is due to his having worked as both gardener and architect for the Duke of Devonshire. It was Paxton who moved the old village of Edensor to its new position to improve the view from Chatsworth.

KATHLEEN KENNEDY, 1948. She was the sister of US President John F. Kennedy and was married to the Marquis of Hartington. She died in an aeroplane crash in France.

Devon

Dean Prior

ROBERT HERRICK, 1674. Poet and clergyman. He held the living of Dean Prior in two lengthy periods separated by the period of the Commonwealth, during which he was ejected. He claimed not to like Devon but tolerated it, sustained by his poems collected under the title *Hesperides*, some of which have a distinctly unclerical flavour:

> Give me a kiss, add to that kiss a score;
> Then to that twenty, add a hundred more:
> A thousand to that hundred: so kiss on,
> To make that thousand up a million.
> Treble that million, and when that is done,
> Let's kiss afresh, as when we first begun.

Lew Trenchard

SABINE BARING-GOULD, 1924. Author and clergyman. He became rector here after succeeding to the family estates, and wrote several books about the area, as well as novels and theological works, adding up to a prolific output, but his best-known work is undoubtedly the hymn 'Onward, Christian Soldiers'.

Littleham

FRANCES, LADY NELSON, 1831. Formerly Frances Woolward, and already widowed, she was married to Horatio Nelson in the West Indies in 1787 but was never the hero-worshipping woman he needed, and they separated after the Admiral's adulterous attachment to Lady Hamilton. After Nelson's death in 1805, his wife divided her time between London and Devon, an unhappy though well-provided-for widow again.

Salcombe Regis

SIR NORMAN LOCKYER, 1920. Astronomer. As director of observatories in London and Devon, he took a special interest in eclipses and made important discoveries about sunspots. He also discovered helium. He was a fellow of the Royal Society and founder of the scientific magazine *Nature*.

Sheepstor

SIR JAMES BROOKE, 1868. See p.129.

Tiverton (St George)

HANNAH COWLEY, 1809. Playwright. Author of successful comedies, though she rarely entered a theatre. She was born here, the daughter of a bookseller, and married a Captain Cowley. Garrick produced her first play. She carried on a quarrelsome correspondence with Hannah More (see Wrington, Avon). Her most famous work was *The Belle's Stratagem*, which was revived by Irving and Ellen Terry.

Dorset

Bournemouth

MARY SHELLEY, 1851. Besides her enduring fame as the author of *Frankenstein*, she was the daughter of William Godwin and Mary Wollstonecraft, authors of *Enquiry concerning Political Justice* and *Vindication of the Rights of Women* respectively, and the wife of the poet Percy Bysshe Shelley. Their remains are here as well, Shelley's heart having been re-interred with his wife after its recovery from his funeral pyre at Viareggio (see p.181) in 1822 and its original burial in the Protestant Cemetery in Rome. Mary Wollstonecraft Godwin died in giving birth to her daughter in 1797. William Godwin died in 1836. They were both originally buried in London (St Pancras) but were re-interred here in 1851.

Came

WILLIAM BARNES, 1886. Poet and philologist. A farmer's son and schoolmaster, he eventually took holy orders and became rector of Winterborne Came. Best known as a dialect poet, he has been called 'the Dorsetshire Burns'. His grave is marked by a tall Celtic cross.

Highcliffe

HARRY GORDON SELFRIDGE, 1947. American businessman and founder in 1909 of Selfridge's, the famous London department store. Born in Wisconsin, he became a naturalized British citizen in 1937, at the age of eighty.

Lyme Regis

MARY ANNING, 1847. Geologist. When she was only twelve, Mary Anning discovered the first complete fossil of an ichthyosaurus, and went on to find fossils of the plesiosaurus and pterodactyl, now to be seen in London's Natural History Museum. There is a memorial window to her in the church, presented by the Geological Society.

Mappowder

T.F. POWYS, 1953. Author and member of a remarkable literary family, Theodore Francis Powys was more original in his novels and stories than his brothers, though neither he nor Llewelyn had quite the gift that distinguished their elder brother, John Cowper. T.F. lived in the cottage near the churchyard entrance for his last ten years.

Moreton (churchyard extension)

T.E. LAWRENCE, 1935. The legendary Lawrence of Arabia. The military hero and author of *Seven Pillars of Wisdom* was buried here after his death in an accident on his motor-cycle. A perpetually enigmatic character, who changed his name by deed poll to Shaw and declined both the Victoria Cross and a knighthood in apparent disgust with postwar British policy in the Near East, his beautifully lettered headstone describes him with infinite tact as T.E. Lawrence, Fellow of All Souls, Oxford. Basil Liddell Hart (see Medmenham, Buckinghamshire) was among his many biographers.

Stinsford

THOMAS HARDY, 1928. Only the heart of the poet and novelist was buried here (see p.170), notwithstanding the full-length tombstone set here among those of his ancestors. He was born at Higher Bockhampton, the son of a stonemason, and became an architect

Moreton, Dorset. The grave of Lawrence of Arabia in the churchyard extension

himself at first. His many famous novels such as *Tess of the d'Urbervilles* and *Jude the Obscure*, works brooding on the struggle of man against the cruel forces of nature, have recognizable Wessex locations and are marked by a frankness and pessimism that shocked many of his contemporaries, and he gave up writing novels in favour of poetry. He was awarded the Order of Merit in 1910. Hardy was a friend of T.E. Lawrence in his last years.

C. DAY LEWIS, 1972. Poet and novelist. Born in Ireland, he was a schoolmaster before becoming a professional writer, when his work reflected the same left-wing sympathies as his contemporaries Auden and Spender. His later poetry was much influenced by Thomas Hardy, and he is buried close to the heart of the man he admired so much. Under the pseudonym 'Nicholas Blake' he wrote detective stories. He was appointed Poet Laureate in 1968, succeeding Masefield.

Worth Matravers
BENJAMIN JESTY, 1810. A farmer, he was a rival claimant to Jenner in being the first man to experiment with cowpox as a preventive of smallpox, his tombstone recording that in 1774 'from his great strength of mind' he inoculated his wife and two sons. No credit is given to them for *their* strength of mind! In any case, Lady Mary Wortley Montagu had introduced the remedy from Turkey much earlier.

CECIL
DAY·LEWIS
1904-1972
Poet Laureate

Shall I be gone long?
For ever and a day
To whom there belong?
Ask the stone to say,
Ask my song

The grave of C. Day Lewis
at Stinsford, Dorset

Essex

High Laver

JOHN LOCKE, 1704. Philosopher. He was also a lecturer in classical subjects, a doctor and a political secretary and adviser to the Earl of Shaftesbury, but his fame rests on his *Essay Concerning Human Understanding*, published in 1690, and on his advocacy of religious freedom, and his work was extremely influential. Modesty led him to request burial in the churchyard here, and his grave has since been protected by railings.

Ongar

JANE TAYLOR, 1824. Poetess. Wrote highly successful verses and hymns for children, mainly in collaboration with her sister Ann, and is remembered for one of her own works, 'Twinkle, Twinkle, Little Star'. She died when only forty.

Gloucestershire

Daylesford

WARREN HASTINGS, 1818. Governor-General of India. The name and date as given here are all that appears on the classical stone monument to this mighty administrator of Bengal. In 1788 he was impeached for cruelty and corruption, and his trial before the House of Lords took place in Westminster Hall. This *cause célèbre* lasted seven years, drew some of the greatest oratory of the age from Burke, Fox and especially Sheridan, his chief accusers, and cost Hastings £76,000, his entire fortune, for his defence. In the end he was acquitted on all charges and retired here on a pension from the East India Company which enabled him to recover the old family estate lost in the Civil War. A fine portrait of him was painted by Romney (see Dalton-in-Furness, Cumbria).

Painswick

SYDNEY DOBELL, 1874. Poet. Son of a wine merchant, he lived in his youth at Cheltenham and in his last years at Horsley, with much time abroad in between. He belonged to what was derogatorily called the 'Spasmodic School' of poetry. His grave is marked by a Celtic cross.

Sapperton

ERNEST GIMSON, 1919. Craftsman. Gimson came from a great engineering family of Leicester, which helped to found the Secular Society there, though originally they were Quakers. A disciple of William Morris, he turned to furniture-making and set up a crafts

The tomb of Warren
Hastings at Daylesford,
Gloucestershire

workshop at Sapperton with the support of Lord Bathurst. One of his
colleagues was SYDNEY BARNSLEY, who is buried close by him,
both graves having typical brass plates on their ledger stones because
the soft limestone of the area offers no hope of long-term legibility.

Hampshire

Binsted

VISCOUNT MONTGOMERY OF ALAMEIN, 1976. The legendary
Field-Marshal Bernard Law Montgomery became a soldier in 1908,
when he was twenty-one, and he was appointed commander of the
British 8th Army in 1942, when he completely routed the German
forces under Rommel in the North African desert campaign, then led
the Allied armies in the Normandy campaign, 'Operation Overlord',
which he had planned – the prelude to victory in Europe. Modesty was
not one of his virtues, though he was the son of a bishop, and marked
eccentricities earned him some ridicule, but his touch of military
genius was beyond question.

Boldre

WILLIAM GILPIN, 1804. Clergyman and author. He was vicar here for nearly thirty years and recorded his travels in the Lake District, Scotland and elsewhere in books illustrated with his own drawings, being one of the precursors of the new Romantic appreciation of landscape. His own inscription is on his tombstone.

East Wellow

FLORENCE NIGHTINGALE, 1910. Pioneer of nursing. The 'lady with the lamp' became famous for her nursing of the wounded in the Crimean War, and she revolutionized hospital practice throughout the world in the face of much opposition from officialdom. She was the first woman to be awarded the Order of Merit. Her tall Gothic monument bears only her initials and dates of her birth and death.

Eversley

CHARLES KINGSLEY, 1875. Author and clergyman. The author of *Westward Ho!* and *The Water Babies* was vicar here for over thirty years. He was also Professor of Modern History at Cambridge and wrote on social reform. Nervous and hot-tempered, he was considered too 'nosey' by some of his parishioners, but he was a man of only good intentions. A white marble cross marks his grave.

Fordingbridge (churchyard extension)

AUGUSTUS JOHN, 1961. Artist. A notorious Bohemian in his earlier years, John had become 'respectable' by the time he made Fordingbridge his final home. He was re-elected RA, having resigned earlier, and was also awarded the Order of Merit. He was a superb draughtsman but will be remembered most for his striking portraits of such as Dylan Thomas (see Laugharne, Dyfed) and W.B. Yeats.

Hursley

JOHN KEBLE, 1866. Poet and churchman. Appointed to the living of Hursley in 1836, when he was Professor of Poetry at Oxford, he remained as rector until his death and rebuilt the church with profits from his works, which included hymns, sacred poems and theological works. He was a saintly and influential man, and Oxford's Keble College is named after him. His grave is marked by the low-mound-type of memorial known as a 'body stone'.

Lyndhurst

ALICE HARGREAVES, 1934. The daughter of Dean Liddell of Christchurch, Oxford, Alice Liddell was the original of Lewis Carroll's immortal Alice. She married Reginald Hargreaves. The shy and stammering Carroll (the Reverend Charles Dodgson) had a fixation on little girls which has given rise to a continuing crop of psycho-analytical interpretations in books and films. Alice's mother destroyed all his letters to her daughter, and Mrs Hargreaves became reluctant to talk about her relationship with Carroll.

Minstead

SIR ARTHUR CONAN DOYLE, 1930. Novelist. His gravestone describes him correctly as 'Patriot, physician and man of letters', but his enduring fame is as the creator of Sherlock Holmes and his side-kick Dr Watson, who first appeared in *A Study in Scarlet* in 1882. Doyle also wrote historical romances and *The Lost World*, however, and became thoroughly sick of Holmes. Towards the end of his life, he became obsessed with psychic phenomena. He was knighted in 1902.

Otterbourne

CHARLOTTE MARY YONGE, 1901. Author. She was born in this village and lived here all her life, teaching in the Sunday School from the age of seven until her death. She was influenced in her youth by John Keble (see Hursley). She wrote novels and a great many books for children, as well as a biography of Hannah More (see Wrington, Avon).

Selborne

GILBERT WHITE, 1793. Naturalist and clergyman. Only his initials and the date of his death are on the tombstone of the famous author of the classic *Natural History and Antiquities of Selborne*, published in 1789. He was born here and came back as rector in 1755, remaining for the rest of his life. Thousands visit the village minutely described in his great work, and his former home, Wakes, is now a museum.

West Meon

GUY BURGESS, 1963. Spy. The 'Burgess and Maclean' affair rocked Britain in the 1950s and set off reverberations which have scarcely yet faded away. Burgess was an Eton-educated homosexual diplomat who defected to the Soviet Union with Donald Maclean in 1951, soon to be followed by Kim Philby. Burgess died in Moscow, aged fifty-three and disillusioned, and his body was brought back for burial by his family.

THOMAS LORD, 1832. Sports entrepreneur. The founder of Lord's, headquarters of the MCC and 'capital' of cricket, in 1814, when he moved to St John's Wood from an earlier ground in London, taking the turf with him, according to legend. A Yorkshireman, he was trained as a wine merchant, but he always loved cricket and was a passable bowler.

Hereford & Worcester

Bredwardine
FRANCIS KILVERT, 1879. Clergyman and diarist. A white marble cross marks the grave of the vicar whose notebooks, kept for the last nine years of his life, recorded parish events of the time and the pleasures of the countryside. He died a month after his marriage, at the age of thirty-eight. See also p.139.

Grimley
SIR SAMUEL BAKER, 1893. Explorer. With Speke and Livingstone, he was one of the great Victorian explorers of East Africa. He and his wife discovered the Murchison Falls in 1864, and he was knighted two years later, after a year of great hardship in returning to his base. He was Governor-General of Equatorial Africa for four years and also built a railway from the Danube to the Black Sea.

Little Malvern (St Wulstan, RC)
SIR EDWARD ELGAR, 1934. Composer. A self-taught musician, except for a few violin lessons, he became a church organist and band-leader at the county lunatic asylum. As his compositions, such as the *Enigma Variations* and the oratorio *The Dream of Gerontius*, earned him increasing recognition, he was honoured with a knighthood (1904), the Order of Merit (1911), appointment as Master of the King's Musick (1924) and a baronetcy (1931), but ironically the work for which he is most famous is the *Pomp and Circumstance* march later savaged, to his dismay, as 'Land of Hope and Glory'.

West Malvern
PETER MARK ROGET, 1869. Scholar and physician. Best known as the compiler of that indispensable reference work the *Thesaurus of English Words and Phrases* first published in 1852, Dr Roget was also in his time Secretary to the Royal Society, Professor of Physiology at the Royal Institution, and one of the founders of London University. He died here whilst on holiday, at the age of ninety.

Hertfordshire

Aldbury
MRS HUMPHRY WARD, 1920. Novelist. Descended from Dr Arnold of Rugby, Mary Augusta Ward was the niece of Matthew Arnold (see Laleham, Surrey), mother-in-law of the historian G.M. Trevelyan, and

aunt of Aldous and Julian Huxley. She lived at the house called 'Stocks' in the village and wrote many novels, most famous of which was *Robert Elsmere*, in which she attacked Evangelical Christianity. She did good work for the poor in London and was one of the first women magistrates.

Ridge

EARL ALEXANDER OF TUNIS, 1969. Soldier. The Second World War army commander whose strategic skill served the Allies in Burma, the Middle East and Europe, General Harold Alexander was promoted to Field-Marshal in 1944, knighted and raised to the peerage after the war, when he was appointed Governor-General of Canada. His headstone bears the name 'Alex' by which he was known to his friends and his men.

Humberside

Hull

JOHN WARD, 1849. Artist. The son of a master mariner, he became an accomplished marine painter, and there is a large collection of his work in the city's art gallery. He died of cholera.

Rudston

WINIFRED HOLTBY, 1935. Novelist. Born here, she served in the First World War and then lived in London with Vera Brittain, who wrote *Testament of Friendship* as a tribute to her. She died of overwork at thirty-seven after completing her best novel, *South Riding*. A marble book at the head of her grave has the inscription:

> God give me work till my life shall end
> And life till my work is done.

Isle of Man

Maughold

HALL CAINE, 1931. Novelist. A tall Celtic cross with characters from his novels marks the grave of Sir Thomas Henry Hall Caine, the son of a blacksmith, who made a fortune from his popular work in the last decade of the nineteenth century. He was knighted in 1918 and made Companion of Honour in 1922.

Isle of Wight

Bonchurch (new church)
HENRY DE VERE STACPOOLE, 1951. Author and physician. Remembered chiefly for his novel *The Blue Lagoon*, he also wrote verse and translations, as well as many other novels, after practising as a doctor for a few years.

ALGERNON CHARLES SWINBURNE, 1909. Poet. Closely associated with the Pre-Raphaelite Brotherhood in his youth, Swinburne was a prolific poet, but his work, though technically brilliant, was rather too precious to appeal to a wide public. He was intoxicated with language when not with wine and was almost totally deaf towards the end of his life.

Kent

Birchington
DANTE GABRIEL ROSSETTI, 1882. Artist and poet. The son of an Italian political refugee in London, he was one of the founders of the Pre-Raphaelite movement. As poet, one of his best works is 'The Blessed Damozel'. His paintings, mainly of medieval subjects, are in important galleries throughout the country. The death of his wife Elizabeth Siddal (see p.96) affected his mind and he became a recluse. Swinburne, Hall Caine and William Morris (see Kelmscot, Oxfordshire) were among his friends, and his monument was designed by Ford Madox Brown.

Dover
CHARLES CHURCHILL, 1764. Clergyman and poet. He was an accomplished satirist, who fell into dissipated habits and had to resign his ecclesiastical preferments. A member of the so-called Hell-Fire Club, he subsequently left and attacked it, along with his friend John Wilkes, who was with him when he died in France, aged thirty-three. His best-remembered line is most quoted by schoolmasters teaching English – 'Apt alliteration's artful aid'.

Groombridge
W.H. WHITE, 1913. Novelist. A civil servant for most of his working life, he published novels under the pseudonym 'Mark Rutherford' from the age of fifty onwards, as well as a biography of Bunyan and some critical works.

Hythe

LIONEL LUKIN, 1834. Inventor of the lifeboat. A London coachbuilder, he built the first insubmersible lifeboat in 1785, with encouragement from the Prince of Wales, but had to fight naval prejudice and rival claimants. He also invented an adjustable reclining bed for hospital patients, and a rain gauge.

St Mary in the Marsh

EDITH NESBIT, 1924. Children's writer. Her first success came with *The Treasure Seekers* in 1899. After the death of her first husband, Hubert Bland, she married Thomas Tucker, whom she called 'the Skipper', and he carved the wooden name plate on her grave.

Shoreham

LORD DUNSANY, 1957. Author and soldier. Edward Plunkett succeeded to his father's title as eighteenth Baron Dunsany in 1899. A sportsman, six feet four inches in height, he served with the Coldstream Guards in the Boer War and with the Inniskilling Fusiliers in the 1914-18 war. He wrote fantastical novels, plays and short stories as well as verse. Buried here, where his childhood home had been, after his death at Dunsany Castle in Ireland.

Leicestershire

Burton Lazars

COUNT ZBOROWSKI, 1909. Racing driver and huntsman. The Polish millionaire count was killed in a motor-racing accident in France. His son was similarly killed in 1924 and is likewise buried here. They belonged to the hunting set centred around Melton Mowbray.

Peckleton

DR ROBERT CHESSHER, 1831. Surgeon. In practice at Hinckley, he was a celebrated specialist in spinal disease and numbered William Wilberforce and George Canning among his patients.

Lincolnshire

Stamford

DANIEL LAMBERT, 1809. Gaoler. Famous as the heaviest recorded Englishman, weighing fifty-two stone at his death, he followed his father as keeper of Leicester's town gaol. He was an affable fellow, a hunting and cock-fighting enthusiast, who walked and swam regularly and drank only water. He died in a Stamford inn whilst on a visit for the races. See also p.156.

London

Barking ('Friends' burial ground)
ELIZABETH FRY, 1845. Prison reformer. She was the daughter of a Quaker banker and married into the Quaker cocoa family of Bristol. Her great work began with her successful efforts to relieve the miseries of women prisoners in Newgate, and thereafter she continued working for better prison conditions throughout the country and in Europe.

Chiswick
WILLIAM HOGARTH, 1764. Artist. The brilliant satirist of eighteenth-century England was a genuine original. He began his working life as an engraver. He was once arrested as a spy for drawing the defences of Calais, and he was probably a member of the Hell Fire Club for a time. He helped to establish copyright protection for artists and was indirectly involved in the foundation of the Royal Academy. His monument is a pedestal tomb with an urn, surrounded by railings.

PHILIP DE LOUTHERBOURG, 1812. Artist. Of Alsatian descent, he came to Britain with an introduction to Garrick, who engaged him as his scenery painter, and he made significant innovations in scenery design. He became a painter of landscapes in which his theatrical background is often evident. His monument is a small mausoleum.

J.A. McNEILL WHISTLER, 1903. (In the churchyard extension.) Artist and wit. American-born, he settled in Britain after studying in Paris. His portrait of his mother was really entitled *Arrangement in Grey and Black*. He brought a famous libel action against Ruskin (see Coniston, Cumbria), which ruined him though he won it, and he wrote *The Gentle Art of Making Enemies*.

Edmonton
CHARLES LAMB, 1834. Essayist and poet. The tomb of Lamb and his sister Mary, buried beside him thirteen years later, remains *in situ* in the levelled churchyard whose other monuments have been lined up along the sides. The gentle author of *Essays of Elia* spent most of his life caring for his sister, who had killed their mother in a fit of insanity. Together they produced *Lamb's Tales from Shakespeare*.

Great Stanmore
SIR W.S. GILBERT, 1911. The 'words' half of Gilbert and Sullivan, William Schwenk Gilbert spent most of his long and eventful life as a humorous writer. As a child, he was kidnapped in Italy and ransomed for £25. His first collaboration with Arthur Sullivan was *Trial by Jury*

Eulogy over the grave of a French refugee, St John's Wood, London

produced in 1875. They eventually parted after constant quarrelling. Knighted in 1907, Gilbert died from a heart attack after rescuing a young lady from drowning, and his ashes were buried here.

Ham

SARAH SMITH, 1911. Author of *Jessica's First Prayer*, she wrote popular moral tales under the pseudonym 'Hesba Stretton'. It is said that her most famous work was compulsory reading in Russian schools under the Tsar. One of her stories had the title *The Doctor's Dilemma*, which Bernard Shaw appropriated with her permission. She was a founder of what was originally the London Society for the Prevention of Cruelty to Children.

Hampstead

JOANNA BAILLIE, 1851. Scottish dramatist and poetess. She was related through her mother to the Hunter brothers, the famous anatomists, and her work was admired by Sir Walter Scott, among others. She spent most of her long life in London.

SIR WALTER BESANT, 1901. (Churchyard extension.) Author and reformer. Wrote several novels influenced by Dickens. He was the founder of the Society of Authors and did much good work for the poor in London. He was knighted in 1895.

JOHN CONSTABLE, 1837. Artist. The great painter of natural landscapes, and one of England's greatest artists, he was not recognized as such during his lifetime, when his pictures were attacked by many critics, including Ruskin. He spent most of his life in his native Suffolk but died in London where he had lived for nine years.

KAY KENDALL, 1959. (Churchyard extension.) Actress. The wife of Rex Harrison, she was best known as a comedienne in films, her most popular success being *Genevieve*, in which her co-stars were Kenneth More and an old car. She died of leukemia, aged only thirty-two.

SIR JAMES MACKINTOSH, 1832. Philosopher and historian. Sometime Member of Parliament and professor of law, he championed the French Revolution against the arguments of Edmund Burke, though he subsequently changed his mind. He wrote several volumes on English history, and works of philosophy.

GEORGE DU MAURIER, 1896. (Churchyard extension.) Novelist and artist. Born in Paris, he wrote several novels, of which the best known is *Trilby*. He became a *Punch* cartoonist, despite having lost the sight of one eye, and satirized the *nouveaux riches* and the aesthetes of his time. His monument is a simple wooden headboard.

SIR GERALD DU MAURIER, 1934. (Churchyard extension.) Actor-manager. Son of the above and father of Daphne du Maurier, he was knighted in 1922 for his services to the theatre. He was the original Captain Hook in *Peter Pan* and a commanding and versatile stage actor who also appeared in a few films, though he never liked cinema.

SIR HERBERT BEERBOHM TREE, 1917. (Churchyard extension.) Actor-manager. Became famous as a character actor and producer of spectacular Shakespeare revivals, and was proprietor of Her Majesty's Theatre, where he had a notable success as Svengali in *Trilby* adapted from du Maurier's novel, and as Fagin in *Oliver Twist*. Knighted in 1909, he was one of the founders of RADA.

ANTON WALBROOK, 1967. (Churchyard extension). Actor. Born in Vienna, he acted on both stage and film, his work in the cinema making him famous on both sides of the Atlantic and an irresistible heart-throb. His most notable films were *The Red Shoes* and *Dangerous Moonlight*, in which he was a pianist who played the famous *Warsaw Concerto*.

Keston

DINAH MULOCK, 1887. Novelist. The wife of a partner in the Macmillan publishing firm, Mrs Craik wrote novels, children's stories and poems but is best known as the author of *John Halifax, Gentleman*, published before her marriage.

Kew

THOMAS GAINSBOROUGH, 1788. Artist. The great landscape and portrait painter was much influenced by Dutch landscape artists, but his lasting importance rests on his accomplished portraits, which he painted only to earn a living. He was one of the first members of the Royal Academy, and a rival of Reynolds, to whom he was technically superior. His last words are said to have been: 'We are all going to heaven, and van Dyck is of the company.' He was buried here at his own request, beside his friend Joshua Kirby.

Lambeth

WILLIAM BLIGH, 1817. Naval officer. He travelled with Captain Cook before becoming captain of the *Bounty* and provoking the mutiny led by Fletcher Christian. Later he was deposed as Governor of New South Wales because of his severe rule and imprisoned for two years. He was promoted to Rear-Admiral and then Vice-Admiral on his return to Britain. He lies beneath an ornate chest-tomb, 'beloved, respected and lamented', so it says, and there is no question that he was a courageous man and an able navigator.

Marylebone (Former churchyard of Marylebone Chapel.)
CHARLES WESLEY, 1788. Minister and hymn-writer. An obelisk marks the grave of John Wesley's brother in a formal garden that was the original parish churchyard, bombed in the war and demolished in 1949. He is said to have written more than 6,000 hymns, of which the best known is 'Hark the Herald Angels Sing'. His nephew Samuel Wesley, the composer and organist, is also buried here.

Mortlake (St Mary Magdalen, RC)
SIR RICHARD BURTON, 1890. See p.131.

Soho (St Anne's, Wardour Street)
WILLIAM HAZLITT, 1830. Essayist and critic. Some redevelopment after wartime bomb damage has left the ruined church tower in a formal garden of rest, but Hazlitt's grave is preserved. He was one of the most stylish writers and perceptive critics in the language. He died at fifty-two, and though the evidence seems to be against it, he said on his death-bed that he had had a happy life.

Whitechapel (St Mary Matfelon)
RICHARD BRANDON, 1649. Executioner. He followed his father in the profession, serving his apprenticeship by chopping off the heads of cats and dogs. Generally thought to have been the executioner of Charles I, his other distinguished clients included Archbishop Laud and the Earl of Strafford.

Norfolk

Aylsham
HUMPHRY REPTON, 1818. Landscape gardener. He succeeded Lancelot 'Capability' Brown as the foremost expert on landscaping and collaborated with John Nash in designing new houses in landscaped grounds. Sheringham Hall, Norfolk, was designed in collaboration with his son John. He died as a result of injuries received in a coach accident.

Lamas (old Friends' meeting house)

ANNA SEWELL, 1878. Novelist. An almost lifelong invalid, she lived in poverty and is remembered for her only book, the children's classic *Black Beauty*, published in the year before her death.

Langham

CAPTAIN MARRYAT, 1848. Naval officer and novelist. Frederick Marryat served in the Navy from the age of fourteen and later wrote many stirring novels and boys' books based on his experiences. Best known for *Masterman Ready* and *The Children of the New Forest*, he was a Fellow of the Royal Society and a Member of the French Legion of Honour.

Norwich (Cathedral)

EDITH CAVELL, 1915. Nurse and war heroine. She was nursing in Belgium at the outbreak of war in 1914 and in the following year was arrested and charged with assisting 130 Allied personnel to escape from Belgium. Condemned to death, she was shot by a German firing squad on 12 October 1915. Her body was brought back to Britain after the war.

Northamptonshire

Weedon Lois (Churchyard extension)

DAME EDITH SITWELL, 1964. Poet and biographer. The striking female of the Sitwell clan, dressed habitually in Plantagenet fashions and appearing distinctly eccentric, was a distinguished poet and the author of several fine critical works. Her monument is a headstone designed by Henry Moore, but the stone was not well chosen, as it is already badly worn.

Northumberland

Bamburgh

GRACE DARLING, 1842. Heroine. The famous daughter of the Longstone lighthouse-keeper, whom she urged to row out with her in a frightful storm to rescue survivors from the wrecked ship *Forfarshire* seen clinging to rocks at dawn in September 1838. She died of consumption, aged twenty-seven.

Randolph Churchill, the
journalist and biographer
of his father Sir Winston,
is buried with other
members of his family at
Bladon, Oxfordshire

Oxfordshire

Bladon
SIR WINSTON CHURCHILL, 1965. Statesman and author. As well as the Prime Minister and leader of the Allied cause in World War II, his parents, Lord Randolph and Jenny, Lady Randolph Churchill are buried here, and his son, the journalist Randolph Churchill, as well as other members of the family. The most visited graves in Britain in the past twenty years. Randolph wrote his father's biography (but did not live to complete it), as Sir Winston had written those of his father and his ancestor the first Duke of Marlborough.

Burford
JOHN MEADE FALKNER, 1932. Novelist and industrialist. He became chairman of the armaments firm Armstrong Whitworth but is remembered chiefly as the author of *The Lost Stradivarius* and *Moonfleet*.

Elsfield
JOHN BUCHAN, 1940. Author and statesman. He became a Conservative MP in 1927 and in 1935 was made Governor-General of Canada and raised to the peerage as Baron Tweedsmuir. He wrote a war history and biographies of Cromwell and Sir Walter Scott but is best remembered as the author of novels such as *The Thirty-Nine Steps, Greenmantle* and *Prester John*. See also p.133.

Ewelme
JEROME K. JEROME, 1927. Author. He worked as railway clerk, newspaper reporter and schoolmaster before he became famous with the classic *Three Men in a Boat* in 1889. He wrote further novels and some plays, of which the best-known is *The Passing of the Third Floor Back*.

Kelmscot
WILLIAM MORRIS, 1896. Poet and artist, Socialist reformer and printer, designer and manufacturer of furniture, wallpapers and tapestries, translator and novelist – it is impossible to get the measure of William Morris in a short paragraph. His influence was brief but enormous, born of his love of beauty and hatred of ugliness. He was the founder of the Society for the Protection of Ancient Buildings and owned the Elizabethan manor house in the village, where he entertained his Pre-Raphaelite friends, including Rossetti (see Birchington, Kent). Morris died in London, and his body was brought here in a farm cart for burial. His monument is a stone imitation of the wooden grave-board.

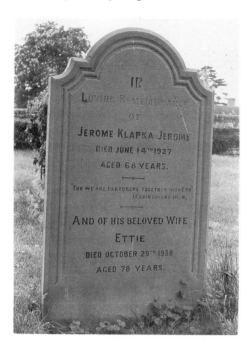

The grave of J.K. Jerome
Ewelme, Oxfordshire

Long Wittenham

ROBERT GIBBINGS, 1958. Author and typographer. He was the proprietor of the Golden Cockerel Press from 1924 to 1933, and as well as producing volumes illustrated with his own wood-engravings, he commissioned Eric Gill and others to illustrate books for him. He was a founder-member of the Society of Wood Engravers. He also wrote many travel books, of which the most successful was *Sweet Thames Run Softly*.

Mapledurham

LORD AUGUSTUS FITZCLARENCE, 1854. Vicar. He was one of the illegitimate offspring of William IV and the actress Dorothea Jordan and was vicar here for a quarter of a century. He built the vicarage in 1830.

Nuffield

LORD NUFFIELD, 1963. Industrialist and philanthropist. Another 'William Morris', the pioneer motor-car manufacturer was made Viscount Nuffield in 1938. He used his millions to promote education, social work and especially medical research. He took his title from this quiet Chilterns village, and he lies beneath an unpretentious flat ledger stone, beautifully engraved.

Oxford (St Cross)

H.W. GARROD, 1960. Poet and classical scholar. He was a Fellow of Merton College and held the chair of poetry at Oxford and at Harvard. He wrote several books about the writing of poetry and edited the works of Latin and English authors.

KENNETH GRAHAME, 1932. Author. A secretary in the Bank of England from 1898 to 1907, he wrote essays and other works, but his immortal work is the children's classic *The Wind in the Willows*, written in 1908 to entertain his son Alastair but which made him a fortune. His son, who died at twenty, is buried in the same grave. Kenneth Grahame was a cousin of Sir Anthony Hope Hawkins (see Leatherhead, Surrey).

(St Giles)

WALTER PATER, 1894. Critic. He made his reputation as a critic under the influence of Ruskin and wrote both art and literary criticism, being primarily concerned with aesthetics and a proponent of 'art for art's sake'. He wrote stylish prose and seems destined to be remembered for his famous purple passage on Leonardo's *Mona Lisa*, not inappropriate here: 'She is older than the rocks among which she sits; like the vampire, she has been dead many times, and learned the secrets of the grave ...'

Eric Blair was 'George Orwell' and he lies in the churchyard at Sutton Courtenay, Oxfordshire

Sutton Courtenay

HERBERT H. ASQUITH, 1928. Statesman. Liberal Prime Minister, 1908-16. His Government introduced old-age pensions and unemployment insurance, but doubts about his leadership in the First World War led to his replacement by Lloyd George. He was made Earl of Oxford and Asquith in 1925. His second wife, Margot, was a descendant of Robert Burns and was famous as a brilliant and witty hostess.

ERIC ARTHUR BLAIR, 1950. Author. Better known as 'George Orwell', author of *Animal Farm, 1984* and other satirical novels, and Socialist essays and studies such as *The Road to Wigan Pier*. He was born in India and died of tuberculosis in London at the age of forty-six. His burial here was arranged by the Hon. David Astor of *The Observer*, Orwell having expressed a surprising objection in his will to cremation.

Swinbrook

NANCY MITFORD, 1973; UNITY MITFORD, 1948. Two of the famous daughters of Lord Redesdale, buried here beneath rustic headstones (see also p.133). Nancy was the eldest, a novelist and biographer well known for *Love in a Cold Climate, The Sun King*, etc, and concerned exclusively with aristocratic life. Unity Valkyrie Mitford, on the other hand, had a tempestuous ride through life, becoming a friend of Hitler and shooting herself in the head in Munich, in a suicide attempt which resulted in her death at thirty-three after nine years of brain-damaged existence.

Unity Mitford's grave at Swinbrook, Oxfordshire

Shropshire

Bromfield

HENRY HILL HICKMAN, 1830. Doctor. He had his practice in Tenbury and was one of the pioneers of anaesthesia, experimenting with nitrous oxide (laughing gas), in attempting to alleviate the tortures of surgical operations on the fully conscious. He demonstrated its effects before learned societies in London and Paris but was dismissed as a madman, and it was left to later workers, notably the American dentist William Morton, to make the breakthrough in what has been called 'the battle for oblivion'.

Ludlow

A.E. HOUSMAN, 1936. Scholar and poet. He was a distinguished Latin
scholar and a severe critic but is best remembered as the author of *A
Shropshire Lad,* a volume of poems frequently pessimistic but with a
clear, simple and often humorous lyricism:

> Oh, I have been to Ludlow fair,
> And left my necktie God knows where ...

His ashes were buried here.

Somerset

Combe Florey

EVELYN WAUGH, 1966. Novelist and biographer. The author of
Brideshead Revisited, The Loved One and many other satirical novels
laced with his acid wit lived in the manor house here for ten years. An
eccentric and controversial figure, he put a notice on the gate saying
'No admittance on business' and once remarked of Randolph
Churchill, who was operated on for a non-malignant lung disease, that
'It was a typical triumph of modern science to find the only part of
Randolph that was not malignant and remove it.' A Roman Catholic
convert, he also wrote biographies of Edmund Campion and his friend
Ronald Knox (see Mells, below).

Cricket St Thomas

VISCOUNT BRIDPORT, 1904. The distinguished Hood family of naval
fame owned the estate (there is no village), and their memorials are
inside the church, but the first viscount of the second creation lies in
the churchyard beneath a white stone angel.

Frome

THOMAS KEN, 1711. Bishop of Bath and Wells. He was the
brother-in-law of Izaak Walton and became a chaplain to Charles II,
but was sent to the Tower by James II for refusing to read the
Declaration of Indulgence. He was tried and acquitted but later refused
to acknowledge William of Orange and was deprived of his living. He
wrote many well-known hymns.

Mells

RONALD KNOX, 1957. Priest and author. Monsignor Knox was a
Domestic Prelate to the Pope in 1936. He completed a new translation
of the Bible two years before his death and also wrote detective stories,

religious works and humorous studies. His brother was the humorist E.V. Knox of *Punch* fame. Asked at the age of four what he did to pass the time when he could not sleep, Ronald is alleged to have replied, 'I lie awake and think about the past.'

SIEGFRIED SASSOON, 1967. Poet and novelist. He won the Military Cross in the First World War but emerged as one of the group of war poets who exposed the horror and hypocrisy of the time and became a pacifist. He became famous later for his semi-autobiographical novels, *Memoirs of a Fox Hunting Man* and *Memoirs of an Infantry Officer*. He wished to be buried near his friend Father Knox.

Orchardleigh (St Mary's in Orchardleigh Park, near Frome)
SIR HENRY NEWBOLT, 1938. Lawyer and poet. Remembered as the author of 'Drake's Drum', he practised law for twelve years and was official historian of the naval aspect of the 1914-18 war. He wrote historical romances as well as banal poetry. He was knighted in 1915.

Trull
JULIANA HORATIA EWING, 1885. Children's author. She wrote many books and stories, many appearing first in *Aunt Judy's Magazine* founded by her mother Margaret Gatty. In delicate health all her life, she died at forty-three.

Staffordshire

Newchapel
JAMES BRINDLEY, 1772. Millwright and canal engineer. One of the pioneering spirits of the Industrial Revolution, he was an engineer of genius though barely literate. The Duke of Bridgewater's engineer on the Worsley canal, he built aqueducts and others works which his detractors regarded as the ideas of a madman, and set the great Canal Age in motion.

Suffolk

Boulge (St Michael's in demolished Boulge Hall grounds)
EDWARD FITZGERALD, 1883. Poet and translator. He published translations of Spanish dramas and Greek tragedies and wrote books of his own before producing his celebrated translation of the *Rubaiyat of Omar Khayyam*, which was published anonymously at first, in 1859, and which Rossetti helped to make famous. The rose bush at the head of his grave is a descendant of one that grew by Omar Khayyam's tomb.

Long Melford

EDMUND BLUNDEN, 1974. Poet and critic. Awarded the Military Cross in the 1914-18 war, he wrote *Undertones of War*, still regarded as one of the best books about that war. He taught English in Japan in the 1920s and in Hong Kong in the 1950s and was an authority on Charles Lamb and Shelley, among others, but he was primarily a poet and was Professor of Poetry at Oxford 1966-8.

Playford

THOMAS CLARKSON, 1846. Anti-slavery campaigner. A granite obelisk marks the grave of one of Wilberforce's most effective colleagues, who spoke and wrote against the slave-trade in Africa and slavery in the West Indies and helped to achieve the passing of the Emancipation Bill in 1833.

Surrey

Frimley

FRANCIS BRET HARTE, 1902. Novelist and short story writer. American journalist and diplomat who settled in Britain when he lost his post as US consul in Glasgow in 1885. Not to be confused with Francis Bret Young, the British author of *My Brother Jonathan*.

Laleham

MATTHEW ARNOLD, 1888. Poet and critic. The son of Dr Arnold of Rugby, he became an inspector of schools but published poems, anonymously at first and then under his own name, his work including pieces such as *The Forsaken Merman*. In 1857 he became Professor of Poetry at Oxford and thereafter turned his attention mainly to criticism and theology. 'Poetry', he wrote, 'is simply the most beautiful, impressive and widely effective mode of saying things, and hence its importance.'

Leatherhead

SIR ANTHONY HOPE HAWKINS, 1933. Novelist. He became a lawyer after leaving Oxford, and in 1918 he was knighted for his services in the war, when he was in the Ministry of Information. He is best known, however, as 'Anthony Hope', the author of *Prisoner of Zenda* and other romances.

Limpsfield

Overleaf: the funeral of Admiral of the Fleet, Sir Provo Wallis GCB in Huntingdon churchyard, 1892

FLORENCE BARCLAY, 1921. Novelist. She was born here, the daughter of the rector, the Reverend Charlesworth, and married the Reverend Barclay, a vicar in Hertfordshire. Her greatest success was *The Rosary*, which sold a million copies in about ten years.

FREDERICK DELIUS, 1934. Composer. Born in Bradford of German parents, his music was popularized in this country by the devoted efforts of Sir Thomas Beecham, who read his funeral oration when his remains were brought here after temporary burial in France. Delius had lived in France for many years and had become blind with what used to be called 'general paralysis of the insane' (syphilis), his compositions being transcribed by an amanuensis, the young Eric Fenby. He is perhaps best known for short pieces such as *The Walk to the Paradise Garden* and *On hearing the first Cuckoo in Spring*.

Pirbright

SIR HENRY MORTON STANLEY, 1904. Journalist and explorer. A naturalized American citizen, he was sent to Africa by the *New York Herald* in search of Livingstone, who was believed lost, the immortal greeting 'Dr Livingstone, I presume' taking place at Ujiji in 1871. His books included *How I found Livingstone* and *In Darkest Africa*. He became a British subject again, was a Liberal Member of Parliament and was knighted in 1899.

Sussex (East)

Hangleton

DR E.V.H. KENEALY, 1880. Barrister. An Irish lawyer called to the English bar in 1847, he became notorious as leading counsel for the Tichborne Claimant, an Australian butcher, Arthur Orton, who claimed to be the rightful heir to the estates of the ancient Tichborne family, who was thought to have been lost at sea. After a long and costly trial, the jury found him to be an impostor, and Kenealy's violent and unprofessional conduct was censured, but he continued his campaign and was disbarred by Gray's Inn.

Ripe

MALCOLM LOWRY, 1957. Author. Best known for *Under the Volcano*, he was subject to alcoholism almost from his boyhood and fell victim to manic depression. He came to live in this village to recover his health and write again after travelling widely, and completed the stories collected under the title *Hear Us O Lord from Heaven Thy Dwelling Place* before his death 'by misadventure'.

Sussex (West)

Ashurst

MARGARET FAIRLESS BARBER, 1901. Essayist. She wrote under the name 'Michael Fairless', all her books being published posthumously. The best known is *The Roadmender*. She died at thirty-two from a spinal disease. A tall wooden cross marks her grave.

Cuckfield
HENRY KINGSLEY, 1876. Novelist. The younger brother of Charles Kingsley (see Eversley, Hampshire), he was an adventurer who went gold-digging in Australia and was a war correspondent during the Franco-German war. His best known novel was *Ravenshoe*.

Felpham
WILLIAM HAYLEY, 1820. Poet. He was a biographer of Cowper and Milton, and a friend of William Blake, but although he was offered the Laureateship (which he declined) Southey said: 'Everything about that man is good except his poetry.' As evidence, we may cite him as author of that epitaph to a blacksmith in the same churchyard: 'My sledge and hammer lie reclin'd' etc.

Ifield
MARK LEMON, 1870. Humorous writer. He was a brewery manager at first but became an author with various works for the stage and some novels. But he is best remembered as one of the founders and first editor of *Punch*. He was a close friend of Dickens.

West Grinstead (Our Lady and St Francis, RC)
HILAIRE BELLOC, 1953. Author. Born in France but educated in Britain, he became a British citizen, was a Liberal Member of Parliament and a lecturer in English. Closely associated with G.K. Chesterton, his writings were immensely varied, from nonsense verse to studies of Cromwell, Napoleon and the French Revolutionary leaders. He said of himself: 'His sins were scarlet, but his books were read.'

West Midlands

Birmingham (Oratory Church of the Immaculate Conception, Edgbaston)
CARDINAL NEWMAN, 1890. John Henry Newman was the son of a banker and became a Protestant churchman but was converted to Catholicism in 1845, being ordained priest in Rome soon afterwards. He established the oratory in Birmingham and wrote the remarkable *Apologia Pro Vita Sua*, his autobiography, as a reply to Charles Kingsley's charge that he did not consider truth a necessary virtue. He was a fine preacher and a man of exceptional intellect. His poem *The Dream of Gerontius* was set to music by Elgar (see Little Malvern, Hereford & Worcester). He was made a Cardinal in 1879.

Bread prices set in the w
of the church, Great
Wishford, Wiltshire

Wiltshire

Bromham
THOMAS MOORE, 1852. Poet. A Celtic cross marks the grave of the
Dublin-born poet who wrote a large number of Irish songs and achieved
huge popularity in his time. He also wrote biographies of Sheridan and
Lord Byron, whose memoirs Moore destroyed, having been entrusted
with them before Byron's death.

Hardenhuish
DAVID RICARDO, 1823. Economist. See p.131.

Wilsford
SIR OLIVER LODGE, 1940. Physicist. A professor of physics and
Principal of Birmingham University, he published many scientific
works before the end of the nineteenth century, dealing mostly with
electrical science and the relation between matter and ether, for which
he was knighted in 1902. But he became interested in psychical
research, especially after his son was killed in 1915, and thereafter
devoted his time mainly to spiritualism, on which he also wrote several
books.

Yorkshire (North)

Coxwold

LAURENCE STERNE, 1768 (but re-buried here in 1969). Clergyman and author – see pp.94 and 180.

Masham

JULIUS CAESAR IBBETSON, 1817. Artist. A self-taught painter of picturesque rural scenes, he used to put his new pictures in his window and listen to children passing comments on the them because, he said, 'They never give flattery.'

Scarborough

ANNE BRONTË, 1849. Novelist. A modest headstone marks the grave of the youngest of the Brontë sisters, author of *The Tenant of Wildfell Hall* originally published under the pseudonym 'Acton Bell'. She came to Scarborough with Charlotte, primarily to obtain a little happiness from the surroundings, but died here of tuberculosis, aged twenty-nine.

Scrayingham

GEORGE HUDSON, 1871. Industrialist. A linen draper, he began to promote railways on inheriting a fortune and was so successful that he created the first big monopoly and was called 'The Railway King'. He was thrice Lord Mayor of York, and Member of Parliament for Sunderland before his downfall when he was accused of fraud. He then lived on the charity of friends and died a broken man.

Sharow

CHARLES PIAZZI SMYTH, 1900. Astronomer. He is buried beneath a pyramid surmounted by a cross – a queer notion like Burton's Arab tent. As a professional scientist, he was Scotland's Astronomer Royal, but as an amateur, he was an archaeologist and one of the first to study the Egyptian pyramids, which he considered to have curious properties. His tomb is a model of the Great Pyramid at Gizeh.

York (St Olave)

WILLIAM ETTY, 1846. Artist. He was a native of York, and was the finest English painter of the nude, thereby bringing upon himself much hypocritical vituperation. His last words are said to have been, 'Wonderful! wonderful! this death!' He wished to be buried in York Minster, of which he was very fond and which he had served well but, having made no provision for the necessary £500, he was dumped here instead.

(St George)

RICHARD TURPIN, 1739. Outlaw. A great deal of romantic nonsense has been written about this notorious highwayman. He was arrested at Welton, going under the name of 'John Palmer', and was only thirty-three when he was hanged for horse-stealing. His body was dug up by body-snatchers but recovered by local people from a surgeon's garden, reburied in quicklime and covered with a heavy slab.

Yorkshire (South)

Darfield

EBENEZER ELLIOTT, 1849. Poet. He worked as an iron-founder but became known for his poems denouncing exploitation and oppression of the poor and was called 'the Corn Law Rhymer':

> When wilt thou save the people?
> Oh, God of mercy, when?
> Not kings and lords, but nations!
> Not thrones and crowns, but men!

WALES

Clwyd

Llangollen

LADY ELEANOR BUTLER, 1829; HON. SARAH PONSONBY, 1831. The 'Ladies of Llangollen' were Irish eccentrics who were hostesses to such men of their time as Wellington, Scott and Wordsworth, at 'Plas Newydd', the house in which they lived together from 1779.

Mold

RICHARD WILSON, 1782. Artist. He is sometimes called 'the father of British landscape painting'. He painted English and Welsh scenes in the classical manner of Claude and Cuyp, bathed in melting light. One of the founder-members of the Royal Academy, he died poor and unappreciated.

Wrexham

ELIHU YALE, 1721. Yale University was named after its first great benefactor, who was born in Connecticut of Welsh descent and entered the service of the East India Company. He chose the site of his burial himself, and there is a quaint rhyming epitaph on his tomb.

Dyfed

Laugharne

DYLAN THOMAS, 1953. Poet and broadcaster. One of the outstanding figures of modern poetry, he was a word-sorcerer and a superlative broadcaster of his own material but died in the USA of what the autopsy report called 'insult to the brain' – alcoholism, aged thirty-nine. He was brought back to his last home for burial. Death forms one of the major themes of his poetic work, but he is perhaps most widely known for his radio play *Under Milk Wood*. He wrote a screenplay about Burke and Hare and Dr Knox, called *The Doctor and the Devils*.

Llangunnor

SIR LEWIS MORRIS, 1907. Poet. A lawyer, he helped to establish the University of Wales and was knighted in 1895. His reputation as a poet was made by 'The Epic of Hades', which adopted a modern approach to the Greek myths.

Glamorgan (West)

Oystermouth

THOMAS BOWDLER, 1825. Literary surgeon. Qualifying as a doctor but never practising, he was the Mary Whitehouse of his day, the self-appointed censor of Shakespeare and Gibbon, giving the language the word 'bowdlerize', meaning to expurgate.

Gwynedd

Llanycil

THOMAS CHARLES, 1814. Methodist minister. The Reverend Charles did a great deal to spread the influence of Methodism in North Wales, being a leader of the Sunday School movement and a founder of the British and Foreign Bible Society.

Powys

Llansantffraed

HENRY VAUGHAN, 1695. Poet. Self-styled 'the Silurist'. His work was mainly religious and influenced many later poets from Wordsworth to Sassoon, the latter writing in 'At the Grave of Henry Vaughan':

> Here faith and mercy, wisdom and humility
> (Whose influence shall prevail for evermore)
> Shine. And this lowly grave tells Heaven's tranquillity.

The tomb bears the three-headed family crest of the Vaughans, said to represent medieval triplets born with the umbilical cord round their necks – almost strangling the family at birth.

Newtown (old St Mary's)

ROBERT OWEN, 1858. Industrialist and social reformer. He was born here, the son of an ironmonger, and became a cotton mill manager in England and an owner in Scotland, where he formed a model community at New Lanark, setting a standard of labour conditions which became famous world-wide. He founded the Co-operative Movement and was the leading proponent of the 1819 Factories Act, limiting the employment of children.

Sources

The following books are the more specialized sources of information I have referred to. It would hardly be helpful to the reader to list all the topographical works, guide-books, newspapers and journals which offer relevant information, though I am equally grateful to all of them.

John Aubrey, *Brief Lives* (Penguin edition, 1972)

Bede, *Ecclesiastical History of the English Nation* (Everyman's Library edition, 1975)

John Betjeman (Ed.) *Parish Churches of England and Wales* (Collins, 1958)

George Borrow, *Wild Wales* (Collins, 1955 edition)

Katharine M. Briggs, *The Folklore of the Cotswolds* (Batsford, 1974)

Frederick Burgess, *English Churchyard Memorials* (Lutterworth Press, 1963)

William Cobbett, *Rural Rides* (Everyman's Library edition, 1912)

M.R. Russell Davies, *The Law of Burial, Cremation and Exhumation* (Shaw & Sons, 1965)

Charles Dickens, *The Uncommercial Traveller* (Everyman's Library edition, 1911)

Irwin Ehrenpreis, *Swift (Vol. II)* (Methuen, 1967)

D. Elliston Allen, *British Tastes* (Hutchinson, 1968)

George Ewart Evans, *Ask the Fellows who Cut the Hay* (Faber, 1956)

J.G. Frazer, *The Golden Bough* (Macmillan, 1957 edition)

G.N. Garmonsway (Ed), *The Anglo-Saxon Chronicle* (Everyman's Library edition, 1953)

Sources

Geoffrey Gorer, *Death, Grief and Mourning* (Cresset Press, 1965)

Robert Graves, *The White Goddess* (Faber, 1952)

Paul Hair (Ed.), *Before the Bawdy Court* (Elek, 1972)

Jacquetta Hawkes, *Guide to the Prehistoric and Roman Monuments in England and Wales* (Chatto & Windus, 1973)

Richard Hoggart, *The Uses of Literacy* (Chatto & Windus, 1957)

Christina Hole, *Dictionary of British Folk Customs* (Hutchinson, 1976)

Ronald Holmes, *Witchcraft in British History* (Frederick Muller, 1974)

Doris Jones-Baker, *The Folklore of Hertfordshire* (Batsford, 1977)

Peter Keating (Ed.), *Into Unknown England* (Fontana, 1976)

Lloyd and Jennifer Laing, *Anglo-Saxon England* (Routledge & Kegan Paul, 1979)

Hugh Meller, *London Cemeteries* (Avebury Publishing Co, 1981)

Jessica Mitford, *The American Way of Death* (Hutchinson, 1963)

Iona and Peter Opie, *The Lore and Language of Schoolchildren* (Oxford University Press, 1959)

Nicholas Penny, *Church Monuments in Romantic England* (Yale University, 1977)

Nikolaus Pevsner and others, *The Buildings of England* (46 volumes) (Penguin Books, 1951-74)

Jacqueline Simpson, *Folklore of the Welsh Border* (Batsford, 1976)

Rev. H. Stapleton and P. Burman (Eds.) *The Churchyards Handbook* (CIO Publishing, 1976)

Mrs Stone, *God's Acre* (Parker & Son, 1858)

Lawrence Stone, *Sculpture in Britain: The Middle Ages* (Penguin – Pelican History of Art, 1955)

Keith Thomas, *Religion and the Decline of Magic* (Weidenfeld & Nicolson, 1971)

G.M. Trevelyan, *English Social History* (Penguin edition, 1967)

Laurence Whistler, *The English Festivals* (Heinemann, 1947)

Dorothy Whitelock, *The Beginnings of English Society* (Penguin, 1952)

Dorothy Wordsworth, *Journals* (Oxford University Press, 1971 edition)

Joyce Youings, *Sixteenth-Century England* (Penguin, 1984)

Philip Ziegler, *The Black Death* (Collins, 1969)

Index

Abbey Dore, Hereford & Worc., 46
Abingdon, Oxon., 67, 135
Adderbury, Oxon., 55
Adderley, Shropshire, 67
Addison, Joseph, 60
Aldbury, Herts., 163, 206
Alderbury, Wilts., 104
Aldersgate, Lond., 15
Aldsworth, Glos., 55
Aldworth, Berks., 33
Alexander, Earl, 207
Alexander, Sir George, 190
Alkborough, Humberside, 27
Allen, D. Elliston, 181
Alsop en de Dale, Derbyshire, 61
Alton, Hants, 76
Alveley, Shropshire, 123
Alvingham, Lincs., 40
Amblecote, West Midlands, 123
Amersham, Bucks., 31, 117
Ampney Crucis, Glos., 28, 29
Anderson, Robert, 194
Andrews, James, 121
Anning, Mary, 199
Anstey, Herts., 47, 48
Antingham, Norfolk, 40
Appledore, Devon, 142, 160
Areley Kings, Hereford & Worc., 53
Arnesby, Leics., 152
Arnold, Dr Thomas, 206, 223
Arnold, Matthew, 81, 206, 223
Ashbourne, Derby., 46
Ashby-de-la-Zouch, Leics., 142
Ashford, Surrey, 77
Ashingdon, Essex, 42

Ashleworth, Glos., 29
Ashton-upon-Mersey, Ches., 64
Ashurst, W. Sussex, 226
Asquith family, 135
Asquith, Herbert H., 219
Asquith, Margot, 219
Astbury, Ches., 125
Asthall, Oxon., 128
Aston upon Trent, Derby., 31
Astor, Hon. David, 219
Aubrey, John, 60, 90, 91, 151, 167
Augustine, Saint, 20
Austin, Alfred, 189
Avebury, Wilts., 21
Awliscombe, Devon, 119, 150
Aylesford, Kent, 163
Aylsham, Norfolk, 214
Ayot St Lawrence, Herts., 47

Bacon, Sir Francis, 156
Bagshaw, Harry, 149
Baillie, Joanna, 212
Baker, Sir Samuel, 206
Bakewell, Derby., 28
Bakewell of Derby, 46
Bakewell, Robert, 41
Baldock, Herts., 116
Baldwin, William, 111, 117
Bamburgh, Northumb., 215
Banbury, Oxon., 112
Bangor, Gwynedd, 154
Barradell, Edward, 138
Barber, Margaret Fairless, 226-7
Barclay, Florence, 223
Barfreston, Kent, 31, 32
Barham, Kent, 33
Baring-Gould, Sabine, 197

Barking, Lond., 210
Barnby Dun, S. Yorks., 55
Barnes, William, 199
Barnsley, S. Yorks., 138
Barnsley, Sydney, 203
Barnstaple, Devon, 98
Barrington, Glos., 121
Basset, Hannibal, 155
Bassingbourn, Cambs., 60
Bath, Avon, 154
Bayswater, Lond., 94, 180
Beaconsfield, Bucks., 182, 189
Beckenham, Kent, 47
Bedford, 46
Beddoes, Thomas Lovell, 109
Beecham, Sir Thomas, 226
Belloc, Hilaire, 227
Bepton, W. Sussex, 117
Bermondsey, Lond., 94
Besant, Sir Walter, 212
Beverley, Humberside, 64
Bewcastle, Cumbria, 27
Bibury, Glos., 128
Bideford, Devon, 134, 142, 150
Bingley, W. Yorks., 138
Binsey, Oxon., 71, 73
Binsted, Hants, 203
Birchington, Kent, 208
Birdbrook, Essex, 150
Birkenhead, Sir John, 90
Birmingham, 128, 227
Bishop, John, 96
Bisley, Glos., 73, 76, 117
Bitterley, Shropshire, 29, 166
Bix Bottom, Oxon., 41
Blackmore, R.D., 82, 175
Bladon, Oxon., 135, 184, 216, 217

Blair, Eric Arthur, 219
Blair, Robert, 81
Blake, William, 227
Blewitt, Martha, 150
Blidworth, Notts., 159
Bligh, William, 213-4
Bloomfield, Robert, 188
Bloxham, Oxon., 55
Blunden, Edmund, 223
Bockleton, Hereford & Worcs., 40
Bodmin, Corn., 67
Boldre, Hants, 73, 204
Boles, Colonel, 76
Bolterstone, S. Yorks., 22
Bolton Percy, N. Yorks., 71
Bonaparte, Napoleon, 19-20, 119, 131, 227
Bonchurch, IOW, 208
Borden, Kent, 123
Borrow, George, 71, 99
Botus Fleming, Corn., 174
Boughton, Notts., 60
Boughton Monchelsea, Kent, 47
Boulge, Suffolk, 222
Bournemouth, Dorset, 181, 198
Bow, Lond., 75, 76, 104
Bowdler, Thomas, 231
Bowes, Durham, 145
Boxgrove, W. Sussex, 61
Bradford, W. Yorks., 226
Brailsford, Derby., 28
Bramham, W. Yorks., 144
Brancepeth, Durham, 38
Brandon, Richard, 214
Brasted, Kent, 122
Braughing, Herts., 56, 66, 97
Braunston, Leics., 77. 78

Bray, Berks., 48, 67
Breage, Corn., 28
Bredwardine, H. & W., 44, 139, 206
Breedon-on-the-Hill, Leics., 22
Brent Eleigh, Suffolk, 68
Bridges, Robert, 189
Bridgewater, Duke of, 222
Bridport, Viscount, 221
Brighton, E. Sussex, 144
Brightling, E. Sussex, 130
Briggs, Hezekiah, 138
Brilley, Hereford & Worcs., 166
Brindley, James, 222
Bringhurst, Leics., 40
Bristol, 113, 133
Brittain, Vera, 207
Broadwindsor, Dorset, 105
Brockenhurst, Hants, 33
Brockhampton-by-Ross, Hereford & Worcs., 48
Bromfield, Shropshire, 138, 220
Bromham, Wilts., 228
Bromley, Lond., 104
Brompton-in-Allerton, N. Yorks., 113
Bromsgrove, Hereford & Worcs., 122, 148
Brontë, Anne, 229
Brontë, Charlotte, 81, 87, 193, 229
Brontë, Rev. Patrick, 87
Brooke, Sir James, 129, 198
Brooke, Rupert, 81
Broseley, Shrops., 116
Brough, William, 155
Broughton, Shropshire, 32
Brown, 'Capability', 214
Brown, Ford Madox, 208
Browne, Sir Thomas, 19
Brush, James, 154
Bryan, John, 130
Buchan, John, 133, 217
Buckden, Cambs., 114
Buckfastleigh, Devon, 150
Buckland, Bucks., 58
Buckminster, Leics., 129
Bullington, Hants, 33
Bunhill Fields, Lond., 19
Bunyan, John, 208
Burford, Oxon., 76, 125, 128, 217
Burgess, Guy, 205
Burke, Edmund, 82, 202, 212
Burke, William, 92, 96, 231
Burnham, Lord, 189
Burns, Robert, 105, 219
Burnsall, N. Yorks., 48
Burslem, Staffs., 43
Burton, Sir Richard, 131, 214
Burton Lazars, Leics., 128, 209
Busbridge, Surrey, 135
Butler, Lady Eleanor, 230
Butler, Samuel, 90
Buttermere, Cumbria, 194
Butterworth, Joshua, 53
Bury St. Edmunds, Suffolk, 152

Cabell, Richard, 150
Cadnam, Robert, 144
Caine, Hall, 207, 208
Caldbeck, Cumbria, 122, 194
Camden, William, 27
Came, Dorset, 199
Campion, Edmund, 221
Campton, Beds., 188
Canning, George, 209
Cantrell, Ralph, 67
Capern, Edward, 134
Cardiff, 181
Cardington, Beds., 142
Cardinham, Corn., 24
Carlisle, Cumbria, 194
Carlyle, Thomas, 194
Carrington, Samuel, 122
Carroll, Lewis, 204, 205
Cartmel, Cumbria, 19
Castle Ashby, Northants, 46
Castledine, Henry, 121
Cavell, Edith, 215
Cerne Abbas, Dorset, 185
Chadwick, Sir Edwin, 87
Chalfont St. Giles, Bucks., 47, 190
Chalk, Kent, 55
Chapel-en-le-Frith, Derby., 76, 125
Chard, Dr, 150
Charles I, 214
Charles II, 125, 190
Charles, Thomas, 231
Chatsworth, Derby., 197
Chawleigh, Devon, 33
Chawner, Ann, 161
Cheam, Surrey, 40
Checkendon, Oxon., 23
Chelsea, Lond., 92
Chessher, Dr Robert, 209
Chester, 113
Chesterfield, Lord, 97
Chesterton, G.K., 227
Chewton Mendip, Som., 64
Chiddingstone, Kent, 129
Childwall, Merseyside, 61
Chilton Foliat, Wilts., 129
Chipping Norton, Oxon., 38
Chipping Sodbury, Avon, 155
Chiswick, Lond., 210
Cholesbury, Bucks., 21
Chorleywood, Bucks., 190
Christian, Fletcher, 213
Church Stretton, Shrops., 58, 66
Churchill, Charles, 58, 208
Churchill family, 217
Churchill, Randolph, 216, 217, 221
Churchill, Sir Winston, 135, 184, 216, 217
Clapham, Lond., 129
Clare, John, 191, 193
Clarke, Richard, 55
Clarkson, Thomas, 223
Claverley, Shrops., 29

Claverton, Avon, 129
Cley-next-the-Sea, Norfolk, 123, 125
Clifton, Avon, 171
Clipstone, Leics., 121
Clophill, Beds., 39
Closworth, Som., 134
Clovelly, Devon, 135
Coalbrookdale, Shrops., 46, 116
Cobbett, William, 33
Cobham, Surrey, 129
Cockayne Hatley, Beds., 188
Codicote, Herts., 94
Coleridge, Hartley, 196
Coleridge, Mary, 184
Coleridge, Samuel Taylor, 194
Coleridge-Taylor, Kathleen, 135
Collingham, W. Yorks., 77
Collins, Wilkie, 83, 102
Colman, Dr Edward, 68
Combe Florey, Som., 84, 221
Compton Pauncefoot, Som., 77
Congreve, William, 157
Coningsby, Sir Harry, 53-4
Coniston, Cumbria, 194, 195
Constable, John, 78, 212
Constantine, Emperor, 24, 92
Cook, Captain, 213
Cookham, Berks., 79, 188
Cooper, Sir Astley, 96
Copgrove, N. Yorks., 77
Corbet, Vincent, 131
Corby, Northants, 160-1
Corfe, Dorset, 41
Corhampton, Hants, 33, 71
Cove, Lily, 144
Covent Garden, Lond., 90
Cowden, Kent, 116
Cowfold, W. Sussex, 66
Cowley, Hannah, 198
Cowper, Sarah, Lady, 145
Cowper, William, 121, 227
Coxwold, N. Yorks., 180, 229
Crantock, Corn., 77
Cranwich, Norfolk, 22
Cranworth, Norfolk, 64
Crapp, Joseph, 144
Crawshay family, 122
Cricket St. Thomas, Som., 221
Cricklade, Wilts., 29
Croft, Lincs., 93
Cromwell, Oliver, 76, 78, 190, 217, 227
Cropredy, Oxon., 123
Crosscanonby, Cumbria, 113
Crosthwaite, Cumbria, 194
Crowhurst, Surrey, 32
Croyland, Lincs., 90
Cuckfield, W. Sussex, 227
Culbone, Som., 42
Cullen, Elizabeth, 145
Cuthbert, Archbishop, 20

Daglingworth, Glos., 71
Dale, Derby., 67
Dalton-in-Furness, Cumbria, 196

Danvers, Sir Joseph, 174
Darfield, S. Yorks., 230
Darley Dale, Derby., 31
Darling, Grace, 215
Darrington, W. Yorks., 71
Dartmouth, Devon, 44
Dashwood, Sir Francis, 58
Datchworth, Herts., 38, 71
Davies, John Newton, 145
Daylesford, Glos., 202, 203
Dean Prior, Devon, 197
Dee, Dr John, 101, 103
Deeping St. James, Lincs., 68
Delius, Frederick, 226
Denbury, Devon, 33
Deptford, Lond., 90
Deryck, Robert, 60
Devizes, Wilts., 144
Dickens, Charles, 13, 61, 82, 85, 87, 105, 108, 166, 168, 170, 193, 212, 227
Dishley, Leics., 41
Disraeli, Benjamin, 190
Ditchling, E. Sussex, 116
Dobell, Sydney, 202
Doddington, Northumb., 94
Donington, Lincs., 68
Donne, John, 171, 185
Dorchester, Oxon., 29, 44
Douglass, Clementina, 157-9, 196
Dover, Kent, 108
Doyle, Sir Arthur Conan, 205
Dryden, John, 149
Dublin, 83
Duffield, Derby., 145
Dumfries, 105
Dunsany, Lord, 209
Dunwich, Suffolk, 44, 73
Durleigh, Som., 61
Dymock, Glos., 154

Earls Barton, Northants, 38
East Bergholt, Suffolk, 67, 78
East Coker, Som., 44
East Dereham, Norfolk, 71
East Grinstead, E. Sussex, 116
East Peckham, Kent, 67
East Portlemouth, Devon, 145
East Wellow, Hants, 204
Easton-in-Gordano, Avon, 161
Easthorpe, Essex, 35
Eastwood, Notts., 156
Eccleston, Ches., 40, 44
Edensor, Derby., 197
Edinburgh, 92, 94
Edmonton, Lond., 210
Edstone, N. Yorks., 71
Edward I, 31, 166
Edward II, 104
Edward III, 31
Edward VI, 61
Eleanor of Castile, 166
Elgar, Sir Edward, 206, 227
Eliot, T.S., 44
Elizabeth I, 103, 104
Elkstone, Glos., 55

Elliott, Ebenezar, 230
Elmesthorpe, Leics., 76
Elmley Castle, Hereford & Worcs., 70, 71
Elmore, Glos., 125
Elsdon, Northumb., 38
Elsfield, Oxon., 133, 217
Elsham, Humberside, 136
Elsted, W. Sussex, 41
Elstow, Beds., 67
English Bicknor, Glos., 38
Epworth, Humberside, 76-7, 164
Essendon, Herts., 97
Etty, William, 229
Evercreech, Som., 55
Eversley, Hants, 204
Evesham, Hereford & Worcs., 122
Ewelme, Oxon., 217, 218
Ewing, Juliana Horatia, 222
Exford, Som., 29, 67
Exton, Leics., 38
Eyam, Derby., 28, 42-3, 69, 70, 149, 160, 161

Fairford, Glos., 56
Falkner, John Meade, 217
Falmouth, Corn., 193
Fanu, Sheridan le, 82
Farningham, Kent, 129
Fawley, Bucks., 129
Felkirk, W. Yorks., 68
Felpham, W. Sussex, 227
Fenby, Eric, 226
Finsbury, Lond., 19
Finsthwaite, Cumbria, 157, 158, 196
Fishlake, S. Yorks., 33
Fitton, Mary, 104
Fitzclarence, Lord Augustus, 218
Fitzgerald, Edward, 222
Flamborough, N. Yorks., 61
Fletton, Cambs., 28
Folkestone, Kent, 90
Ford, W. Sussex, 33
Fordingbridge, Hants, 204
Foremark, Derby., 46
Formby, Merseyside, 164
Foster, Richard, 73
Fox, Charles James, 202
Fox, George, 115, 190-1
Foxgale, Katherine, 100
Frampton-on-Severn, Glos., 122
Frazer, Sir James, 166
Frenchay, Avon, 95
Frimley, Surrey, 223
Friskney, Lincs., 68
Frith, W.P., 63
Frome, Som., 221
Fry, Elizabeth, 210
Fulham, Lond., 129
Fuller, John, 130
Funtingdon, W. Sussex, 223

Gad's Hill, Kent, 170
Gainsborough, Thomas, 78, 213
Gandhi, Mahatma, 194

Garrick, David, 187, 198, 210
Garrod, H.W., 219
Gaskell, Elizabeth, 193
Gawsworth, Ches., 104
George I, 159
Gibbings, Robert, 218
Gibbon, Edward, 231
Gibbs, James, 129
Gilbert, Sir W.S., 210, 212
Gilker, Simon, 145
Gill, Eric, 135, 136, 137, 191, 218
Gilpin, William, 204
Gimson, Ernest, 202-3
Glanville, William, 53
Glastonbury, Som., 22
Godalming, Surrey, 135
Godwin, William, 198
Goldsmith, Oliver, 188
Goole, Humberside, 43
Gootheridge, John, 94
Gorer, Geoffrey, 184
Gosforth, Cumbria, 27
Gould, Joseph, 93
Grahame, Kenneth, 219
Grappenhall, Ches., 64
Grasmere, Cumbria, 171
Graves, John Woodcock, 194
Gray, Thomas, 78, 81, 191
Great Asby, Cumbria, 38
Great Baddow, Essex, 61
Great Bowden, Leics., 39-40
Great Budworth, Ches., 71
Great Chalfield, Wilts., 38
Great Chart, Kent, 73
Great Easton, Leics., 40
Great Livermore, Suffolk, 154
Great Stanmore, Lond., 210
Great Torrington, Devon, 148
Great Wakering, Essex, 171
Great Wishford, Wilts., 51, 228
Great Yarmouth, Norfolk, 155
Greeve, James, 125
Gregory the Great, Pope, 20
Grimley, Hereford & Worcs., 206
Grimthorpe, Lord, 149
Groombridge, Kent, 208
Guiseley, W. Yorks., 51
Gumb, Daniel, 121
Gunwallow, Corn., 44, 155
Gurney, Sir Goldsworthy, 193

Hackney, Lond., 64
Hadleigh, Suffolk, 78
Hale, Ches., 156
Hall, Dr Robert, 152
Halton, Lancs., 28
Ham, Lond., 212
Hambleden, Bucks., 129
Hamilton, Lady, 196, 198
Hampden, John, 190
Hampstead, Lond., 46, 212-13
Hampton Lucy, War., 46
Hanbury, Staffs., 42
Hangleton, E. Sussex, 226
Hardenhuish, Wilts., 131, 132-3, 228

Hardy, Thomas, 35, 170, 176, 199-200
Hare, William, 92, 96, 231
Harewood, W. Yorks., 38
Hargreaves, Alice, 204-5
Harmer, Jonathan, 122
Harpsden, Oxon., 45
Harrison, Mary, 194
Harrison, Rex, 212
Hart, Sir B. Liddell, 191, 192, 199
Harte, Francis Bret, 223
Hartfield, E. Sussex, 47
Harting, W. Sussex, 64, 135
Hastings, Warren, 202, 203
Hatfield, Herts., 46
Hathersage, Derby., 159
Hawkedon, Suffolk, 38
Hawker, Rev. R.S., 71
Hawkins, Sir Anthony Hope, 219, 223
Hawkshead, Cumbria, 42
Haworth, W. Yorks., 65, 87, 89, 123, 144, 166
Hayley, William, 227
Hazlitt, William, 214
Headless Cross, Hereford & Worcs., 28
Heanor, Derby., 155
Heanton Punchardon, Devon, 134, 151
Heathfield, E. Sussex, 122
Heaton Mersey, Gtr Man., 48
Helpston, Cambs., 191
Hemingstone, Suffolk, 67
Hendon, Lond., 122
Henham, Essex, 95
Henley, W.E., 188
Henry V, 28
Heptonstall, W. Yorks., 87
Herbert, Lady Magdalen, 171
Hereford, 91
Herrick, Robert, 197
Herstmonceaux, E. Sussex, 122
Hertford, 97
Hertingfordbury, Herts., 145
Hessel, Phoebe, 144
Hexham, Northumb., 64
Hickling, Notts., 151
Hickman, Henry Hill, 220
High Easter, Essex, 116
High Laver, Essex, 202
High Wycombe, Bucks., 46
Higham Ferrers, Northants, 29
Highcliff, Dorset, 199
Higher Bockhampton, Dorset, 199
Highgate, Lond., 96, 98, 129
Hinckley, Leics., 99, 105, 209
Hind, John, 121
Hinderwell, N. Yorks., 73
Hitler, Adolf, 220
Hogarth, William, 210
Hoggart, Richard, 181
Holbeach, Lincs., 33
Holdgate, Shrops., 58
Holtby, Winifred, 207
Hope Bowdler, Shrops., 122

Hood, Thomas, 112
Hounslow, Sarah, 155
Housman, A.E., 17, 38, 81, 221
Howell, George, 116
Hucknall Torkard, Notts., 156
Huddersfield, W. Yorks., 33
Hudson, George, 135, 229
Hughenden, Bucks., 190
Hughes, Arthur, 79
Hull, Humberside, 207
Hunstanton, Norfolk, 145
Huntingdon, Countess of, 76
Huntspill, Som., 46
Hursley, Hants, 204
Hutchinson, Mary, 196
Huxley family, 207
Hythe, Kent, 90, 208

Ibbetson, J.C., 229
Ideford, Devon, 53
Ifield, W. Sussex, 227
Iffley, Oxon., 77
Ilam, Staffs., 28
Iron Acton, Glos., 29
Irton, Cumbria, 28
Irving, Sir Henry, 198
Isabella, Queen, 104
Iseham, Cambs., 48
Itchingfield, W. Sussex, 67
Ivinghoe, Bucks., 77

James I, 61, 64, 98
James II, 221
Jerome, Jerome K., 83, 217, 218
Jesty, Benjamin, 200
Jevington, E. Sussex, 134
John, Augustus, 204
Johnson, Dr Samuel, 187
Jordan, Dorothea, 218
Jordans, Bucks., 115, 116, 190
Joyce, James, 83

Kafka, Franz, 193
Keble, John, 204, 205
Keighley, W. Yorks., 123, 161
Kelly, Edward, 101, 103
Kelmscot, Oxon., 135, 217
Ken, Thomas, 221
Kendall, Kay, 212
Kenealy, Dr E.V.H., 226
Kennedy, John F., 197
Kennedy, Kathleen, 197
Kensal Green, Lond., 129, 177, 180
Kerry, Powys, 33
Keston, Lond., 213
Keswick, Cumbria, 196
Kew, Lond., 38, 213
Khayyam, Omar, 222
Kildwick, N. Yorks., 134
Kilpeck, Hereford & Worcs., 56-7
Kilvert, Rev. Francis, 44, 139, 206
Kingsbridge, Devon, 115
King's Lynn, Norfolk, 46
King's Stanley, Glos., 117
Kingsley, Charles, 204, 227

Kingsley, Henry, 227
Kingston, E. Sussex, 135
Kington, Hereford & Worcs., 179
Kinoulton, Notts., 41
Kirby, Joshua, 213
Kirk Ella, Humberside, 77-8
Kirk family, 121
Kirkby Mallory, Leics., 156
Kirkdale, N. Yorks., 70
Kirkheaton, W. Yorks., 142
Kirkleatham, Cleveland, 129
Knebworth, Herts., 38
Knowles, Arthur, 125
Knowlton, Dorset, 21
Knox, Dr Robert, 92, 94, 231
Knox, E.V., 222
Knox, John, 193
Knox, Ronald, 221-2
Knutsford, Ches., 71, 193

Laing, R.D., 150
Laleham, Surrey, 223
Lamas, Norfolk, 215
Lamb, Charles, 109, 210, 223
Lamb, Mary, 109, 210
Lambert, Daniel, 156, 209
Lambeth, Lond., 213
Landewednack, Corn., 161
Langham, Norfolk, 215
Latton, Wilts., 22
Laugharne, Dyfed, 230
Laughton-en-Morthen,
  S. Yorks., 58
Launcells, Corn., 193
Lawrence, D.H., 156
Lawrence, T.E., 191, 199, 200
Laycock, John, 134
Layston, Herts., 39
Leatherhead, Surrey, 223
Leeds, 43, 87, 129
Leicester, 44, 93, 121, 161
Leland, John, 40
Lemon, Mark, 227
Lenon, Etienne, 142
Leominster, Hereford & Worcs., 46
Leverhulme, Lord, 49
Levisham, N. Yorks., 113
Lew Trenchard, Devon, 197
Lewis, C. Day, 200, 201
Leyland, Lancs., 68
Limpsfield, Surrey, 47, 223, 226
Linby, Notts., 142
Lindale, Cumbria, 131
Linkinhorne, Corn., 121
Little Dean, Glos., 123, 144
Little, John, 159
Little Malvern, Hereford &
  Worcs., 206
Little Marlow, Bucks., 191
Little Ousburn, N. Yorks., 129
Little Rissington, Glos., 142
Littleham, Devon, 197
Livingstone, David, 206, 226
Llandegai, Gwynedd, 130
Llanfair Waterdine, Shrops., 155
Llangennith, W. Glam., 47

Llangollen, Clwyd, 99, 230
Llangunnor, Dyfed, 231
Llanivet, Corn., 28
Llansantffraid, Powys, 231
Llantwit Major, S. Glam., 113
Llanwarne, Hereford & Worcs., 48
Llanycil, Gwynedd, 231
Lloyd George, David, 220
Lloyd, Sarah, 152
Lock, Herbert, 155
Locke, John, 202
Lockyer, Sir Norman, 198
Lodge, Sir Oliver, 228
London, 104, 179
Long Compton, War., 47
Long Melford, Suffolk, 118, 223
Long Preston, N. Yorks., 71
Long Wittenham, Oxon., 218
Lord, Thomas, 205
Loudon, J.C., 131
Loughborough, Leics., 121, 174
Loutherbourg, Philip de, 210
Loversall, S. Yorks., 98, 114, 125
Lowry, Malcolm, 226
Ludlow, Shrops., 38, 221
Lukin, Lionel, 209
Lundy Island, 105
Lutterworth, Leics., 92
Lutyens, Sir Edwin, 135
Lydd, Kent, 161
Lydden, Kent, 67
Lyme Regis, Dorset, 199, 200
Lyndhurst, Hants, 204
Lynton, Devon, 149

Mackintosh, Sir James,, 212
Maclean, Donald, 205
Madeley, Shrops., 111, 112, 117
Maentwrog, Gwynedd, 22
Mallwyd, Gwynedd, 35
Malmesbury, Wilts., 141, 144
Mancetter, War., 66, 67
Manchester, 61, 174, 182
Manning family, 145
Mapledurham, Oxon., 218
Mappowder, Dorset, 199
Marazion, Corn., 24
March, Cambs., 13, 177
Market Harborough, Leics., 39-40
Marlowe, Christopher, 103
Marnhull, Dorset, 105
Marryat, Captain, 215
Marsden, W. Yorks., 64
Marsh Baldon, Oxon., 71
Marston Moretaine, Beds., 67
Martyn, William, 174
Marylebone, Lond., 214
Masham, N. Yorks., 28, 154, 229
Maughold, IOM, 207
Maurier, George du, 212-3
Maurier, Sir Gerald du, 213
Mawgan-in-Pydar, Corn., 142, 155
Mayfield, E. Sussex, 122, 123
Medmenham, Bucks., 191, 192
Mellitus, Abbot, 20
Melsonby, N. Yorks., 113

Melton Mowbray, Leics., 209
Merthyr Tydfil, Mid Glam., 98-9
Mickleham, Surrey, 116, 117
Middlesmoor, N. Yorks., 42
Middleton, John, 156
Middleton-in-Teesdale, Durham,
  67
Milborne St. Andrew, Dorset, 105
Mildenhall, Suffolk, 90
Mills, Bertram, 190
Milton, John, 227
Minstead, Hants, 205
Minster, Kent, 64
Minster-in-Sheppey, Kent, 145
Mitford, Mary Russell, 188
Mitford, Nancy, 133-4, 219-20
Mitford, Unity, 219, 220
Mockham, Devon, 93
Mold, Clwyd, 230
Mompesson, Katharine, 161
Monksilver, Som., 145
Montagu, Lady Mary Wortley,
  148, 200
Montgomery, James, 100
Montgomery, Powys, 145
Montgomery, Viscount, 203
Moore, Henry, 135, 215
Moore, Thomas, 228
More, Hannah, 187, 205
More, Kenneth, 212
Moreton, Dorset, 199, 200
Moreton Corbet, Shrops., 131
Morpeth, Northumb., 94
Morris, Sir Lewis, 231
Morris, William, 135, 202, 208, 217
Mortlake, Lond., 131, 187, 214
Morton, William, 220
Morwenstow, Corn., 71, 145
Much Marcle, Hereford & Worcs.,
  32
Muir, Edwin, 193
Mulock, Dinah, 213
Murat, Caroline, 119
Mylor, Corn., 144, 193

Napoleon, Prince Louis, 155
Narborough, Leics., 121
Naseby, Northants, 78
Nash, John, 214
Navestock, Essex, 35
Nelson, Lady Frances, 198
Nelson, Lord, 196, 198
Nesbit, Edith, 209
Nevern, Dyfed, 25, 30
New Lanark, Strathclyde, 232
Newbery, John, 188
Newbolt, Sir Henry, 222
Newbury, Berks., 48
Newby Bridge, Cumbria, 157
Newcastle-on-Tyne, 94
Newchapel, Staffs., 222
Newman, Cardinal, 227
Newton Harcourt, Leics., 134
Newton-le-Willows, Merseyside,
  148
Newton, Rev. William, 68

Newtown, Powys, 232
Newtown Linford, Leics., 77
Nightingale, Florence, 204
North Stoke, Oxon., 64
Northam, Devon, 142
Northchurch, Herts., 159
Northenden, Gtr Man., 105
Norwich, 215
Nuffield, Oxon., 218
Nuffield, Viscount, 135, 218
Nun Monkton, N. Yorks., 44
Nuthampstead, Herts., 179-80

Oare, Som., 82
Odiham, Hants, 68
Ogbourne St. Andrew, Wilts., 21
Old Cleeve, Som., 68, 71
Oldfield, Elizabeth, 155
Olney, Bucks., 121
Ombersley, Hereford & Worcs.,
  129
Ongar, Essex, 202
Orchardleigh, Som., 222
Orme, Richard, 97
Ormskirk, Lancs., 71
Orwell, George, 219
Ospringe, Kent, 33
Oswestry, Shrops., 48
Otley, W. Yorks., 131
Otterbourne, Hants., 205
Overbury, Sir Thomas, 60
Owen, Robert, 232
Owston Ferry, Humberside, 49
Oxford, 155, 219
Oystermouth, W. Glam., 231
Ozleworth, Glos., 22

Paddington, Lond., 43, 179
Pady, James, 150
Pains family, 161
Painswick, Glos., 33, 51, 125, 128,
  130, 202
Palmer, Dr William, 96-7
Pannal, N. Yorks., 95
Parham, Suffolk, 64
Paris, 129
Parkinson, Norman, 141
Partridge, John, 156-7
Patcham, E. Sussex, 97
Pater, Walter, 219
Patrington, Humberside, 55
Pattingham, Staffs., 77
Paul, Corn., 155
Paulton, Avon, 161
Paxton, Sir Joseph, 197
Pearce, John, 122
Peckleton, Leics., 209
Peel, John, 122, 194
Pembridge, Hereford & Worcs.,
  67, 166
Penn, William, 115, 116, 190-1
Penrith, Cumbria, 113
Pentreath, Dolly, 155, 175
Peter the Wild Boy, 159
Pettrson, Nils, 142
Pevsner, Sir Nikolaus, 177

Philby, Kim, 205
Phillip, Robert, 115
Phipps, John, 121
'Phiz', 87
Pickworth, Leics., 34, 38-9
Pinchbeck, Lincs., 68
Pinner, Lond., 131
Pirbright, Surrey, 226
Pishill, Oxon., 64
Pitman, Isaac, 155
Pitman, Jane, 154-5
Pitt, William, 152
Pitts, William, 133
Playford, Suffolk, 223
Ponsonby, Hon. Sarah, 230
Pope, Alexander, 105, 148
Porlock, Som., 64
Portsmouth, Hants., 73, 94
Potterne, Wilts., 54
Potton, Beds., 123
Powerstock, Dorset, 54, 105, 171
Powys, T.F., 199
Poynder, Mary, 130
Prestbury, Ches., 67
Preston, Leics., 33
Price, Dr William, 181
Purdue, Thomas, 134

Radcliff-on-Trent, Notts., 122
Radcliffe, Ann, 180
Radwinter, Essex, 104
Railton, Martha, 145
Ramsgate, Kent, 152
Ravenstonedale, Cumbria, 64
Rearsby, Leics., 170
Reeves, Mrs Pember, 174
Repton, Humphry, 214
Reynolds, Sir Joshua, 196, 213
Ricardo, David, 131, 132, 228
Richard III, 76, 93
Richmond, Rev. Leigh, 184
Ridge, Herts., 207
Ringsfield, Suffolk, 119
Ripe, E. Sussex, 226
Ripley, N. Yorks., 29
Rocester, Staffs., 28
Rochdale, Gtr Man., 115
Rockingham, Northants, 42
Roget, Peter Mark, 206
Rome, 181, 198
Rommel, Field Marshal, 191, 203
Romney, George, 196, 202
Romsey, Hants, 105
Rossetti, Dante Gabriel, 96, 208, 217, 222
Ross-on-Wye, Hereford & Worcs., 29
Rotherham, S. Yorks., 129
Rothley, Leics., 28
Round, Nicholas, 155
Rudston, Humberside, 23-4, 207
Rugeley, Staffs., 97
Ruskin, John, 194, 195, 210, 212, 219
Rutherford, Joseph, 122

Sacheverell, Andrew, 171
St Austell, Corn., 21
St Dennis, Corn., 21
St John's Wood, Lond., 211
St Just-in-Roseland, Corn., 35, 42
St Leven, Corn., 47
St Mary in the Marsh, Kent, 209
St Pancras, Lond., 129, 198
Saintbury, Glos., 54
Salcombe Regis, Devon, 198
Salthouse, Norfolk, 40
Sancreed, Corn., 28
Sancton, Humberside, 163
Sand Hutton, N. Yorks., 40
Sandringham, Norfolk, 77
Sandwich, Kent, 77
Sandys mausoleum, 129
Sapperton, Glos., 117, 202-3
Sarratt, Herts., 42
Sassoon, Siegfried, 222, 231
Scaife, Thomas, 132
Scarborough, N. Yorks., 229
Scathelock, William, 159
Scott, Sir Walter, 196, 212, 217, 230
Scrayingham, N. Yorks., 135, 229
Selborne, Hants, 33, 205
Selfridge, Harry Gordon, 199
Selworthy, Som., 42
Sewell, Anna, 215
Sexton, Mary, 150
Shakespeare, William, 30, 82, 90, 92, 103, 104, 156, 166, 231
Shalder, Robert, 93
Shallcross, Philip, 154
Sharnford, Leics., 33
Sharow, N. Yorks., 131
Shaw, George Bernard, 47, 134, 183, 212
Shebbear, Devon, 24
Sheepstor, Devon, 129, 153, 165, 198
Shefford, Beds., 188
Shelley, Mary, 91, 198
Shelley, Percy Bysshe, 181, 198, 223
Shelley, Richard, 97
Sheridan, Richard Brinsley, 202, 228
Shillibeer family, 145
Shoreditch, London, 64
Shoreham, Kent, 209
Shotleyfield, Northumb., 129
Shrewsbury, 99, 144
Siddal, Elizabeth, 96, 208
Sidlesham, W. Sussex, 116
Sileby, Leics., 138
Silkstone, S. Yorks., 144
Sitwell, Dame Edith, 135, 136, 215
Skelton, John, 135
Smith, Charles Piazzi, 131
Smith, Richard, 105
Smith, Sarah, 212
Smithfield, Lond., 52, 53
Snell, Martha, 154
Snowshill, Glos., 38

Sobieski family, 157-9
Soho, Lond., 214
Somersby, Lincs., 29
Sonning, Berks., 46
South Elmham St. Margaret, Suffolk, 64
South Molton, Devon, 175, 178
Southey, Robert, 194, 196, 227
Southwold, Suffolk, 129
Sowter family, 145
Spalding, Lincs., 122
Sparrow, James, 122
Speen, Bucks., 136, 137, 191
Speke, John Hanning, 206
Spencer, Sir Stanley, 79, 188
Spring, Howard, 193
Squire, William, 128
Stacpoole, Henry de Vere, 208
Stamford, Lincs., 156, 209
Stanhope, Durham, 33
Stanley, Sir H.M., 226
Stanton-by-Dale, Derby., 70
Stanton Harcourt, Oxon., 148
Stapleford, Notts., 28, 46
Staresmore, William, 159
Staunton Harold, Leics., 35
Stephens, Mr Justice, 181
Stepney, Lond., 130, 131
Sterne, Rev. Laurence, 94, 180, 229
Stevenson, Robert Louis, 96, 188
Stinsford, Dorset, 170, 199, 200, 201
Stogumber, Som., 61
Stoke Gabriel, Devon, 30, 33
Stoker, Bram, 91
Stokesay, Shrops., 38
Storrington, W. Sussex, 60
Stowford, Devon, 155
Stowlangtoft, Suffolk, 22
Stratford-on-Avon, War., 33, 90
Stratton St. Margaret, Wilts., 105
Strong, Valentine, 121
Stroud, Glos., 125
Stuart, Charles Edward, 157-9
Sullivan, Arthur, 210
Sundell, Alice, 64
Sutton, Lond., 95
Sutton Courtenay, Oxon., 114, 219
Swaffham Prior, Cambs., 40, 193
Swallowfield, Berks., 188
Swift, Jonathan, 156-7, 159
Swinbrook, Oxon., 128, 133, 219, 220
Swinburne, Algernon Charles, 208
Swindon, Wilts., 105
Swinford, Leics., 150
Swithland, Leics., 120, 174
Symonds, Rev. Symon, 48-9
Syston, Leics., 121

Tabley, Warren de, 81
Tandridge, Surrey, 33
Tawstock, Devon, 38
Taylor, Jane, 202
Telford, Shropshire, 117
Telford, Thomas, 41, 99

Tenbury, Hereford & Worcs., 220
Tenterden, Kent, 65
Terry, Ellen, 198
Theddlethorpe, Lincs., 55
Thetcher, Thomas, 142
Thixendale, N. Yorks., 48
Thomas, Dylan, 204, 230-1
Thompson, Flora, 90
Thompson mausoleum, 129
Thompson, Sir Henry, 181
Thorney, Cambs., 41-2
Thorney, Notts., 40
Thornton Hough, Merseyside, 49
Thurcaston, Leics., 121
Thurrock, Essex, 64
Thurstaston, Merseyside, 40
Tilberthwaite, Cumbria, 194
Tintagel, Corn., 46, 47, 122
Tintern Abbey, Gwent, 41
Titchmarsh, Northants, 46
Tiverton, Devon, 198
Tollesbury, Essex, 64
Tolstoy, Leo, 194
Totnes, Devon, 98
Town, Rebecca, 161
Travers, Elias, 121
Tree, Sir Herbert Beerbohm, 213
Trelawney, Edward, 181
Trevelyan, G.M., 206
Treyford, W. Sussex, 41
Trimley, Suffolk, 40
Troutbeck, Cumbria, 149
Trull, Som., 22
Turchich, Serafino, 142
Tunstall, Norfolk, 76
Turner mausoleum, 129
Turner, Robert, 30
Turner, Thackeray, 135
Turpin, Dick, 229
Turvey, Beds., 129
Twickenham, Lond., 105
Twynnoy, Hannah, 141, 144

Ufford, Suffolk, 64
Underwood, John, 175
Upper Shuckburgh, War., 38

Vaughan, Henry, 231
Viareggio, Italy, 181, 198
Victoria, Queen, 190

Waddington, Robert, 121
Wadhurst, E. Sussex, 116
Walbrook, Anton, 213
Walesby, Notts., 100
Walker, George, 85, 87
Walker mausoleum, 129
Wall, Matthew, 66, 97
Wallace, Edgar, 191
Waller, Edmund, 189, 190
Wallis, Sir Provo, 223
Walpole, Sir Hugh, 196-7
Walpole St. Peter, Norfolk, 68
Walsoken, Norfolk, 123
Waltham St. Lawrence, Berks., 188

Walton, Izaak, 221
Walton, Suffolk, 40
Walton-le-Dale, Lancs., 101, 103
Wanstead, Essex, 94
Wantage, Oxon., 40
Warblington, Hants, 93, 94
Warburton, Henry, 96
Ward, John, 207
Ward, Mrs. Humphry, 163, 206-7
Warmington, War., 35, 44
Wasdale Head, Cumbria, 33, 142, 171
Waterhouse, Alfred, 189
Waugh, Evelyn, 133, 221
Waxham, Norfolk, 38
Webb, Mary, 167
Webster, John, 151
Wedmore, Som., 77
Weedon Lois, Northants, 135, 136, 215
Wellington, Duke of, 230
Wendron, Corn., 47
Wensley, N. Yorks., 113
Wesley, Charles, 214
Wesley, John, 38, 76-7, 214
Wesley, Samuel, 214
West Grinstead, W. Sussex, 227
West Malvern, Hereford & Worcs.,

206
West Meon, Hants, 205
West Wycombe, Bucks., 58, 59
West, Richard, 138
Westerham, Kent, 114
Westmill, Herts., 71
Westonzoyland, Som., 76
Wetton, Staffs., 122
Whalley, Lancs., 28
Wharram Percy, N. Yorks., 39
Whistler, James McNeill, 210
Whistler, Laurence, 135
Whitbourne, Hereford & Worcs., 48
Whitby, N. Yorks., 91, 144
Whitchurch, Hants., 113
Whitchurch, War., 33
White, Gilbert, 33, 205
White, Henry, 64
White, W.H., 208
Whitechapel, Lond., 14, 91, 214
Whitefield, George, 76
Whitehouse, Mary, 231
Whitstone, Corn., 71, 72, 73
Whittlesey, Cambs., 175
Whittlesford, Cambs., 58
Whitwell, Herts., 92
Wiggins, Joseph, 64

Wilberforce, William, 209, 223
Wilde, Oscar, 108, 190
Wilkes, John, 58, 208
Wilkinson, John, 131
William III, 221
William IV, 218
Williams, Edward, 181
Williams, John, 91
Williams, Thomas, 96
Willingale, Essex, 40
Willocke, John, 174
Wilsford, Wilts., 228
Wilson, Richard, 230
Wincanton, Som., 46
Winchcombe, Glos., 55
Winchelsea, E. Sussex, 38
Winchester, Hants, 142
Wingfield, Suffolk, 67
Winwick, Northants, 22
Wirksworth, Derby., 154
Woking, Surrey, 182
Wollstonecraft, Mary, 198
Wolverton, Bucks., 122
Woodbridge, Suffolk, 46
Woodchurch, Merseyside, 44
Woolland, Dorset, 33
Woolward, Robert, 152
Woolwich, Lond., 154

Wootton St. Lawrence, Hants, 130
Worcester, 85
Wordsworth, Dorothy, 171, 196
Wordsworth, William, 108, 148, 194, 196, 230, 231
Worth Matravers, Dorset, 200
Wotton, Surrey, 53
Wraxhall, Som., 68
Wren, Sir Christopher, 46, 104
Wrexham, Clwyd, 230
Wrighton, Rodger, 145
Wrington, Avon, 187, 198
Wroxham, Norfolk, 129
Wyatt, Benjamin, 130
Wycliffe, John, 73, 92
Wylye, Wilts., 135
Wythall, Hereford & Worcs., 68

Yale, Elihu, 230
Yarm, Cleveland, 43
Yattendon, Berks., 189
Yeats, W.B., 103, 204
Yonge, Charlotte Mary, 205
York, 46, 229
Young, Edward, 81
Ysbyty Cynfyn, Dyfed, 22

Zborowski, Count, 209